The Fast Track to Mastering Ascension

by Alexander Quinn

© 2022 by Alexander Quinn
2nd-2022, 3rd-2022

All rights reserved. No part of this book, in part or in whole, may be reproduced, transmitted or utilized in any form or by any means, electronic, photographic or mechanical, including photocopying, recording, or by any information storage and retrieval system without permission in writing from Ozark Mountain Publishing, Inc. except for brief quotations embodied in literary articles and reviews.

For permission, serialization, condensation, adaptions, or for our catalog of other publications, write to Ozark Mountain Publishing, Inc., P.O. Box 754, Huntsville, AR 72740, ATTN: Permissions Department.

Library of Congress Cataloging-in-Publication Data

Starseeds: What's It All About? by Alexander Quinn -1984-

This book acts as a 360* dot-connector giving a beginner to master level explanation of the starseed phenomenom, which is currently exploding globally.

1. Extraterrestrial 2. Consciousness 3. Starseed 4. Spiritual
I. Quinn, Alexander, 1984 II. Metaphysical   III. Starseed   IV. Title

Library of Congress Catalog Card Number: 2022930886
ISBN: 9781950608515

Cover Art and Layout: Victoria Cooper Art
Book set in: Multiple Fonts
Book Design: Summer Garr
Published by:

PO Box 754, Huntsville, AR 72740
800-935-0045 or 479-738-2348; fax 479-738-2448
WWW.OZARKMT.COM

Printed in the United States of America

To my father, the world would be empty without you. Thank you for being the closest friend I ever had.

To my mother, who died shortly before this book was published, the very last words she said to me before hanging up the phone:

"Alex, the world must have this book. Promise you will get this work out into the world. I'm tired. I must rest now. Talk tomorrow, dear boy."

✦ Contents ✦

Foreword	**i**
1 ✦ Ascension	**1**
✦ DNA	23
✦ The Akashic Record	28
✦ Consciousness	38
✦ Spirituality	49
✦ Shadow Work	55
2 ✦ Starseeds	**59**
✦ Galactic Earth History	61
✦ Indigo Children	70
✦ First Wave: Indigos/Light Warriors	73
✦ Second Wave: Indigos/Lightworkers	74
✦ Third Wave: Crystal, Rainbow, and Indigo Children	77
✦ The Old Soul	85
✦ Extraterrestrial and Soul Origins	95
3 ✦ E.T. Phone Home	**108**
✦ The Arcturians	116
✦ Pleidians	121
✦ Reptilians	126
✦ Anodromedans	142
✦ The Sirians	152
✦ The Anunnaki	156
✦ The Grey's and Zeta Reticulans	164
✦ Agartha (Inner Earth)	184
✦ Angels	198
4 ✦ The Densities Explained	**206**
✦ Third Densities	212
✦ Fourth Densities	218
✦ Fifth Densities	223
✦ Sixth Densities	236
✦ Seventh Densities	240

❖ Eighth Densities and Beyond   244

5 ❖ The Crystalline Grid   **247**

  ❖ Summary   268

6 ❖ The Future   **270**

  ❖ Sovereignty   270

  ❖ Time and Reality   278

  ❖ Disclosure   282

  ❖ Systems   287

  ❖ Food   290

7 ❖ Final Words   **293**

About the Author   **299**

⁂ Foreword ⁂

Increasingly humans are waking up to new realities including dimensionality and spiritual narratives. People on Earth, otherwise known as Gaia in galactic terms, are becoming open to the possibility that there is more to life than the simple 3D or third-dimensional perception we live each day. Who are we really? Where do we really come from and why are we now more reflective and susceptible to finding these answers and accepting the realities behind them? This book is going to run through all the information in an easy-to-understand format that will make it accessible for the beginner all the way to the advanced, with no holds barred and all the facts explored. Upon reading this book you will have a holistic view of our galaxy and various incredible concepts as seen in the list of chapters. Perhaps while pruning the hedge one day, you will bump into the neighbor on the other side of the fence and find yourself speaking like a seasoned master about a world you thought you knew nothing about. This book will glance over a large subject, slowly break down the parts, and link all the ideas together so that they are understandable—thus revealing the bigger picture. There are many in what is called the new age who preach with evangelical tones on what is and what the world should be. Here we are, putting these facts to you and letting you decipher them for yourself. You must have your own sovereignty over what you believe and what resonates with you.

At this time, it is important to mention that as the author of this book, I am not part of any occult or organization nor do I believe you should be in either in order to live and feel the items that we are going to discuss. Discernment and diligence are needed in this day and age, as cults and organizations do use the information found within these pages to entrap humans and control the experience we have in our lives both in the physical and nonphysical world.

On reading this book you might find surprising threads or unseen commonalities that you have yourself already experienced somewhere on the journey that we call life. However, if you find yourself being part of a structure where you are enlisted and encouraged to give money in structured ways in order to entertain similar information, or are controlled in your use of time or the amount of information that is given to you, then we suggest you ask your inner being if that reality resonates with you and your own free will. The best way to absorb the type of information within these pages is as a person of complete free will, using your own discernment and spiritual sovereignty to feel what is correct for you–for your higher self knows better than anyone else what your highest truth is.

Spiritual sovereignty is a feeling inside which no one can control or take away from you spiritually or financially. You are a free being and that is how you should continue, so I urge you to enjoy some of the elements of the starseed movement and the concepts around it, but to be careful not to become enslaved or entrapped by it in any way. There will be parts of this book that might seem implausible should this be a new field for you. If this is the case, I ask that you look at these ideas from a conceptual basis in understanding the true nature of human consciousness, which is rapidly increasing at this present time, which was calculated by the ancients.

There are many books on the market at the moment that discuss various elements of these chapters, but few take you through all the elements, linking the dots together in an easy-to-understand fashion, so you can have a full holistic view of the story. Keep reading these pages and I shall enlighten you to truths that might open your mind to concepts you potentially had never even conceptualized, which will mysteriously start to make sense, and in doing so will make you want to ask more.

Do you find yourself awake at night, with a ringing in your ears, wondering what this life is all about? Do you wonder why you are here, what your purpose is, how we came to be here in life, and why on Earth at this time? Were you born into this world to have a career, make money, create a family, and then die? Or is there more? Is there a much higher purpose for souls being on Gaia at this time? Perhaps the trappings of daily life are currently disguising a higher purpose unknown to yourself until you awaken to stand in the light and understand old deceptive dark energies which have plagued you in both present and past lifetimes? Perhaps they are even stopping you from becoming your true self and achieving who you really want to become as a sovereign being?

The information before you is not fictional. It has a basis in esoteric, scientific, and spiritual findings mostly found across the Internet and books confirmed by various spiritualists, ET experts, scientists, and government officials. "Starseed" is a term that you will come across in this book among other universal ones. In the multiverse are many universes, galaxies, and solar systems with various stars. We are not alone, and there are many beings, entities, and energies that surpass our currently limited field of vision within the six senses we use in these human bodies. Governments and influential individuals have been aware of this for decades. Many of you will be aware of ghosts. Perhaps you have discussed angels with your neighbor, or you know of people in the military who have seen strange things in the skies or even found themselves accidentally flying alongside craft defying all laws of our current known physics. There are evidently energies that are all around us with some existing in the field just beyond our field of vision and comprehension. It is said that due to the infinite and overwhelming size of our universe alone there are more stars (suns) than all the grains of sand on all the beaches in the world. Once you understand that, you begin to interpret just how big the universe is and how great the possibilities really are. The proportion of Earth-like planets that would easily hold life are many, and that is just in our galaxy. The chances of finding intelligent beings are higher than winning the lottery, and yet someone wins the lottery every year somewhere around the world!

Starseeds: What's It All About?

In Area 51, there once worked a well-known security guard by the name of Charles Hall. He has written books about ETs and beings he spent time with at Groom Lake, which is nestled in the desert. Mr. Hall explains how he had direct physical contact with beings on a regular basis. Upon one of those contacts, he was with a being that he called a "Tall White." Hall mentions a quote that one of these beings said to him telepathically while they were working together. The being looked directly at him and said, "Look at the stars in the night sky. Look how many there are. Did you really think you were truly alone in this universe?"

Due to the enormous size of the universe, the mathematics are so stacked against the idea of being alone, that a scientific probability calculation concludes we would be mad to believe so. Why is it the case that we have been conditioned to believe that we are alone then? And if so, who would be the darkness or the power behind separating humanity from our galactic neighbors? And what do they have that is so precious in which it must be hidden from us? What have they got to lose? Governments have covered up and even lied to taxpayers around the world since the start of time. Why listen to government and large corporate rhetoric when we can have sovereign thoughts based on what we believe is true without being fed a narrative? Narratives are delivered to the masses to control and silence questions that confront a reality that is being carefully sold upon which many have no idea they have already bought.

The truth of it all, however, is that you are a spiritual being, incarnated on Earth and loved more than you can imagine by those you can't see. You are infinite, important, so special at this time of enlightenment, and always loved by the universe and the creator. But more about that later. You are a creator of realities and can achieve and make dreams come true when you believe! So, where are we from? Are we from the stars?

⁂ 1 ⁂
Ascension

Across this universe, beings, spiritualists, and starseeds have one word first and foremost upon their lips and thoughts during this great time of purification and transformational healing: Ascension. We have moved spiritually, metaphysically, and scientifically into a new era of energy along with a new consciousness that humanity will upgrade to along its journey back into light as we become the forerunners of an ascended planet. For far too long, our planet has existed within an inverted matrix where everything energetically was spun and tipped upside down as to propagate the vantage points of abusing human free will via the control of bloodlines and negative galactic interference that have gripped the reality matrix we all have waded through. Throughout this time, humans have also had the abilities to use their own free will but with little foresight in a low-density vibrational construct in which Gaia (Mother Earth) has tolerated for so long. There has been a time of descension. A period of quantifiable time when resonance, energy, and acoustic magic was cast into lower doldrums.

The world of separation from who we really are and hidden truths is coming to an abrupt end. Can you feel it? Earth (known as Gaia) is transforming exponentially along with the way systems and our understanding of the planet and its history has been delivered to us. For a long time humanity has existed at a fraction of its potential not understanding that the world of forced rulers, dependency, and systems in which we have been integrated were all in an attempt to keep humankind in a box that said "controllable" while being moved around like cattle on a game board played by unseen and unimaginable forces both physical and nonphysical.

For too long we have survived in a matrix that told us how to live, when to die, and more while reinforcing and creating man-made structures in society that if spoken against landed one in grave and sometimes perilous predicaments. Humans have throughout time forgotten their light and divinity, relinquishing these traits of freedom for subservient and submissive mindsets never questioning the narrative given or whether the truth even existed in the first place. The greatest mind-control game of all time was that the inmates never realized they were even in a prison until now.

There are incredible powers and energies at play as of this very moment that are undoing these great atrocities that bring the human back into his and her own sovereignty and abilities, some of them otherworldly! Now is the time of great change on Earth predicted by the ancients and natives around Gaia that have lived before explorers set foot and when the lands and oceans were untouched. This is the time humanity takes the reins once again and walks into the journey of light in thousands of years on this planet. In this process, every man and woman including Earth herself transform mentally and physically into a new vibration of freedom, abundance, and joy. The process is called . . . Ascension. As a sweeping generalization, some in the new age prefer to call it "going into 5D!"

What is it to ascend? you might ask. There are many undertakings that need to be addressed in exploring what this really means and how souls will accomplish this in a new energy. Let us explore the canvas of ascension and paint our way into its picture with the colors needed to understand the most beautiful story ever told—moving from a dark vibration to one of light and high frequency. A remembrance of who we really are!

We see this term used often in biblical texts sometimes stated as "Entering heaven alive without dying" or "becoming an ascended being/master," which is a belief held in various religions. Historically, death is the normal end to a life on Earth and the beginning of the afterlife. Entering Heaven without dying is thought exceptional, becoming a sign of a deity's special recognition of the individual's piety, or in other words, being multidimensional through vibratory growth in various elements in one's life, climaxing throughout the work or many lifetimes, this one being the payoff regarding humanity as a whole.

There have been many conversations regarding the subject of ascension in religious texts throughout human history. There are various scriptures that discuss both Mother Mary and Jesus ascending.

In Hinduism, Yudhishthira is believed to be the only human who can cross the plane between mortals and heaven while still in a mortal body with his brother Arjuna, who has been to heaven already living there for five years in a human body, also. It seems many kings including Nahusha have been admitted to heaven still in their human body as well.

The religion of Islam states that Muhammad ascended into heaven alive at the site of the Dome of the Rock.

In Judaism there are potential accreditations to ascension regarding Enoch and Elijah although it is arguable. In Genesis 5:24 there is a mention of Enoch, who is described as having "walked faithfully with God, then he was no more, because God took him away." However, there is no hard evidence that he was dead at this point, and it does not say where God took him either. The Book of Kings details Elijah being carried toward "shamayim" within a great wind, but the word can mean both heaven and "the abode of God."

You can begin to see a pattern forming here why there is a general conscientious belief that an entity regardless of religion is able to transcend into a higher state sometimes within the body and other times out of the body; sometimes through lifetimes and sometimes within a single lifetime. More interestingly still is the ability to ascend while still in the body as a "physical," which leads us to the terminology known as becoming an "ascended master." Examples of this range widely; however, there is a group considered ascended masters such as Jesus, Buddha, Krishna, and many more. There is an understanding that to become an ascended master you are raising your energy in the universe and potentially lifting up through portals of vibration otherwise known as dimensions and densities having cleared and transmuted all the elements of lower vibrational humanism and its previous limited consciousness restraints within the meridians of the body. In the later stages of this book, we will discuss the characteristics of the various dimensions and how they work. Could it be that these religious deities had previously ascended from lower 3D consciousness into a higher state of being into fifth dimensionality? A place of pure thought, unconditional love, and light?

Earth is at a very special crossroad in our evolution in various ways. It is widely discussed among spiritualists, ancient astronaut theorists, and quantum specialists that Earth itself is going through a unique spiritual evolution that has not been seen before in our universe. This evolution is not for just the privileged few, but for the coming of age for every soul on Earth. The idea where all humans enter the heavens while still in their body raising consciousness and spiritual awareness, not only for themselves but for the soul of the Earth herself. In other words, raising up through the limitations and lack of the 3D world into the 5D world having transcended through 4D. It is widely disclosed from various mediums and ET contacts that there is a message coming through that has a very similar tone each and every time regards the ascended masters and other energies that are alive on the other side of the veil. It seems that "All eyes are on Gaia" at this moment in time. Those in the heavens, those of physical and nonphysical appearance, and even the creator itself seem to have an extraordinary involvement in Earth's path currently. The Earth is at the beginning of a mass ascension led by a shift in human consciousness on a global scale. Eventually all humans will ascend depending on various timelines, and this will be achievable by staying in the human body without having to die and reincarnate. In other words, instead of dying and finding a new body and being born into the new energy or higher vibration, it will be achieved in the same lifetime within the same body. Ascension will not be a matter of dying, it will be an experience in a body that is also transforming energetically to keep pace with the incoming energies in which it operates. Within the spiritual community there is often a misconception that one must have an outer body experience in order to facilitate a feeling of being ascended often through only living in the higher chakras while negating the lower ones. In a new energy 2012 onward, it will be the opposite. The desired effect will be about carrying your physical body into 5D with you and grounding incoming energies into Gaia.

There are complexities to this, of course, and many different theories have come to light on how this might happen. One theory is the duality idea that those ascending will live in a super-embossed reality on top of the old 3D world while beings struggling to ascend will have to enter the life/death cycle with some souls reincarnating on another planet that will be their new home. There will be souls with contracts and pre-agreed-upon missions who have taken on unconditional responsibilities carrying out actions that will heal karma, resolve unfinished business, and uncover issues within bloodlines and not ascend as a result of some of these actions in order to facilitate these agreements. Brave souls who came at this time to facilitate other projects will be left behind, but they knew this before coming. There is a great plan for souls on Gaia at this time with many complexities. The creator's plan is one of compassion and love for all souls on Gaia. Often this is why upon having a reading or speaking to one's spirit guides, they refer to the plan and ask you to trust it.

Within the new-age and spiritual communities there are those who speak of fearful revolutions that should a soul not ascend there will be repercussions with some souls becoming stuck for the next thousand years. As a general rule of thumb within the new-age field it is healthy to be mindful of fear-based philosophies and to be guarded when hearing these seemingly scary ideas regarding ascension. All souls will ascend in the end without limitation or consequence with none being left behind. It is only a question of when and where. The idea is that those who do not manage it in this lifetime, will have a much larger potential in the next and so on depending on their soul path and Akashic trajectory.

Accounts from loved ones who have passed, messages from angels and ETs including people under hypnotherapy all around the world are expressing recently that this has never been done before like this. Earth seems to be writing a new chapter in the history of the universe and everyone on both sides of the veil is greatly interested to see how it will work out. There are many beings also greatly interested in actively taking part. Is this perhaps what has led to the highest recorded levels of people channeling and having spiritual contact? Just look on Facebook. These days the groups within the new-age and spiritual community are more abundant than ever before and growing considerably each year. This is not a fad or popular trend due to become extinct any time soon. Something within the fabric of peoples' being is awakening and expanding. The old souls are being inquisitive and soaking everything up that they can come across like an enormous sponge. Old souls are absorbing and seeking out new and ancient knowledge like moths to a flame. It is a sign of the times as we move through the ages and into the new.

It has been debated that we reincarnate over various lives and go through the birth and death cycle. Earth then it seems is currently hosting this procedure of learning without a death clause this time. The ultimate spiritual party approaches, if you will, and that is why there is such a presence of energies and beings all coming to Earth and rushing to get here at this moment in time. Could this explain the rapid onset of growth regarding global population since the Second World War and the baby boomer generation?

With regards to Gaia's current ascension, it would be like a spiritual fast-track system unlike anything ever seen before, not only in this galaxy but in this universe! This is essentially the move from dark to light, from control to freedom, from being divided to being one, from being alone to being a collective while respecting individualism. Does this, however, suit all perspectives? There are plenty of dark energies of the pre-ascension era that are doing everything in their ability to stop this rise in world consciousness for their own manipulative gains and profits. We will cover this as we continue. However, rest assured, that as you are reading this book in your now, the time in the future from when this book has been written, that light will be even further on its merry way to winning no matter how much the dark on Earth fights back until its timely death. Let us explore the prospect of someone who has been tracking this phenomenon for a while in order to further open up what ascension is about from a creator God perspective first.

Robert Aaron Gulick III was an architect, educator, and feng shui practitioner living in the United States with over forty-five years of experience. His work has focused on all kinds of projects with many receiving awards for design excellence. He was a noted lecturer and consultant in sacred geometry and has also worked in special projects within the movie industry such as the cult movie *The Lawnmower Man*, starring Pierce Brosnan. He has written his ideas on the subject of ascension. The statement below (from Gulick's website, mind-matrix.net) shares forty-five years of research, experience with beings, and the understanding he has gained.

Every universe, every galaxy, every being is created with a program for expression and experience for consciousness and a path of return to the Source-Creator which is called The Plan. Each is unique and in a sense an experiment. Once set in motion the Creator/God normally does not interfere but recedes to witness in order to know itself.

So without these sources available to us now, we are left with what has been given to us either telepathically or in direct contact with ET's with varying intentions and agendas or from higher dimension beings who generally are interested in our survival and awakening to join the galactic community of evolving intelligent species. ET civilisations have different ways of telling time, thus tracking history, based on life cycles rather than orbital periods. ET's are either positive, serving the light, or negative, serving their dark self-interests. The negative operate a control agenda to keep humanity from advancing and do not want us to know our true history. If we were to awaken to our true nature and potential as spiritual beings we would not tolerate their mind control games. Positive ET's hold back because of the non-interference rule and wait for our request for assistance. Those in between are here to witness the ascension event or to harvest our DNA for hybridisation experiments.

In our duality universe, the specifications include 12 dimensions, duality, frequency, and certain universal and systemic laws, one being free will choice. Our history then is the record of how that plan unfolded, the sequence of choices made, causes and effects. With the initial separation of the light and the dark, a history of conflict was set in motion that was leading the world into a state of chaos and destruction that was affecting other universes of creation, requiring an ad hoc adjustment in the Plan. This activity of the fallen dark was causing un- anticipated major disruptions, i.e. imbalances, in the Creator's Plan. The empire had taken free will beyond the bounds of possibilities and had run amuck, requiring some ad hoc adjustments lest the whole universe fall into chaos. Free will is risky business. The prime directive is the return to Source over cycles of existence but duality allows us free will-choice of the path of evolution, growth, experience, and learning.

With the fall of the Empire, the plan for Earth was modified. It was to become a grand experiment in spiritual evolution, blazing a fast track return to Source while redeeming the fallen light and rebalancing the karma of the galactic wars, otherwise the whole Orion drama would be replayed again and again on Earth. As a planet of unsurpassed beauty in the galaxy, Earth holds a special place in the experiment in spiritual evolution that could change the entire universe. A call for volunteers went out again and the first wave of souls arrived, 144,000. They would become the humanity of Earth. The Creator made a covenant with them for their service, the conditions of agreement or a sort of rules of the game to be played.

This adventure serves a great service to the Creator's Plan with all the rewards that entails, and it also serves as an unparalleled opportunity for fast-track personal spiritual growth available nowhere else in the galaxy. Earth would be the hardest school in the galaxy and its graduates would be highly respected and sought after by worlds transiting through the dimensions. Earth is a conscious being in service to this Plan, as are all humans and all stars and galaxies. Earth is evolving with humanity. As humans move into higher dimensions [densities] Earth is ascending and leaving her physical body, and will become uninhabitable in the 3rd dimension.

Humans developed a physical body along the genetics of the human archetype, combining the genetics of 22 of the most advanced races in the galaxy. This afforded humankind the highest possible spiritual powers and qualities needed for the task. Codes for the universe are recorded in human DNA. Such knowledge gives humans the potential for interstellar, inter dimensional, and time travel using just the physical body without technology. Also, human light energy bodies are encoded with the knowledge, laws, harmonics, and experiences of the entire universe in a microcosm which is projected to the outer sheaths of the aura. Human DNA is of such advancement humans are considered royalty by those ET races that know. Humans were created to be peers of Creator, equal and identical in every aspect, and are evolving to become creators of universes themselves.

Those souls that agreed, descended from an Angelic state not fully realizing what they were getting into. Protection from outside interference didn't quite work as well as it was supposed to. The dark did not follow the agreement but continued to usurp human free-will through genetic engineering and mind control.

A cabal was created by the dark to rule the Earth for them through a hierarchy of elite families, generation after generation. Outsiders, mostly Reptilians, were allowed in and began manipulating the human DNA for their own purposes (allowed in a free-will zone). They blended DNA from evolving Homo Sapiens with Reptilian forms plus original human etheric genes. The genome had great promise but portions of the genetic code were modified further or simply switched off (junk DNA). All humans are hybrids of both human and ET genetics.

In essence, Robert Aaron Gulick explains that Earth's harmonious evolution didn't go quite to plan, and in effect we have a huge restoration job in the works to restore humans back to their true origins and cosmic powers! The great clean-up has begun. This also mirrors our sociological and environmental systems on Earth at this time. Old systems are changing and being broken down to serve the many as opposed to the few. This is especially present in the pharmaceutical world who by stealth keep the majority in sickness for financial gain and various world banking systems that lend monies nonexisting in the first place and charge for the privilege. As we ascend, there will be a more harmonious structure whereby all can be abundant without taking away from anyone else, in turn serving the all.

It is now important to travel back in time. Many great civilizations on this Earth that are well documented such as the Mayans were aware of a great time of change, the end of the world as we know it, the end of an era. This was predicted by the Mayan calendar in the fifth century BC. Within this calendar was a component called the long count that differs from the Gregorian calendar.

In effect what you have is the end of an old era and the beginning of a new one in which old souls around the world are waking up to this idea of ascension and spiritual fast tracking. There are other tribes around the world with similar ideas; however, the Mayan calendar is the most well known. It was the ancients who predicted the rise again of light on the Earth and the fall of darkness and interruptive forces keeping us in the lower realms of consciousness and DNA suppression as discussed by Robert Aaron Gulick in the previous passage.

Modern-day astronomers believe that the only feasible way the Mayans could have known about these coming times of change was through the precession of the equinoxes. At the time of the Mayans this would have been extremely advanced knowledge which was incorporated into the way the Earth moved through the heavens using the various constellations like road maps. Their system was different to the modern system we have today. Within modern astronomy this means that if you stand at any point on the Earth, an hour before dawn and look to the east, you will see a constellation sitting on the horizon in the place where the sun is about to rise, and for the last 2,160 years or so that has been a Pisces. However, that is almost completely at its end and many believe we have already transitioned into the constellation of Aquarius. It has been named the Golden Age as it represents unity, integrity, freedom, abundance, and love as well as incredible technological and spiritual innovation. Pisces has been associated with more traits such as control and suppression in times gone by with an emphasis on masculinity being the dominant vibration often leading to many imbalances in the way that society has been structured.

It is debated among astronomers when the age of Aquarius begins, however. Some say the beginning of Aquarius starts in 2012 or thereabouts. Different accounts by astronomers give different figures and dates although they are roughly similar, agreeing that to move through all twelve constellations in the sky takes 24,000–26,000 years with 2,000 years or so for each individual star sign to come and go within our heavens. As you can see from the below figures we are able to time the movement of each constellation. Aquarius is the age we are moving into currently. Below shows the order of constellations working in linear time. However, you can see the end of Pisces concluding in 2160 and yet the Mayan long count calendar comes to an end on 21 December 2012. Could it be that the Mayans predicted the time we would enter the Photon belt in space, or is the 2160 count per constellation incorrect? There are different accounts. We have only given a snapshot here of seven of the twelve constellations for the sake of example. All twelve add up to 25,920, often rounded up to 26,000.

Leo	(Lion)	10800–8640	BC	(2,160	Years)
Cancer	(Crab)	864–6480	BC	(2,160	Years)
Gemini	(Twins)	6480–4320	BC	(2,160	Years)
Taurus	(Bull)	4320–2160	BC	(2,160	Years)
Aries	(Ram)	2160	BC–0	(2,160	Years)
Pisces	(Fish)	AD	0–2012?	(2,160	Years)
Aquarius	(Water jug)	AD 2160–4320		(2,160 Years)	

The precession of the equinoxes therefore translates to the observable stars in the sky which rotate in a cycle which spans a period of approximately 26,000 years. The great predictions of the past all seemed to come to an end in 2012. There have been mystics that thought 2012 was the end when in fact it was a great spiritual fast track whereby Earth and its inhabitants reboot all time fractals, release all old energies, and reboot the quantum and spiritual energies with all negative attachments cleared, including karmic energies. Imagine Earth's energies like a large computer operating system. Then 2012 came and the reset button was pushed. Could the 2012 prediction also revolve around the passing into a photonic area in space linked to the Pleiades system?

It is understood that our solar system makes a revolution around Alcyone (Pleiadian central sun) every 22,000 years (approximately) with Earth going through a photonic belt every 11,000 years. This would mean that we pass through this ring of photonic light twice in each cycle each 11,000 years as we go round hitting the edge of its ring each time. The photonic belt has also been referred to as the great monastic ring which circles the Pleiadian star of Alcyone. It is said that there are 2,000 years upon which it takes to pass through this area of space, or some call it the 2,000 years of light. Could this be what the Mayans were also referring to? Scientists have in fact examined and known about this area of space upon which we are moving into and to some degree have kept it hidden from the general public. Either way, we are moving through as of 2012 roughly an area of space tightly packed with phonic light particles not seen on Earth in a very long time. When your neighbor who is a new-age junky explains that there is more light on Earth than ever before, they are unwittingly relating to scientific fact also!

In effect we are entering a much higher vibrating part of the universe where frequencies are affecting various things on Earth like electro and magnetic frequencies which some aspire to the "ringing" in the ears sensation which people are waking up to. The idea of the ringing being that you are becoming receptive to higher energies and hearing what is inaudible, otherwise known as the ability to have *clairaudience*. More on that later. Space and its weather react with the Earth's fields electromagnetically, but could that affect the way our brains and bodies work also? Therefore, it could be said that as Earth moves through a high photonic belt in space, this would affect the partials in the ionosphere (measured as the Schumann resonance) changing the electromagnetics of Earth, in turn rewiring the bio-circuitry not only of the brain but of our human DNA and cellular activity leading to a change in consciousness. If everyone were to evolve a very high consciousness in a short space of time this might not be convenient to the rulers of the 3D world as all humans would stand up overnight and the game would be over, so to speak. The charade would be up!

Perhaps the old rulers might try to invent a way to change the DNA and cellular coding back and stop it from evolving so that humans would be more controllable, again allowing for the old paradigm to exist further. Perhaps in the future they might invent an injection used on mass and have everyone take it to stop ascension and created an event of mass hysteria whereby the people of Earth would rush of their own free will to have their arm injected. It would be an experimental DNA/RNA jab you would have to take in order to keep your civil liberties and freedoms propagated by people adopting this through fear choices. In this way the rulers would not create karmic or negative consequences upon their own timelines avoiding cosmic laws. Earth is after all a free will planet and divine laws must be adhered to. Or perhaps that is just another bedtime story. It is for you to ponder, dear reader.

Science has proven that we are moving through a more energetic part of space with experts at the highest levels discussing this. It has effects on our sun, which are easily measurable, as the sun is calming down and giving off less heat. Weather specialists are aware of the cycle the sun is coming into, and it is not the first time we have gone through a solar minimum. Have we reached a pinnacle of temperatures slowly shifting on a downward scale of things now? Does this mean that the forecasts of a mini ice age are still on the table? Many of you will have noticed that the sun is far whiter in recent times. In years gone past it had a more yellow hue to it. The very light that our sun is emitting seems different. Again there are more changes in the external world outside of the Earth. Are they all linked? Over time, however, you will notice coronal mass ejections known as CMEs, and other solar activities growing as our sun become stimulated in other ways by the area of space we are moving through. In time we will receive more and more intense space weather, which will be felt as ascension symptoms including heart palpations, extreme tiredness, and feeling spaced out or not present as the human body adapts.

If the energetic area of space we are traveling through affects electromagnetics, then surely there would be evidence of this unfolding on Earth, and if so, what would this look like? As of late the very magnetics of the Earth also have been changing vastly beginning at the top of the world. The north magnetic pole has been moving away from Canada and toward Siberia. This is known science. Is there going to be a pole shift? As the author of this book, I do not believe that is the case. This is because a pole shift on Earth would have devastating consequences for all life on Earth and an extinction event on Earth is not on the cards or in any timelines. In fact, we have avoided the sixth extinction event. More dangerous, though, would be a pole shift for the believers in the flat-Earth theory as this would eliminate the idea of the Earth being flat due to the way the Earth would operate if that event did happen.

Ascension

Subtle changes are indeed underway so much so that it has forced the world's geomagnetism experts to examine this whether they like it or not. As of recently experts in this field have updated the World Magnetic Model, which describes the planet's magnetic field upon which all modern navigation is based, from the systems navigating ships at sea to Google Maps on smartphones and cars. In 2018, the World Magnetic Model was in need of a major rethink as it had become archaic. Researchers from the National Oceanic and Atmospheric Administration including the British Geological Survey in Edinburgh began to come to some startling realizations. Upon annual checks of the magnetic model and magnetic fields, they realized that it has become so erroneous that it was about to "exceed the acceptable limit for navigational errors."

One must ask, is the media owned by a small group of hyper-wealthy psychopaths? Few saw this information on the news which is owned by that same small group of ultra-wealthy individuals who control the vast amount of information the global inhabitants digest. If you didn't see it on the news, it doesn't exist, right? This mentality of discernment is partly to blame for the level of obedient behavior humanity has kept itself enslaved by. When you turn on the TV and watch the news every day, you might think that the mundane issues discussed are trivial compared to the changing magnetics that affect everyone on this Earth. The same is said for the Schumann resonance. W. O. Schumann was a professor who experimented with measuring the electromagnetic waves in the atmosphere. In 1952 he finally measured frequencies between the surface of the Earth and the ionosphere and it became known as the Schumann resonance.

The ionosphere is densely layered with electrons, molecules, and ionized atoms that stretch from approximately thirty miles above the surface of the Earth to the edge of space and beyond for hundreds of miles. The area of this region grows and shrinks depending on various solar conditions and interactions between the sun and the Earth, which are variable. The ionosphere has also been labeled as a celestial power station that makes radio communications possible. It serves many purposes and, with this in mind, we return to Professor Schumann.

❖ 15 ❖

It wasn't until 1954 that Schumann and another doctor in the field by the name of H. L. Konig finally concluded Schumann's theories when they began measuring frequencies of 7.83 Hz in the ionosphere, solidifying the given name "Schumann resonance." This was further established by measuring global electromagnetic resonances, which can be altered by lightning discharges in the ionosphere.

It is important to bear in mind that we ourselves live in this charged atmosphere, be it on land depending on your altitude range, and the frequencies produced are a measuring stick in terms of what humans call home. The 7.83 Hz has been the approximate standard frequency that humans have been born into since records began and long before. If we were to go to another planet, for example, and this frequency was many times larger, it could have a dramatic impact on the human physiology and the wiring of the brain, especially as the brain uses electrical impulses to send messages throughout our synaptic pathways. So there is some importance in the effect this resonance has on our biological circuitry. The frequency itself is also similar to the range between theta and alpha waves in the brain, which are also associated with meditation, relaxation and reflection. It has been studied that cerebral blood-flow levels increase while in this frequency. It is also why native Indians and Tibetan monks have used humming or ohm sounds in order to help activate this frequency while using breathing techniques and meditating sometimes also referred to as toning which is incorporated by those who speak light language and other spiritual practices. Could there be a connection between this and the third eye idea, or is this another way to vibrate the pineal gland (third eye) into certain frequencies that connect and manifest things?

Therefore, is it possible that the Earth's electromagnetic field is able to have some kind of a say over the way the human nervous system operates? It seems quite possible. There are millions of people that live in cities across the world. Humans are constantly being bombarded with man-made electromagnetic frequencies that can cause anxiety and stress which are often seen in the beta brain at higher ranges. It is not until one leaves the city and escapes these waves that a more relaxed state can be obtained with alpha waves that are far more rejuvenating while in a more natural surrounding like a lake or grassy field in nature. So then the electromagnetic field not only affects our physical and mental well-being, but it also has a direct link to consciousness itself, which manifests directly to both. Therefore, as the energy around us is fluctuating more often, we are being pushed into potentially involuntary fields of brain waves that continue from Alpha, into Beta and then up into Gamma, Gamma being a brain function linked to heightened awareness and expanded consciousness.

As we discussed earlier, the Earth itself swinging on the Orion arm within the Milky Way galaxy has moved into a much higher frequency part of the universe that is much less dense and heavy in energy, a place where Earth has been before, but not with humans living on it as we know it now. Could it be that if a human is subject to quantum forces such as much higher naturally according electromagnetic fields (EMFs) paired with new and unusual sun activity emitting different energies encrypted with different light codes, that it would directly affect our consciousness, raising it to match new levels? It's not so far a stretch to imagine. Science has on many levels proven that the intense Gamma and plasma photons hitting out planet at this moment in time do in fact impact mental and physical compos mentis. While the new-age community speaks of light codes and activations, there seems to be a very plausible scientific explanation that works hand in hand with these ideas that is explainable and logical.

Vitamin D is synthesized from sunlight interacting with the body. We are also able to send very advanced light information across long distances with a technology that seems almost archaic in this present day: fiber optics. We use light technologically and biologically every day. Would it be such a stretch to imagine a new photonic area in space affecting our sun, our atmosphere, and the relationship we have with them and our consciousness?

Something very strange happened in January 2017, when for the first time in history, the Schumann resonance peaked at frequencies of 36+ Hz. Prior to this in 2014 this frequency rose from its usual 7.83 Hz to somewhere in the 15–25 Hz levels, which was considered at the time just an anomaly. A jump from 7.83 Hz to 36+ Hz was considered quite incredible! According to neuroscience, frequency recordings of 36+ Hz in the human brain are more associated with a stressed nervous system than a relaxed one. Could it be that higher consciousness comes with growing pains, such as a newborn baby teething for the first time, and is this why people in the spiritual community who have an awakening develop what is known as "The Coming Feeling" which is a sense that something is imminently about to happen. Does moving into a higher frequency require better ways of living, eating, and looking after oneself in order to facilitate these changes that might not be affecting only our mental state but increasingly our physical state also? Within the spiritual community adverse effects to these measurable changes have been known as ascension symptoms, something we will cover in detail in due course.

For a long time now, medical science has proven that consciousness itself can affect EMFs and even electrical components, although the establishment has been fearful to give this credence. It seems there is a two-way relationship in these energies. Tests in the US at Princeton University were engineered to set a computer to generate random sets of zeros and ones, in much the same way a coin might toss heads or tails. They created a scenario where the generation of these numbers happened continuously over and over in random patterns. It wasn't until humans were invited to sit in front of the machine and use their thought and intention to bias the machines output, that they found many more zeros than ones were generated, thus the machines output was not random anymore. It had somehow become entangled with human consciousness. In essence, the power of the human mind affected the machine. This is no constant of just human consciousness but all lives on Earth. The plant light experiment also shows incredible similarity in respect to living things affecting its surrounding environment. In one experiment, a plant was placed in one corner of a dark room under a ceiling that had a matrix of bulbs fitted to it. The lightbulbs were set up to operate independently of each other but given orders by a computer to shine randomly for short periods of time focusing light on the room below. It was not until the plant was introduced into the room that the random acclimation of light began to miraculously change. It seemed that more of the lightbulbs seemed to trigger in the corner where the plant had been placed, giving the plant an advantage in what it needed for life. It seemed that the plant and its cellular needs had interacted with a field in the room which in turn manipulated the outcome of the light matrix making it less random but seemingly tailored to making sure the plant receives more light.

It is greatly suspected that our consciousness with intent can manipulate the magnetic fields around us and create anomalies and vice versa, especially at moments of heightened states of emotion, negative or positive. This type of phenomena has been recorded with events such as 911 in New York where there were measurable jumps in magnetic frequencies that day. We live in times of very heightened emotions regarding political and social polarizations as humans begin to evolve past old ways and into new ways of thinking. Beliefs are becoming more polarized. Could the extreme rise in frequency also be affecting time fractals? As a generalization, many people feel that time is speeding up and that the day isn't as long as it used to be. Hypothetically, an Anunnaki being vibrates at such a high frequency of physicality and mental consciousness that their time is passing at an extremely high rate to the very slow time elapse of a human who is vibrating at a lower level especially at a cellular level. If humans are starting to vibrate higher, could it be that we are energetically vibrating more than time as we knew it before? Days and years seem shorter than ever. As we vibrate higher, so does time. Studies have shown that during the release of THC into the lungs via smoking marijuana that the user seems calmer and time elapses more slowly. Perhaps this is why nonhuman beings who vibrate at a very high vibratory rate live many years longer than humans as their cellular consciousness affects the field/physics around them in the same way the plant and the random number generator tests did.

As we know from science, the higher the frequency, the more highly diversified the information those frequencies carry.

Since we are organic creatures made of matter and susceptible to electromagnetic fields, and because our lives are inseparable from the Earth, then if the Earth's frequency is rising, shouldn't that also raise our frequency and ultimately human consciousness itself? Everything is getting faster, lighter, and higher over time. Time also might be getting faster and lighter. Perhaps an event horizon will eventually be reached where human time has sped up so much (or our perception of it) that we become fully multidimensional like other beings who view the past, present, and future all at the same time!

As with any sentient life form, be it a virus, a bacterium, or a squirrel in the forest looking for nuts, if you change the parameters of the environment it allows for evolutionary changes to begin occurring often with new benefits and adaptations that were stronger than before. Therefore, if the Earth's electromagnetic field is rising, then shouldn't that allow our brain and body to be able to pick up greater frequencies that are even higher? If so, is there a range of brain frequencies that would allow for more awareness, consciousness, and in turn abilities such as creativity and intuition? A place that stimulates more right-brained activities or perhaps both at the same time? The brain cannot live without the body, and therefore where the brain goes the body will follow upgrading itself also. We have lived in an energy of linear left-brained logic. Is it now time for the right brain to unlock latent or new evolutionary abilities?

Increased consciousness would therefore give us a higher state of being. Higher states of awareness have been associated with Gamma brain waves, which are the fastest brain-wave frequency with the smallest amplitude. When your brain is working with these Gamma waves, it is said to be "firing on all cylinders." These waves have also been associated with spiritual euphoria and feeling at one with everything, which are reported by experienced meditators, such as monks and spiritual practitioners and those that have their crown chakras fully open. Gamma waves are associated with peak concentration and high levels of cognitive functioning, also. The Earth, as we have explored, is moving through a part of space where photonic Gamma plasma is passing through us and the Earth more than ever before. Is this also leading to higher levels of Gamma-like activity in the mind, perhaps allowing us to have abilities thinking outside of the laws of physics that we are aware of, perhaps interfacing with the field around us and manipulating synchronicities around us in our everyday lives? Throughout my life personally I have always had the ability to think of a friend whom I have not spoken to in recent weeks or years and they will call me on my phone within seconds! To have this happen throughout a lifetime is more than simple coincidence. In conclusion the atmosphere we are living in super charging due to external helps from the cosmos, which is also affecting our sun's activity and then the relationship we have as humans with these new energies pouring in. It is affecting us at a cellular level. Is this why the new-age and spiritual community speak of leaving 3D carbon bodies and transmuting to crystalline bodies similar to that of an ET? Therefore, we are moving at lightning speed from *Homo Erectus* (upright man) to *Homo Luminous*, a transitioned human capable of all clair abilities, including *clairvoyance, clairaudience, clairsentience, and claircognizance,* and does this have something to do with what science calls junk DNA?

Historically, we have been a 3D-stimulated creature playing with the external world with regard to things we can only see and touch. Would a much more connected and evolved human drive the road maps of inner knowing and intuition as much as the external map systems which have already been explored?

By default, the human has lived in a world stimulated by things and thoughts that arrive firstly from the external world, which has then governed one's inner standing and direction. The opposite of this would be a new human who lives in symbiosis of the soul within which it is then used to affect the external world creating a higher sense of oneness with self and more rewarding reality. A person who does not wait for the external world of advertising and other projections and expectations, but navigates one's soul from intuition and divine connection alone. Therefore, a person who would walk through life never feeling lost as it was always connected to him or her while listening to the navigation within instead of the external world and its old paradigms. This would create a new human who would intuitively know what to do with life and where to go from the get go.

Would a different new upgraded human therefore be more in touch with its quantum self and the laws of the 5D+ quantum realm that exist on the edge of what current science predicts? Humans therefore are driving a new conscious road that could change the way we see our reality, which in turn would sharpen our senses and intellectual capabilities. It might not be too far-fetched to say that we are having a fast-track evolutionary jump, but would it be more in line with current acceptable thinking that we are having more of an initiation maybe, what some might call a rite of passage, a coming of age as predicted by the Mayans and other natives all that time ago? Is this the ascension that is so widely spoken of in recent times that people feel as ascension symptoms?

With all this comes pushes into different layers of dimensionality and density, going from third to fifth speeding through the turbulent fourth polarities. This would lead not only to true awareness of the universe and our part we play in it, but also to awareness of self-expression and eventually group/unity consciousness.

It seems the veil is slowly lifting. The cracks of the old paradigms are being wrenched open. The human in the playground has had its rose-tinted spectacles taken off and is blinking in the wonderful daylight prior to the eyes adjusting. The human has graduated, you could say, into a higher existence, but is still standing in their graduation robes wondering what might come next and how it will determine the future like a graduate in a new job looking for instruction.

There are parallels between technological advancement, also, which came at an astonishing rate within just the last hundred years or so. Consciousness has visibly been rising on this quota, and it can be openly seen around the world. You might ask yourself why all of a sudden in just the last hundred years we have had such incredible advancement. Where did it come from, after what has been a very murky state of advancement for a very long time, especially in comparison to what we possess today and what the industrial military complex secretly possesses, which is somewhere of 100–200 years of advancement? Ultimately, we could find ourselves doing away with lower consciousness such as living to survive and survival of the fittest, to thriving in high consciousness abundance without lack or fear-based thought processes. Fear and suspicion then would not be a driver in situations, but instead compassion and love as natural human endeavor. Would this change head energy into heart energy consciousness? These are the basics of ascension. However, let's break them down into smaller components like DNA, consciousness, and spirituality. As we become more integrated with our souls or higher selves, we move away from ego and the psychology of the collective becomes more entangled with that of serve to the all.

DNA

Deoxyribonucleic acid, known as DNA, is the critical building block for life. Within the DNA are various codes and instructions that serve for the healthy function and development of all things that are biologically alive. It can also be equated to being a very intricate storage structure holding vast amounts of information and in turn keeping the blueprint for the creation of other cells and their components. DNA is the formula that makes up who we are, both on an individual basis and as a species. It could be argued that mental, physical, and character traits of an individual are the relationship to the blueprint within the DNA. Furthermore, it is becoming widely theorized that DNA could also hold a record of our journey on a spiritual level including past lives and who we were. This has been given the cosmic term Akashic record. We shall discuss more on this shortly.

On a scientific level, there is a record of who we are in our DNA that tells a story. That story keeps passing through reproduction. Everyone at some point has been with a parent and someone else's children while the mother or father looks at them having an epiphany, saying, "My gosh, that's quite incredible, you are so like your mother/father (for example)." You can see how characteristics are passed through the DNA like information from lifetime to lifetime. DNA is constantly cycling through the human living experience as we come and go in the life-death cycle. What if medical science were to peer much deeper into the DNA and read past lives?

For a long time, the medical establishment has explained that we have two active strands of DNA with a staggering 90 percent or more of DNA that is said to be junk or dormant. Why would evolution create something as complex and incredible as the human body to leave so much waste or discarded genetic detail doing nothing at all? These dormant parts of the DNA have been under scrutiny for a very long time and it appears that we have had junk DNA within our makeup for hundreds if not thousands of years, just sitting there. Within our bodies, therefore, it can be agreed that there are codes that can be used to replicate, copy, or create new forms of intelligent life. Dormant DNA could be considered as a living data storage containing the instruction sets for our greater human potential. Within the starseed universe are varying theories regarding the ideas of DNA. There is an idea that increasingly DNA is changing with more strands becoming active with an evolution of up to twelve strands eventually becoming available. One strand for every density that exists or more coming online as your body physically adjusts to the vibratory rate your vessel has arrived at. The belief is that as we ascend our DNA, we activate all twelve strands bringing us back into full Christ consciousness, one is considered "Christed." This is important to understand. When we arrive in an older energy pre-2012 (as a generalization), we come with a hard drive that genetically carries only a fraction of self-remembrance of who we are. As the DNA and RNA begin to work together to initiate the so-called junk DNA, it expands our sense of self but begins to allow us to read parts of our genetic coding and Akashic records. Within our DNA is the history of who we are galactically also. Having your records slowly switched on begins to unlock memories about who you were in past lives and other places you have been including off Earth and the talents related to those times. What has always been inside you begins to stir. This can come through in many ways, but dreams often are some of the first. You begin to dream about existing on other planets and so forth as if you had always been there.

Those "ascending" experience bodily symptoms because the very coding within your body is changing. This sometimes can present itself as flu-like symptoms or becoming tired halfway through the day and needing a short nap that is unusual for you. The necessity of some starseeds to want to drink a lot more water facilitates incoming energies as a conduit but also flushes out the toxins and dead cells in your body during the transformation process. Hydration is important. You will notice in the spiritual community people increasingly becoming meticulous about the water they drink, and you will see them loading up their cars with high-alkaline water for fear of going anywhere near the fluoridated water that comes out of the tap in the home.

It does not end there, either. Also in the running is the idea regarding Lemuria, which was an ancient and very spiritual land before Atlantis. The Pleiadian civilization helped seed genetically and spiritually what should have been the new human today before we entered descension and went backward after Atlantis. The Pleiadians are said to have mixed their genetics with us. This would equate to humans having twenty-four chromosomes, twenty-three visible, and the twenty-fourth a quantum part that is yet unseen within the human body. Our DNA does indeed have quantum characteristics that are fascinating to watch when proven in a scientific setting. We will look at real examples of this very shortly.

In galactic terms, Earth has been a center point within the universe for a long time. Different beings coming and going and intersplicing their genetic codes with ours while trading other commodities and resting here before leaving to continue their journey to visit other places. Our galactic history is rich with the manipulation from Anunnaki and Reptilian interference both good and bad.

Here are three case studies that have piqued interest

among even the strongest of skeptics that could shed light on the operation of quantum DNA and the way it affects its environment.

The Phantom DNA Effect

This experiment was carried out by physicist Dr. Vladimir Poponin, who was interested in light energy (in this case photons) with human DNA and their relationship. In simple terms, he created a vacuum within a small tube of glass ensuring that the tube was completely clear of any pollutants of any kind, albeit light particles which were still present. The first part of this experiment was to measure how these photons were dispersed around the tube with findings showing particles dispersing randomly all around the tube bouncing off each other. In terms of particle patterns, it was like a gas filling a void.

The second part of the experiment is more interesting. Upon putting a human DNA sample into the tube, there was an unusual effect on the photons with them becoming aligned instead of random, which shows that genetics can affect our surroundings on a quantum level.

The third part of the experiment was still more interesting. Upon removing the DNA sample and measuring the patterning and structure of light particles, it was discovered that the photons remained aligned in the absence of the DNA sample. In essence, DNA creates a field that is relational to light particles and potentially matter itself.

The second experiment was carried out by the US military whereby DNA was taken from a donor and transported to another room in the same building, the donor and the sample becoming separated. Scientists put the DNA sample in a machine that was able to measure any effects that might occur on the sample when prompted. While in the other room the volunteer was then given various emotional stimuli to evoke happiness, sadness, or other human expressions, which were recorded as various peaks and troughs on a scale depending on the response. The DNA was being monitored at the same time for any environmental response, and astonishingly, the DNA was also measuring peaks and troughs that were coinciding on an identical recorded scale at the same time as the volunteer. Not only were the DNA and the volunteer having the same results, but it was happening instantaneously in real time while being separated. Something was gluing the two together in order for there to be a connection that was transcending time and space. Some scientists have called this the "New Field," although it's greatly believed that it has always been there, but not seen until now. This work was then followed on by Dr. Cleve Backster, who carried out a similar experiment but with a distance of four hundred miles separating the volunteer and their DNA sample. The results were the same. Despite having a four-hundred-mile separation there was no time lag and the results were instantaneous.

The third experiment was taken to another level when the institute of HeartMath carried out further studies of this nature in the early 1990s, finding that the emotion of the volunteer was affecting the efficiency of the DNA. Happiness, forgiveness, and compassionate emotions were seen to have a scientific effect on the DNA equating to better operation and in turn attributes leading to much better cell efficiency and immune systems. Negative emotions like hate and jealousy degraded the health of the DNA and in extreme cases began to shut down the DNA completely. On a dimensional level, it can be said that emotions contributed to the fifth density idea allow for better health, while emotions that are more characteristic of the lower third realms such as fear and hate result in health issues. As you think, you are, in mind and body.

In light of this, it is possible that DNA could carry information not only on a soul level and a biological level, but also on a cosmic level. If it is the case that DNA links to past lives, could this be the reason for more and more souls on Earth being able to feel strongly about past life expressions and, if so, why are so many of them becoming younger in the age at which they recall this information? Alfie Clamp is a two-year-old boy who has become the only person in the world to be diagnosed with an extra strand in his DNA, giving him three. The case is so rare that it didn't have a name at the time of it being reported in 2011, and it is believed there are other children around the world also potentially unreported that are being born with similar characteristics. Within the starseed universe is this idea of past life records. Let us delve deeper into the spiritual attributes that are said to be held by the quantum DNA.

The Akashic Record

If we are to discover what this record is, then we need to uncover what it means. Some of the following information has been inspired directly from the teachings of Kryon (YouTube), who helped me further my understanding. The Akash (in human terms) could be translated as the representation of all the energies and past lives experienced to date. This could be concluded as having experienced consciousness on other planets or places in the known multiverse. Some Akashic readers will highlight your very first universal incarnation and others will uncover your pre-universal origins. In other words, who or what you were before you ever entered into this known universe. This is taking into account that there are multi-universes. However, we will focus just on experiences we had on Earth for now.

Often you will hear this explained as the Akashic record, which contains the personal accounts of each individual. Therefore, everyone has a personal cosmic record stored within them and this is known as your Akash. There are different ways in which the Akash can be stored, but one of the most important is within the DNA. With this in mind the Akash can also be representative of potential future events as it highlights the inherent makeup of distinctive individual lifetimes that have been experienced and their future effects. In turn, this shapes future lives with the promise of latent or unrealized talents and abilities yet to be lived or expressed during a lifetime and future lifetimes not yet had. In other words, what happened in a previous life might shape the next and so on with varying degrees of outcomes stemming back to previous events experienced. As the Akashic record is related to the past, it is important to remember how it is related to the future also as time is in a circle, not linear. The past, future, and present are all occurring at once.

Within Akashic remembrance we can begin to pinpoint elements that have shaped our soul and led us to where we are today including our personality, attributes, and even health issues, which often can relate to unresolved energies and unfinished business that have created blockages. This is why ascension and personal work is so important, as these issues and blockages need to be resolved in order to move fully into the ascension timeline. That is why a great deal of healing is occurring on Earth at this moment in time and things are coming up to the surface that can no longer be suppressed so that they can be fully realized and let go. One can't walk into the promised land holding all the baggage of a lower vibration that is held at a subatomic level within you.

Effectively you then have something called Akashic inheritance, which is carried over into your current life. This, in turn, could affect outcomes that might stop you from fulfilling various things or become a trigger driving you back into experiences or pursuits. Either way, as the vibration of Earth begins to dramatically increase, unfinished business and negative Akashic inheritance must be dropped as the new energies will not allow for its presence. This can manifest in many ways. When there is a struggle to let go of such attributes both in this life or in previous lives, a reset is often activated. The universe will push this button in our lives, and this is a message to say, the old way wasn't working. You are ready for something better now. Currently on Earth we are seeing a global reset for many people's lives and the way in which they operate on a daily basis. This is part of the restructuring that will allow humanity into a new and improved Earth. It is happening in your DNA, also.

Within the new-age world, practitioners will often discuss Akashic records. You might find yourself in a crystal shop and one of the shop assistants might lead you to a crystal that deals in Akashic remembrance or work of this nature. Sometimes this might incorporate Akashic healing or past life healing. This is where the DNA part and spirituality become combined and where we see just how deep the rabbit hole really goes. Akashic work has been known within the starseed and new-age movement for a long time, but where does it play a part?

On Earth at this moment in time there is a subgroup which many identify with as the old souls. There is an overwhelming feeling among this group of people around the world that they were once here a long time ago.

This feeling coincides with sinking island syndrome or dreams connected often to the Atlantis idea or Lemuria and often this can play out Akashically as trauma. Old souls are feeling the big changes and Akashically some are thinking, oh no, it's all going to fall apart again like Atlantis did. This could be through past life feelings, or just a knowing from dreams that uncover you being part of an advanced civilization in Earth history. This could also be said of feelings that perhaps you were in a past life more recently and it seems that more people than ever are suddenly experiencing this in a stronger way. How can this be proved without a time machine? The answer is the Akash. Often these can be the most energetic moments you experienced. This doesn't happen in a linear way, showing itself year per year, but in a dimensional way.

The Akash is outside of the logic and purview of things that might make sense, especially if you are left-brain heavy in your rational thinking. The human brain is complex, but it is only able to analyze based upon what it already knows. It struggles to analyze things that it doesn't already know about. So where do we go in order to seek these answers?

In order to answer these questions, let us back track for a short while. We have discussed that the ionosphere and magnetics of the planet are greatly changing and that these changes are likely also becoming responsible for the activity of a changing consciousness. It could be argued that DNA and the enlightenment of the human consciousness is potentially tied into the magnetic grid of Earth. It altered in recent years, and in ten years it moved more than it has over the last hundred years! This can be found in the history of the magnetic grid on Earth after 1987. This has also been known as the harmonic convergence, a very important shift in preparation for something that is coming: ascension.

This was the preparation for the Earth moving into a less dense photonic part of space that we are currently entering, becoming the first time human consciousness has ever been where it is headed. For the last 10,000 years or so we have been floating in a denser bubble of radiation that the energies of our sun have cooperated with accordingly. Suddenly it's now changing. Have you noticed anything about the sun and its activity recently? It's changing alongside global weather patterns, too. There is a relation to where the solar system is headed and traveling through in space.

This area of space has a very interesting radiation to it. Many government scientists secretly think it is dangerous or could be hazardous for humans. It is known about in high circles. What it will do is alter the magnetic field of the planet in a multidimensional way to enhance human development in evolution. It's going to change our intelligence. Just like we did with the incredible rise of technology within the last fifty years but on a much bigger level. The magnetic grid is now ready for this through its vast changes since 1987 in order for us to evolve. We needed to have the correct energetic structures in place for it.

At about 11,000 years ago at the end of the last glacial age, which was a mini ice age, there was unusual plasmic activity in the atmosphere and the magnetic grid was very different. There were mass ejections from the sun that hit the planet's magnetic field charging it with different types of plasma. It is everywhere to see. It is in the scientific ice core samples taken; it is in the magnetics that are recorded in the layers of the Earth. It's been recorded in various ways even in the rings of the core samples of ancient trees. The unbalance of Earth at that time was not able to survive, and there was an extinction event. With a mixture of scientific and spiritual understanding it is believed that humanity has gone through at least five of these events where life has tried to advance but was held back or there was a cataclysmic event. Humanity currently stands as the sixth civilization getting ready to take the great leap one last time. This planet had an atmosphere that was alive in a different way to what it is now. Through the sun's activity it charged humanity to a degree that it awakened our DNA to around 50 percent activation, it is believed. Currently it is estimated that our DNA is now active at somewhere between 30–35 percent, but opening rapidly.

Within you is an Akashic pattern fast tracking the human through again, but just in a new environment. So the newborns coming into the planet who seem much more full of wisdom and growing up faster with elements of spirituality are this way because they are naturally picking it up from their Akash. They are having a cellular remembrance and returning to the way we once were. Our Akashic records are filled with all these things and more. We have the building blocks of the past backed up by the Akash pushing us into the future. As you look into the new souls coming onto Earth at the moment, they are coming in with a confidence as light beings not stained by the older energies as the veil lifts further and further. With this, you will notice that the younger crowd will sail through the ascension energies with more grace as they arrive with an already encoded Akash and cellular composition within their DNA.

For some of the older beings on Earth at the moment who are thirty years of age or older, it is somewhat harder. Their Akashic record is more biased. It isn't going to read past lives like you look at a book in a linear way. It will begin with dreams, also. If you wonder why you are feeling the way you are feeling, it is because it is giving you things to process. Things to clear and release that were not releasable before because they need to be cleared in order to move into the new consciousness of ascension. This could be the various ascension symptoms and grand changes that so many people have gone through in the years going up to and after 2012. Things that don't serve you anymore will come knocking on your door, saying, this needs to be cleared now! No more time for delay. It could even manifest in jobs and relationships. In your DNA, that which is most profoundly affecting your life based upon the past is going to come up and face you and ask for dismissal. You will have repetitive dreams about things, people, places. That is why it is so important to not go into fear at this moment. Fear takes away your high consciousness.

Let us say hypothetically that in a previous life something

bad happened to you, or even in this life, it could be that you nearly drowned in water. You have this dream many times and you wake up at night panicking because you feel it will become a prophecy. You fear it will become your future that you will drown again. So then you stop going near water at all costs. In fact, what the dream is really about, is something that affected you before in this life or the last, and the Akash is bringing it up for you, personally handing it to you and asking you to let it go and dismiss it out of your consciousness and have it buried once and for all. This might be the same for mothers around the world who dream of their baby or child dying. Many mothers have experienced this in many lifetimes. It's coming up because it wants to be buried. Let it go. Say the words out loud if you need to. Anything that is going to create fear or problems in your dream state, it needs to be released or it is going to hold you back and slow you down. Do not reside in fear around it or decide it is prophecy. It is not. It's yourself working with yourself to get you to a better place. Next time you have that nightmare, wake up, face it, laugh, and say, thank you, Akash, for bringing this up and getting me through it. What's next?! And then go about having a fantastic day. Others will say that this is the subconscious working its magic. At this moment in time, it isn't necessary what name is given to it, working through these issues is key as dense experiences built into the cellular library won't hold light well in a higher vibratory rate. Some who cannot let go of very dense energy will change back to their nonphysical being and exit.

Old souls often have Akashic dreams with the quantum memories stored in the DNA linked with the soul. It is the classic linear human condition to take something that isn't understood and then project fear onto it. Instead project it into a metaphor. What might it mean? The Akash is conceptual, not linear. Look at your dreams in a metaphoric way, not a literal way.

In lifetime after lifetime in old energies we have had war after war and killed each other. We have lived in survival and slogged through life after life often with difficulty. Some of us have been kings and queens, but those are few and far between and we carry these things around in dreams. Just because it happened before, it doesn't mean it is going to happen again. It's old energy and you're past this now. That is why it is believed that some people on the planet at this time came here to raise the frequency and work through the old energies prior to 2012 and thus they are called lightworkers, or starseeds, but more on that in the chapter titled "Starseeds." That is why this is happening, because you can't go to an advanced place with a dark remembrance on your consciousness. You also cannot carry 3D into 5D and expect the results to work the same!

When the bad dreams come, comprehend what happened, then dismiss it and celebrate. You just cleared something and now it's gone! Do you have the courage to celebrate a bad dream? Can you handle it? Clear the ugly feeling of the dream; use the words, "I dismiss it." Once you clear your bad dreams, then you begin to move into magnificence. Get rid of the old before you get into the new. This is the same for waking dreams. That is the power of the human in these times. The consciousness of an evolved spirit. Whatever change is happening in your life, celebrate it, for it is the old souls that are the ripest for the ascension because they have been through more lifetimes garnering earthly experience. The newer souls are just getting the hang of being here for the first time. There is a soul matrix at play and different souls perform different missions at this time.

It will be the old souls who will start making the leaps of consciousness, the ones who have struggled in previous lives, perhaps even for half of the current lifetime. As we move swiftly into the new energy, the old souls will find their place in the world and manifest ideas and dreams they never thought were possible, with things finally working out when in years gone by, it just didn't seem possible to get ahead no matter how hard you tried. Nothing worked and you didn't know why. Those days are coming to an end. This is partly why souls dread doing shadow work as they feel it will be more of the same. This is an Akashic bias that is changing. It will be easier than ever going forward.

The Akash also works in other mysterious and wonderful ways. In the same way, it can bring up past abilities that might be triggered for different reasons. You might suddenly take up something creative like cooking, painting, music, writing; it could be that you enjoy working with crystals and meditating with them. All of sudden you have new hobbies or things you like to do in your spare time that literally came from nowhere, and if you had to explain where it came from you might find it hard. It could also be that you came from a soul group who all share the same attribute. Perhaps you had a brother and you were separated at birth and lived in different parts of the world and yet you both became chefs cooking the same food mysteriously. It's in your Akash, the memory in your DNA.

These experiences are not just exclusive experiences to Earth, but also experiences that you might have had away from Earth. Perhaps you were somewhere else. These Akashic records are fairly well hidden; however, more enlightened souls dream about off-world experiences. The majority of people experience the Akash in mostly earthly ways. Most human beings have no idea it is there and yet are driven by it. You might find yourself asking, so why then if I have this record inside me am I not able to access it, what is it that is stopping me? A very good question. Even the most spiritual of people on Earth have difficulty discussing past lives unless through a regression that was filmed perhaps.

The Akash is not in your brain, which is where the synapse of memory happens. So you would be trying to find this thing in a consciousness that works in a structure of brain. The Akash is not in your brain. It's in the DNA. You have a communication issue that is not conducive to the human because it is not linear, it's not able to be remembered, and there it sits regardless.

The Akash has triggers. It pushes things into your brain that allow you to feel something. So the Akash is not necessarily broadcasting who you were or when you were. The main triggers have been fear, drama, and unfinished business. They can drive you into action, or at other times inaction. This is partly due to the very low 3D energies previously experienced, but imagine an Akash that is realigning its triggers in the new energy consciousness. The higher the consciousness you allow to come through and vibratory rate in which you reside, the more the communication is changed and allowed through. This is part spiritual and part biological.

There are also spectacular exceptions to the rule. Imagine a child who is coming into their craft early on, a prodigy on a musical instrument perhaps. It could be anything but let us stay with creative forms. This child is not triggered by fear, drama, and unfinished business. The child performer who plays their instrument like a master at a young age is triggered purely by their craft, the same for an artist who at a young age paints like a master.

Psychologists would say there is no possibility of having remembrance of something that is 3D that they never experienced in their current life; however, in Akashic terms the DNA is pushing it to the synapses of brain in relation to the level of consciouness that person has. This is somewhat of a special scenario, but we see it enough to know that it doesn't fit with the synapse in the brain and memory. It is the Akash pushing something to the child which is conceptual. Lifetime after lifetime the soul will come back and take off from where they left things. There will be an unseen voice in their head saying, okay, back to the piano, off we go again, back to it! As we go up in vibration more and more Akash will come to the surface also as conceptual emotions that want to be felt and released.

For a lot of people on Earth the Akashic record can be labeled as karma. There are various forms of it, but Akashically, it is an emotional response that has been felt so often in lifetimes that you intrinsically feel you want to do it again. Karma doesn't necessarily feature the attributes of unfinished business or completion. The feeling will come back regardless. Lawyers will become lawyers, teachers will become teachers, free diving champions will go back to diving deep again, and mothers become mothers again because it is what they did in the past, it's in their DNA.

We take the example again of a family being separated at birth or even before. Imagine the grandchild becoming a military man and finally years later meeting the family he never knew he had, and it turns out the grandfather was a great military leader when he was alive. It's in the DNA the Akash is pushing through. This is also related to soul groups. Groups of souls with similar Akash. So often souls come back, and this is what they energetically remember and then they go and do that thing in their life.

Imagine a lifetime where you felt worthless in an older energy. It stores itself in the Akash. So when you come back in this life, you feel worthless and that you don't deserve to be here on Earth as validation in some form of abuse to confirm this lack of worthiness. Perhaps you know people who have gone through one abusive relationship after another over and over. Families might say that they are crazy, but on an Akashic level they are responding to prerecorded instructions, in that way, they are not crazy at all!

Past lives carry these concepts into the Akash, and they are inherited, otherwise known as Akashic inheritance. If you were a tailor or a seamstress and you love material and the feel of it and see life in terms of fashion and clothes, it's possible you did this in a previous life. It's carried over. Some of you can go to a clothes shop and feel the very essence of how those clothes are made or designed and you will know that there is something there, but you are unable to put your finger on it and it goes right into your nervous system. A knowing.

Regarding fear and drama and unfinished business, we enter a magic age now. In with the new, out with the old. Being a soul doesn't hold nearly as much weight in the world as it does now as all the energies and consciousness recalibrate. There will be a mixture of old and new talents and possibilities coming to the surface with old cycles becoming discontinued if that is where intent goes so that new patterns can be created for the new Earth that arrived in 2012. Coming into Earth now is a time where the energies will change the way we think about things, especially as our Akashic inheritance begins to clean itself up and prepare for love and light in a way never seen before. It is written in the stars.

As we begin to rise in human consciousness awareness, we begin to find ourselves playing in a new landscape. What is that landscape and how is it measured? Is there a way we can pinpoint milestones in this new landscape to navigate where we sit within it? The answer is yes. This is where we begin to vibrate up into higher levels of existence and consciousness. In understanding what these higher levels of vibration are, you begin to look at the road map and find your place within it. This is called dimensionality, and it is key to understanding the road map we are headed on.

Consciousness

With changes also come symptoms of the ascension variety. These can be uncomfortable. Imagine the lobster swimming in the ocean. For some a beautiful animal living in our oceans, for others a tasty meal! The lobster is ever slowly growing. For protection it grows a tough outer shell. As the lobster begins to outgrow its old shell the symptoms can be quite uncomfortable and even painful. It is not until this sea-going crustacean completely releases the old shell that it can breathe again and begin to grow to the next stage. This is the same with ascension in the form of challenges, emotional struggles, mental or even physical pain as you transform from a dense and lower vibrational carbon-based body into a higher vibrational being with more crystalline resonance.

It is at this time or around the year 2012 that more people all over the world began to feel these ascension symptoms and many have begun in numbers larger than ever before to document their experiences. They often manifest in various ways. Things that no longer serve your highest and greatest good will fade away or disappear in order for new experiences in your life that serve your highest path. These occur in various forms such as beliefs, routines, habits, changing jobs, relationships, or even where you live in order to search for a greater you and environments that serve who you are about to become. You may have feelings that include wanting to move to another part of the world and start a new relationship there. New beginnings and doing away with the old that often served others and not yourself are underway. In an older energy it was easy to maintain energetic pursuits that seemed right but were far from serving your highest outcomes, while in the new energy there will be more than ever a voice speaking to you, saying, "Hmmm, maybe this wasn't what I thought it was, after all. There's a light shining on where I need to be that wasn't there before."

Here are a few commonly found ascension symptoms when discussing with spiritual people from all walks of life that explore the depths of these changes. The following cannot be directly associated with ascension, and if you have a medical issue it is always advised you see a professional doctor. Despite that, these are the following "occurrences" that are happening to people all around the world since ascension began with the argument being led by those who associate having an awakening regarding the symptoms which give them their place in this list. For those of you seeking help in real time there is now an array of excellent social media support groups that are growing in numbers every month. Salvation might be found in speaking to others who are experiencing these following attributes.

1. You feel at times that you are going slightly crazy. The way you are processing life and assimilating your internal and external world seems to have changed drastically. The way you are cognizing your reality has seemingly changed and yet you are unaware of why this has begun. There might even be confusion of what has triggered it in the first place and wonderment regards how you have arrived at this very new feeling that helps you navigate a new world you are stepping into.

2. Your mental and physical state are changing including the routines and systems that you put into place that allowed you to operate in a certain way for large period of your life. There seems to be a slowly increasing awareness that structures you created for yourself depending on how you reacted to the external world are changing, with the result being that you feel you are stepping into unfamiliar territory regarding your day-to-day activities and the relationship you have with them now. There is a feeling of needing to break free from the old ways but also a wanting for things to return to the way they were before. How does one find a balance and where is this headed? one might ask!

3. There may be strong feelings of wanting to return home or go back to another indescribable place but you are not sure where. You just know this place doesn't feel right and you're not from here. In turn you begin to experiment with the idea of there being other life in the universe and explore the stars on maps on the Internet late at night. You get interested in the cosmos and find deeper meanings to life itself.

4. Synchronicity in your life is suddenly happening all around you. Coincidences that occur frequently when you least expect them that seem almost directed at you without you feeling fearful. This could include numbers. You could be driving, at work, in bed, and around you are phones, clocks, or in a book you are reading you see 22:22 number sequences repeating. Repeating number sequences such as 333, 14:14, and so on or other number patterns that are significant or meaningful to you are popping up in your day-to-day life. It could be that there is a continual alignment of events or chance encounters or happenings. This could also be the case with people you meet or reconnect with in ways that meet odds that are very small or are almost impossible. You might start seeing the relevance of messages coming through this way and through synchronistic happenings begin to encode messages, some of which could be multidimensional, an ET trying to reach you, your star family, or an angel. Often, they work this way.

5. Your diet begins to change. You have a lower desire to eat meat, especially red meat. You crave lighter and raw foods including vegetables. Your eating habits change and you have new intolerances that you didn't have before, some food or drinks you are not able to have as of late and your eating routines have changed. Processed foods and sugary drinks you liked before just don't click as they are becoming intolerable now.

6. You begin to have more moments of being at one and feeling connected with the universe. Feelings of gratitude. Appreciating more moments of calm and stillness away from the crowd. Being able to enjoy moments alone more and especially the small things in life. You desire more to be out in nature, walking among trees and the animals feeling the fresh breeze on

your skin. You develop a higher connection with animals, and they warm to you more freely than before.

7. Your physicality begins to change. There are strange aches and pains that were not there before. Stiffness in joints and skin conditions begin to change. Perhaps rashes or spots appear that you never had before. The spine, neck, and shoulders are stiffer and more fragile than before; perhaps you have experienced pressure in the head.

8. Visual abilities begin to manifest as flashes of light, orbs, or little circles of different colors appear around you. You see things out of the corner of your eye, perhaps dark shadows. You are more sensitive to light. You begin to slowly see into the parts of the visual color spectrum not seen by you before. This could include other people's auras or just etheric light wherever you are or out in nature.

9. Strong sense of feeling lost and not knowing who you are anymore. You feel the old part of yourself has gone and you don't know where it is. You want to get back to who you were, but you don't know how anymore. A sense of ego death and old belief systems are fading away along with old personal identities. You feel disassociated or fragmented as you grow into a new higher consciousness and become a multidimensional being as if you are invisible to others, or as if you are a total stranger. Strange moments where you feel others can't hear you, or you can't hear or see them, not relating to others in the same way as before and craving people who are similar or who understand you better. In other words, as you vibrate higher, you become less visible to some people as they are stuck in a lower reality and vice versa.

10. Your vibration especially in heightened emotional moods causes interference for electrical appliances such as lights flickering, bulbs blowing up, batteries suddenly dying, or your computer at work not functioning, the more stressed you get. In the same vein electromagnetic frequencies such as phone masts and inner-city frequencies leave you feeling drained and anxious.

11. Time begins to distort, and it seems there are unusual shifts in relation to time itself and the events and memories within it. There are moments when you feel time both slows down and

Starseeds: What's It All About?

speeds up within your day or year with the resulting feeling that you are not able to complete or conclude all that you wanted to achieve and that time is running out. In turn this is producing a sense of urgency. Other feelings include that you are ready for an event, something unforeseen is drawing close and you must be ready for when it happens. You experience more déjà vu and other similar happenings.

12. Headaches and migraines that are hard to relieve. Experiencing odd feelings in the head/skull area, on one or both sides of the head. A pressure in the head that can leave you feeling lightheaded with a pulsating heat near the crown area as if your head was in a vise that day. Other sensations include jolts of energy, static electricity, pinpricks, pins and needles, tingles, or suddenly feeling that you have just felt a tremor or a jolt on the ground where you are standing.

13. Erratic sleep schedules or disrupted sleep. You have become more of a night person, perhaps with unsettling awakenings often between the hours of 2 a.m. and 4 a.m. for no apparent reason. You may even experience insomnia and fatigue, followed by huge bouts of sleeping. Suddenly experiencing lucid dreaming or astral projection. Your dreams are more intense than ever. Your subconscious is working through a lot more issues and ideas in your dream state than ever before.

14. Your emotions are more erratic than before. You go through more swings of happiness and sadness and everything in between. The highs are much higher, and the lows are very low. Things seem to be at either end of the spectrum with more work needed to get a balance.

15. Your environment or surroundings can feel like a dream world or alternative reality. Things can seem out of place, distorted, or unusual, leaving you feeling confused, spacey, or ungrounded. It feels safer to be in your inner world and feeling more introspective in an environment with familiar things or pleasures like music, art, books, film, or just a comfy bed or room with safe memories. Time away from family, friends, or the world around you begins, partly because you don't relate to them or their ideas in the same way anymore. You have stepped outside or past

that moment, including hobbies or past pursuits that no longer serve you. You seek sanctuary more than ever before and the noise of the world drains you more. Even the thought of spending time with people that might take from your energy is too much; you would rather stay at home and feel at one with yourself with a good book or a loved one. Inner self-reflection has become a lot more important. You struggle to see the level of importance that people in your life put on pointless or mundane activities or behaviors that now seem somewhat childish to you, including political views and the importance of the way others think the world should work from their "lower vibrational viewpoint."

16. Your chest and heart especially seem to go through an almost frightening period lasting anywhere from two to six months of palpitations and thumping inside your chest, including electrical like pulsations that shoot through your chest especially when energies are intense. There are even times you think you are going to have a heart attack so you visit your doctor and have tests with nothing being found.

17. Ringing in the ears. This is a very interesting phenomenon that is occurring more than ever. It is important not to get this confused with a condition called tinnitus, which is associated with the damage of the apparatus of the ear itself. People on Earth are currently experiencing a very high-pitched frequency that can be explained as hearing a tone almost inside the head itself. There are many cases of visits to the doctor with reports of this ringing, and upon checks, there is no sign of ear damage at all. As a note from the author of this book, if you feel you have ear damage, do see a doctor, but do not rule out this ascension symptom. As we discussed earlier, the Earth is moving through a part of the universe not traveled before. As we journey through new energies and magnetics, photons pass through us creating what is in this case, clairaudience or the supposed faculty of perceiving, as if by hearing, what is inaudible. This is not something to fear or be worried about. It means you are transcending, gearing up, and moving through the frequencies. You're hearing the higher dimensions and receiving downloads. As large energies arrive to Earth from the cosmos the ringing

in the ears can begin. Many starseeds have coincided periods of ramped-up ringing within the head as space weather approaches.

This has been experienced also by those who are not awakened but who have entered a pocket of vibration. Imagine that you have driven high up a mountain or been on a plane and as you travel through altitudes your ears "pop" and then return to normal. The same is happening here. You are going through pockets of energy picking up new frequencies as actual audio. It can be said that the cellular and nervous systems are like a tuning fork that resonates to what is broadcast to us with our antenna translating the sound as a very high-pitched buzzing or ringing. This can be amplified by astrological events, solar flares, or energy shifts. It is important to remember you are part of the universe and not just Earth. Often in our daily lives there is so much noise, especially in the modern world, that we do not hear these frequencies. More often than not they come at times of reflection and connectedness.

This can be triggered by various things. Perhaps you have a religious or spiritual experience. It could be that you had a powerful meditation, and the ringing began shortly thereafter. Others have reported having enlightening experiences using drugs such as marijuana or other hallucinogenic drugs that have activated this ringing after coming back to their normal state. There are also experiences to this phenomenon that can be linked to electromagnetic frequencies (EMFs) which are not natural. Living in a city there are EMFs being blasted at you on and off throughout the day. Some people are very sensitive to EMFs and can feel them in their physical body, which can cause agitation. EMFs can also manifest as a different type of ringing. As we pass through new energies, it has been argued that we are receiving not just clairaudient downloads, but also other levels of conscious downloads, which can be the energetics of the multidimensional realm, which are shifting at all times, changing the frequency that you are in. This is why it is so important to ground the natural EMFs from the cosmos into the physical body—moving away from WIFI and 5G cell towers and phone masts. Either way you will be more sensitive to EMFs as they increase from both

Ascension

categories which are both natural and unnatural. Use the ringing in the ears to navigate as a signpost for what is incoming.

For individuals who are first experiencing this, it is a hard visualization to represent; however, it can be explained as walking through waves all the time, some cosmic, some EMFs, and even your WiFi. In turn you are passing through different waves of consciousness that are energetically being emitted in the fields around you depending on what is happening on an energetic level and what is available within the cellular body itself. This is being amplified by the photonic light realms we are passing through in space, which are actively passing through our magnetosphere to the surface of the Earth and, in turn, giving us the high-pitched sound that will ring, and then dissipate. More often than not, the ones that come in and are more of an irritation feeling, which does not dissipate, are EMFs of unnatural origin. These also do eventually go away; however, they are a longer wave. The frequencies coming from the photon belt dissipate faster because as they land, they connect to the Earth differently and are absolved more economically in a way that could be argued as being far more natural. EMFs from radio towers and phone masts are not as "natural" and thus cause irritation to those of us that are more sensitive, and dare I say it, sometimes you might be getting both. This is why it is best to get out of the city and be in nature so that you can connect in a purity of state that is less bombarded with external noise and interference while encoding natural cosmic radiation.

It is useful to understand the anatomy of the ear itself and how this works regarding the brain. There is an important part of the ear called the cochlea. The cochlea is the part of the inner ear involved in hearing. It is a spiral-shaped cavity in the bony labyrinth. It has been theorized that this part deep in the ear might be part of the hearing of these frequencies alongside the acoustics of the head and brain itself. In each the left and right ear sits the cochlea deep inside. It's widely agreed that the right and left ear both have different parts to play in the interpretation of this ringing with its relation to the brain itself.

In esoteric terms, the left ear, which works with the left

part of the brain, is a radio receiver and anchor for translating frequencies to do with the Earth plane, which is more physical, while the right ear is receiving and coding data at a cosmic/God level (photons from space), which is more to do with spirituality and multidimensionality. For those who are awakened, a combination of one or the other or both can be experienced. It has been said that angels or nonphysicals who are trying to contact you or give you a signal can do this through the ringing in the ears. If this is the case, then this would be a controlled ring in the right ear, which is connected to the more spiritual, less logical right side of the brain. In more scientific terms, this translates to the nervous system and the brain working together through various neural pathways affecting the ears and cochlea, causing a vibration/ringing. This can activate such parts of the brain as the pineal gland while transmuting messages of light photonic energy, which is heard as the language of sound. Other names also express this as the language of light. This is not to be confused with spoken light language, which is more commonly channeled verbally. Spoken light language can have a tonality mixed with some Eastern and African sounds with strong Rs and very fast vowel and consonant sounds. It is said that the brain does not need to understand the meaning as it is felt at a soul level regardless which is helped in by the higher self.

It is important for those who are having changes in their life at the moment or might go through changes in the future, to align yourself if you do experience any of these symptoms. There are many healers, shamans, and such like people on Earth who since 2012 or around that time seem to have lost their abilities to heal, or don't read the energy as it was before and wish a return to the old energy in which they were embedded. This of course isn't possible as we can only move forward in global consciousness and not back. You just have to tune into the new frequency. It's there and it's improved. Likewise, it can also be said for some entertainers and comedians who simply didn't know how to be funny anymore as the feedback from the new energy was not the same.

Once you have reached a higher level of being mentally

and physically, there is an issue in going back for this would result in a lack of ease, hence the word disease, which is when the body falls into a lower vibration and becomes susceptible to negative energy externally while internally controlling your biological sovereignty. There have been those who have experienced higher states of consciousness and feared the enlightened ideas it showed them and decided to go back to old ways and found ill ease or dis-ease. Returning back to a less enlightened way of living such as before will open you up to illness. Once enlightened there is no going back. This is why some souls fear enlightenment. They know that intuitively it will change them forever into a high consciousness, but they prefer the safety of the same familiar old energies to the point whereby some souls will have to exit Gaia early as the hardware (the body) has not shifted to the incoming energies. The mind and the body work hand in hand.

In the same vein, spontaneous regression in cancer patients has been seen in patients on the other end of the spectrum. The individual managed to reach a higher state of consciousness, unconditional love, belief, or even reach just a few seconds of fifth-density existence in which these destructive cells are unable to live. As with other beings in the universe, disease is something of the past as fifth-density beings live in a higher state of joy and consciousness that lower forms of consciousness cannot exist in, such as cancer. Cellular activity in a lower consciousness energy has more prevalence to become active when the mind and body are not connected and diet is not carefully regulated. One also attracts to them what they most fear and think about! If you fear catching a virus and believe that you are prone to doing so, on an energetic level your consciousness is programming your listening body into readiness to receive these thought-provoking desires.

One must stay in a state of awakenment or thinking about new ideas for the future, listen to your inner being, the voice in your head, and see where the positive ideas lead. This is how the higher self works. It is best to stay calm and understand that better things are to come. If you are in a place where you do not feel the energies, or your life is not as it was, try changing up your routines or practices and have a little fun with them until it clicks. Grounding will help facilitate this. When souls speak of leaving Earth and this being their last time here it is often because they are not grounding to Gaia. When you are fully in your body and grounded that is when the magic seemingly is introduced to you again and you wish to remain here having worked through stagnant energies in the lower meridians of the body or chakras as some people call them.

All that you need and want is in front of you, and with some turning of the dial on your inner radio, you tune into the new station, finding life experiences that are better than before. The same is said for healers, for example. Many healers around the world tuned into the new radio station and found better rewards. So be open to new paths and new ventures, new possibilities, and the letting go of old structures that do not serve you anymore while listening and trusting that inner voice.

There is importance in the state of your mental being. Joyfulness and happiness are literally felt by the cells in your body. You will also be more of a vibrational match for your star family and angels in these mental states with messages coming through more easily. A joyful happy person resonates at a higher frequency and attracts more synchronicities than other people or experiences resonating on a lower frequency which are naturally brought to you through the powerful laws of attraction, which has been characterized by the Hawkins scale of enlightenment. Beginning to view change as a blessing is key in leading to something greater than you could have imagined. Change is good as is learning new things in life. Let go of negative emotions and thought patterns blocking you going into a new energy and learn to live in the now because living in the past is depression and living too far in the future is anxiety.

As higher consciousness is achieved, the very cells in your body will listen to you. The more you fear getting spots on your face, you manifest your fear into reality and spots appear. Where you put your intent and focus is where you will manifest especially when going into fear and anxiety. It is important to manifest from a positive state of being that is balanced. The human body is also evolving in these times. Have you ever considered talking to it?

The very cells in your body are just waiting to connect to you personally and have you take command of your own wonderful vessel. Perhaps give your body thanks in the shower every day and speak with it, you might see interesting results! When the soul enters the body, it is awaiting direction from the boss so that there can begin a relationship that keeps you in health.

It is important as we move forward to try new things and see life in ways never cognized. The air we breathe itself is alive and the world is ready and listening to your every command in order to give and let you receive the things you want. There is a field that surrounds you at all times. It is in the universe and doing all that it can to bring a positive outcome to you. Believe in miracles everyday as part of your consciousness and embrace life changes because as you evolve your life will change around you very fast going into these high incoming energies. The past of least resistance will flow like water and find its way to the ocean eventually.

Spirituality

There is a very important question. It negates all religions, races, and ages. The question is, who am I? It can be argued in many ways. Here is a simple explanation in spiritual terms of who we all are. We are spirit. A soul. We came to Earth using a physical vessel to have an earthly experience and grow. This is done through a journey gaining experience while accessing scenarios that teach us life lessons for the soul's development in order to expand. Earth for a long time has been a lower density experience, and often these are the hardest schools for souls to learn through. Perhaps you have heard the saying, that person is an old soul? There are people on Earth who have a knowing; it could be that they feel they have been here before or perhaps lived in a specific place before or feel like they were a particular personality before.

Usually this can be triggered by people and places. Perhaps there are lessons still unlearned and when you move to a new town or city, your heart begins to feel that light, like a moth being drawn to the flame, that feeling of coming home without the comprehension of understanding why. These are some of the parameters of the "who am I" question. You sometimes intuitively know you are in the right place at the right time, but you aren't sure how you got there and this is partly Akashic also. Is humankind an anomaly randomly evolved on Earth and all alone in the universe? Is there a reason we are here and what is that plan, if any, and why would we be on a beautiful planet, in a universe with more stars and lights in the sky than all the grains of sand on Earth? What is our purpose?

Ascension is the light that is switched on in the room which begins to unravel these questions. Earth is a free will planet spiritually. Possessions do happen, for example, but on the whole, universal law says spirit, or even beings of extraterrestrial origin, are not to interfere. "Who am I" is the ultimate question people begin to ask themselves when they question the reality around them and wonder if there's more. Ascension is not about becoming a superhuman, it is about letting go of your human limitations and unlearning what society deems you must be, do, or say through centuries of religious, political, and cultural programming that have put everyone into a linear box so that they can become controllable. The soul is divine, timeless, and limitless, but has been put into boxes because of lower human consciousness. The soul does not arrive with labels or preconceived imagery. It has immense purity.

Ascension is freedom of the soul to be yourself in any way that you choose and to create in any way that you desire. It is letting go of anything limiting that you thought defined who you were in an archaic world in order to blossom into the new you in your world. It is the unlearning of everything you thought you knew or have become while transcending the ego which is forever trying to keep you in that protective box. In an older energy the ego only felt safe with firm ideas relating to self and title, for example. In the new energies coming it will be the opposite. It is at this point that you begin to discover the meaning of life when you completely let go. It is the freedom to walk into the light. The absence of a life that is petty, mundane, boring, repetitive, or confusing bound by parameters that we feel must be in place in order to keep us safe and sane. It is discovering the true joy of life, a life worth living, and a feeling of worthiness of being on Earth at this time and the confidence to go forth and manifest anything you wish on your terms and have your needs met in abundance while enjoying both the physical and nonphysical world. So many in the spiritual world came from a place where the physical world did not meet their needs so they turned to the nonphysical. The new energy is about coming into that balance and unlearning polarities created by lower density often disguised as spiritual bypassing.

It's an expression that manifests in the person feeling and knowing that, yes, they are a beautiful soul, this is my time, I am meant to be here, and my presence is so very important on Earth. It is the thing you have been longing for deep within yourself, the thing you have been crying for, and the thing you have been praying for at night when you couldn't sleep, which now comes into manifestation with ascending. There is no school, exam, or formula to this. It is about choice, this choice to go through the ascension process, and get out of the many cycles of lifetimes on Earth that had you coming back learning difficult lesson after difficult lesson and releasing all the things you have believed in the past so that you can move into a new freedom of self-expression. As you move up in vibration, these levels begin to unlock for you as you effectively see through the matrix and the veils it has blinded you with. Your reliance on the external world matters less and the inner world becomes more important. Addicts often need constant stimulation from the external world, whereas the ascended masters took everything from within. This is because you are a part of the God creator. It is inside you.

As you raise your spiritual awareness and energy, you center more divine light into the physical vessel where it is anchored, dissolving darkness. In spiritual terms this includes the expansion of the aura which often boasts wonderful colors depending on your own signature. The more light your aura holds, the more you will light up a room and people will choose to be in your presence as you light them up, too. A high consciousness is attractive. This is why many followed and sat with the masters.

As you grow, so will your light body and people will be drawn to your 5D energy without you having to explain the ascension process or do anything at all!

The auric field can be up to eight meters wide like a huge bubble around you. It is for this reason that in the past you may have been in a room with someone else and there was an unexplainable feeling that you didn't feel compatible with them and left the room, or perhaps switched seats on a train or plane as your field entered theirs and a discord manifested. Your new improved light body will be interacting with those around you in a profound way unseen that quantum physics will catch up with.

Next is the chakras. These are spiritual energy points of the spiritual body. Often people in trance or the spiritually advanced see and express these parts as colors. This is why spirit will identify people on Earth first by their energy frequency signature, while on the other side of the vale being able to see the quantum array of colors that are out of our visual light spectrum. We have energy around us at all times. These are anchored in different ways. Aside from being spiritual or not, you can see the relation that these things create in real life.

Below is the universal chakra system that ethereally maps out the energy points on the body and a basic analysis of these meridians. However, our consciousness precedes us at all times and you begin to see a pattern of how it shuts down the energetics of the body or opens it depending on free will.

Crown (Cosmic Energy) Violet Blocked by – Ego attachment

Third Eye (Insight/Seeing) Indigo Blocked by – Illusion (trapped in the matrix)

Throat (Your Voice/Truth) Blue Blocked by – Lies

Heart (Love) Green Blocked by – Grief

Solar Plexus (Will Power) Yellow Blocked by – Shame

Sacral (Pleasure) Orange Blocked by – Guilt

Root (Suvrvival) Red Blocked by - Fear

As you can see from the above, negative and limiting ideas greatly take away from our power and slow us down from being who we really are. In keeping these parts of yourself in check, you begin to open and evolve; this is when DNA becomes activated as you move into alignment with divine synchronicity so that all around you things begin to mysteriously "click" into place like never before. Or for those that do not believe in spirituality, it could be said that you are "in the zone," completely connected to everything, you can't put a foot wrong, everything you touch turns to gold all the time. Aligning and healing all your chakras is a good way to heal and get spiritual focus.

There are a multitude of ways to align your chakras which can be found in books and on the Internet. It's well worth practicing. Upon doing this it unlocks all the energies in your body allowing you to spring out of bed in the morning without needing that large coffee to get you going. It also bangs out all of the bent parts of your radio antenna which connects you to the stars and more.

The ancient religion of Hinduism has known about these great practices for thousands of years, and practitioners have had the ability to awaken themselves into higher beings using breathing techniques, yoga, and meditation. They believed and taught in the power of the kundalini, which means in Sanskrit "coiled one," a divine energy believed to be located at the base of the spine associated with the power of the divine feminine. The Sanskrit word kundal means circular and it has been referred to as a coiled snake. Imagine the chakra system as existing on a single electrical circuit that runs lengthwise up the spine with lights at spaced locations of each of the chakra points. As the kundalini rises and travels up the spinal column, it passes through each of the chakras on its way helping align them and work together. Where masculine energy has been about doing and action, the kundalini is the creative feminine energy linked to creative wisdom and evolution. It has been portrayed as a snake coiled three and a half times around the spine. The kundalini can lie dormant at the base of the spine for a lifetime. When awakened and aligned this powerful experience helps to dissolve blockages, and in turn frees up cosmic energy. As blocks are freed in the body, so are they in the mind.

Kundalini awakening is a very mystical thing triggering physical, emotional, and sometimes even psychic capacities causing major shifts in your perspective. It is the process of releasing negative programs running in the mind, limiting patterns, and delusions of separation of self.

However, understanding this is important as those journeying through the awakening of the kundalini often experience levels of ego death and similar mental structures loosening or fading away entirely. Expanding into the unknown too fast is often disorienting, causing an unfamiliar feeling in which people lose grip on reality as they knew it. On the other side of the argument, it could be that they are awakening to who they really are, experiencing baby steps into becoming a higher sentient being or just evolving into the better half of their life which doesn't have the old limitations. Imagine the power to experience new levels of perception in your job, in relationships, and to begin behaving like an ascended master! A place where you don't spin drama, do not react to dramas, and live in balance as you float above it all. Did you ever notice people with low vibration constantly attract drama in their lives and the ones who are in higher consciousness seemingly float above it all with more ease?

Living in balance is felt by the very cells in your body. Stress, anger, and anxiety for prolonged periods are ways of living in unbalance felt by your cellular structures, which can result in illness. Your body is listening to you all the time. This includes the ownership of health problems you concrete into your reality such as, "I have this problem, I have this illness, I have that issue." As you take ownership of these negative energies they manifest into reality and the universe then confirms that which you are thinking and speaking. Be careful of what you take ownership of, especially with your words. Words increasingly will manifest faster in a new energy. In conclusion to all of this, going into a high consciences will all be about balance in all areas of your life, but within the physical and nonphysical.

Shadow Work

Why is shadow work so important, and why is practicing only love and light so disadvantageous? We have been programmed within the 3D matrix to be disconnected from the world, source energy, and ourselves, which in turn allows us to become more easily influenced by the external reality often sold to us without our permission. We have lived in a very low consciousness reality for so long that we have amassed a huge undeleted folder in our subconsciousness ruled by the ego called the shadow self. This can represent latent or hidden attributes, some powerful, but many which are attributed to the parts of ourselves we do not wish to acknowledge as they have stemmed from adulthood, but usually childhood trauma.

To access 5D we must become whole, so that there are far fewer of these subconscious blockages and 3D programs running that rule our lives from hidden places that we are not in control of and often hidden in the root and sacral meridians. We cannot carry these heavy bags into a higher density and if anything they will slow us down. This is part of ascending so that we can heal karmic, ancestral, and Akashic issues within this lifetime and previous lifetimes that are coming to the surface for dismissal now. Creating a reality of only love and light is denying your traumas both in this life and other lives that your higher self is now forcing us to deal with so that we can become enlightened spiritual beings. To live in only love and light is to live in an illusion based on denial of issues caused living in lower densities and the resonance it still carries. While it is exciting and fun to live only in love and light and feel the euphoria of this plane of existence, it is also a very difficult balancing act which, when toppled, comes with a heavy fall that creates far more unbalance than balance. This is why some lightworkers and starseeds within the spiritual community become so triggered and unbalanced by anything that is not light. Light is blinding and knows no limitation. As light energy and vibration arrive on Gaia it is shown within us. This can be unnerving, but very rewarding.

The masters were creators of realities and champions of duality. They knew that inside themselves darkness had been mastered so they never never triggered. With this knowledge they did not need to maintain a forced level of light and love, and there was nothing to fear in the void or absence of love and light because they had fully conquered themselves becoming whole. It was not necessary to overcompensate with more light and love to feel better about the darkness they had not conquered either from past lives or childhood trauma. This is what we must do as we move into higher densities; we must become balanced, neither indulging in either side so that we can become masters within the only planet of free will in this galaxy—Planet Earth, otherwise known as Gaia. One must not drown in the darkness but one must not be blinded by the light. Polarity will not help in the great reset and unlearning that the human brain needs as it ascends as polarities become blocks for new cosmic energy and learning. Those who will find mastery fastest going into these higher energies will be those of compassionate detachment and observational neutrality, who stay balanced and spend more time observing then reacting.

In an older energy our shadow selves were so deeply buried and hidden by the ego that in some cases it became hard to even trigger them. As light grows, life and the people within your reality will trigger our darkness more and more so that it can wave a flag at you, saying, "Finally, you brought me to the surface, here I am, you can see me now, I'm ready for acknowledgment and dismissal!" Love and compassion are so important in a higher vibration because they allow us and others to do our shadow work without judgment and reach higher consciousness, offering a safe platform upon which to carry out this work while still receiving intuition from our star family and spirit who are working with us at all times.

If we are not giving ourselves and others a platform of nonjudgment, then we are not only denying something inside of ourselves, but also the space for others to grow. The result of this is that planetary ascension slows down and the realization of a 5D collective consciousness in unity is not achieved in a timely manner as more separation has in fact been created. This is partly why it is also so important to love yourself to facilitate the light that is needed in shadow work so that you can direct more light into shadowy places. Dark cannot be defeated with more dark.

In achieving and practicing shadow work it gives us a greater sense of self and thus the world that is around us. As our personal awareness increases so does our awareness of the outer world for what it really is as opposed to the other way around. A higher knowledge from the inner world gives us perception of the outer in terms of density perception, also. It becomes clearer at which density we are fluctuating within. In very simple terms, the outer world begins to trigger us less as the inner work has been done. People of a high consciousness can work in very stressful situations and thrive without the external being internalized as stress. You can watch a master work in an arduous situation and yet always maintain a smile, compassion, and other higher states of being. People of high consciousness do not sweat the small stuff and allow for the small dramas of life to grow from seeds into trees.

Our shadow is always with us and we can never disconnect from it. It is also much easier to observe someone else's shadow forgetting that when light shines on us no matter where we are, our own shadow is cast whether it is in a room or outdoors—that we cannot escape. So to try and escape something that is unavoidable is to live in the illusion of denial. This in turn leads us to further egocentric issues and other seeds that can grow into depression and disease. The other polarity of this is spiritual by passing in a state of permanent light and light accelerated by activism in trying to take you out of your body, all the time not withstanding that we will be taking our physical vessels with us into the new Earth. Accepting our shadow opens up portals into greater 5D attributes such as authenticity, creativity, energy, and personal awakening which is the frontier upon which mastery begins. The shadow is the "dark side" of our personality because it consists chiefly of primitive, negative human emotions and impulses like rage, envy, greed, selfishness, desire, and the striving for power. Negative emotions like these can be used positively when we realize we consciously have them.

Carl Jung, the great Swiss psychiatrist and psychoanalyst who founded analytical psychology, wrote, *"There is no light without shadow and no psychic wholeness without imperfection."*

When we come to terms with our shadow self it improves relationships, creativity, perception, physical health, and energy and removes repression of self, allowing psychological integration and maturity, something our angels and the ETs want for Earth badly! All of this is achieved through cultivating self-compassion, grounding and centering, nurturing self-awareness, being honest with yourself, and for the very brave, recording your own personal discoveries! These are all tributes that are real work for the soul that are felt by the body and the DNA. A low consciousness paired with self-esteem issues removes years from your life. Look in the mirror every day and tell yourself how wonderful you are, how necessary you are, and remember to allow your shadow self to be present without it controlling you or others. This is 5D work at its finest—the quantum characteristics of lightworkers performing in an ascended planet. Many starseeds wish to bypass through to the crown (seventh) and third eye (sixth) meridians of the human vessel having negated the very first one, the root, where all these issues happily fester waiting for dismissal! I am using the chakras as a way to paint a picture here, but used metaphorically, the meaning is the same. Entire books have been created on the art of shadow work. Before carrying out this magnificent and rewarding effort, one must understand what it is first and why it is important. Without the why and what, shadow work especially more than many spiritual practices becomes void. Starseeds come to Gaia raising their vibrations at this time, but they also came to do the other 50 percent of their mission—to work through and release dense Akashic and emotional issues trapped in the subatomic make-up of your body and cellular DNA. You cannot go into a high consciousness with a dark remembrance, be it subconsciousness or consciousness.

⋆ 2 ⋆
Starseeds

We have touched on ascension and how that might work and the experience you might find yourself undergoing. It is a truly great subject that has many intriguing levels. However, ascension can't happen by itself, and there is work to be done in order to get the rise in vibration fully into play on Gaia. The following is an accurate representation of something that millions of people around the world are feeling at this moment in time. It is a phenomenon that can be observed on social media globally with groups expanding daily. It is a "feeling" not a religion. Something governed from the internal not the external. Starseeds do not have a leader or doctrine or rules in which they must operate. No one can enter the "church" of starseeds, it is simply a knowing or a feeling you resonate to with only one goal, light overcoming darkness and healing the human collective and Gaia restoring it back into its true self and the golden age that should always have existed as we return back into Aquarius. That is the starseed ethos. Starseeds cannot be controlled and it is neither a cult nor an organization.

Historically a religious person will do what they are told, no matter whether it is right or wrong. The spiritual person (starseed), however, will do what is right, no matter what they are told. This is why ultimately they cannot be governed by religion, because no man-made construct can put a cosmic soul in a box, read its rules, and expect it to become formatted in a way that diminishes its divinity and grand nature. Starseeds are born with this inside of them. They are the system busters coming in at this time to change systems on Gaia.

Mother Earth (Gaia) will help with ascension, but

someone has to get in the driver's seat. This is the work of the starseeds. Starseed is a general term that encompasses many of the souls coming to Earth at this present moment; however, there are other names and we will cover these, also. Often there will be one of these in a family unit that society calls the black sheep, or the odd one out. They are from the stars planting seeds of energy and knowledge; hence, starseeds. It is important to understand that Earth has been visited by many souls and beings for billions of years and souls have been coming to Earth's free will lower dimensional experiment of separation from self and God experience for long periods that our galactic neighbors call eons, a quota of very large proportions of time often relational to one billion years, although some claim it is 0.5 billion.

Before we begin fully on current transitional news, there are some important honorable mentions that need to be addressed such as how seeding works and how within starseed folklore the Pleiadians took a leading role in helping seed Earth.

Seeding is a galactic responsibility of sorts and is often addressed when a civilization reaches a certain level of advancement both spiritually and technologically by which they are able to seed a part of themselves onto another planet. It is widely expressed that the Pleiadians were the seeders of Mu, otherwise known as Lemuria, and they crossed their genetics with ours giving us the potential quantum part of our DNA that is dormant. This is expressed as twenty-three pairs of chromosomes with the twenty-fourth being quantum as we discussed earlier.

The Arcturians, who are a very distant expression of Earth people in the future, reached a stage in their evolution and dimensional awareness whereby they seeded the Pleiadians. The Pleiadians are approximately one million or so years in advance ahead of Earth and are often seen as our cosmic brothers and sisters while looking very much like us with their humanoid features, albeit a little taller. In much the same way that an Earth parent might lovingly give birth to a son or a daughter, advanced civilizations do the same looking at their creation lovingly from afar without interference. Parents give birth to children and civilizations give birth to civilizations. When this becomes advanced enough, it becomes interplanetary. This is how the Arcturians over a million years ago seeded the Pleiadians, who in turn were granted access by what is known as the Galactic Federation, who gave permission to seed Earth. Often in seeding there is a transference of genetic coding much like Earth parents giving birth. However, in early seeding stages often there will be way showers and originals who will stay from their home planet and offer themselves to the birth process and become inhabitants, which is noted as being very honorable. Some have referred to the very first being the 144,000. Let us begin with some galactic history, the kind they don't teach in school.

Galactic Earth History

There is a great deal of debate regarding Earth history and the events that have transpired over millions of years in our galaxy and specifically our solar system. Earth science has estimated that our universe is 13.8 billion years old with the Earth being 4.5 billion years old. As far as awareness goes, it is understood that in a multidimensional setting, there are various universes, hence the term, the multiverse. It is possible that there are infinite universes and that many are far older than ours. ET contactees and humans that have had contact with otherworldly beings put the universe at much older. It is said to be anywhere from 20–27 trillion years old with Earth being older at 7.5 billion Earth years. As ever with Earth science it seems to be limited to beliefs held only at this present state of understanding of self-contained humanism.

There are a great number of accounts in literature and stories across the world regarding Earth's hidden history including a variety of dates and differences in terms of Earth years and durations of time in which "things," "beings," and "people" happened. What is consistent, however, is that the wider picture generally explores the idea that humanoid species of various different types have been battling Draconian/Reptilian forces for as long as records go back. Regards the Earth, a mixture of all of these beings have visited, fought each other, or left some trace of themselves, be it DNA or other traces that are genetically stored within the human genome. Other remnants exist of nuclear fallout such as various particles found on Mars and on other continents on Earth that are of radioactive nature usually only found after the explosion of a nuclear device.

Mars and especially Earth hold clues to what scientists refer to as weapon signature isotopes including uranium, thorium, and radioactive potassium, which allude to a timeline long before man having nuclear abilities or at the least experiences of this nature.

An article published via Fox News, April 1, 2011, spoke with scientist Dr. John Brandenburg, who stated, "The Gamma ray spectrometry taken over the past few years on Mars shows spiking radiation from Xenon 129, an increase also seen on Earth after a nuclear reaction or a nuclear meltdown, including the one at Chernobyl in 1986 and the disaster in Japan earlier this month. There seems to be a reasonable closure between the number of fissions required to produce the Xenon 129 enhancement and the amount of energy required to toss material to that point on Mars. This massive nuclear explosion on Mars seems to defy natural explanation."

When you look at Mars but especially the Cydonia region on Mars, you can clearly see perfectly shaped geometric pyramids and structures that allude to there being a settlement there. You have the famous face structure that exists and various astronauts who were skeptics have publicly spoken out that the chances of these structures being natural are almost impossible. Buzz Aldrin openly talks about there being monoliths on the moon of Mars, Phobos; you can search for this clip on YouTube. On top of all of this there are the countless past life regression recalls from people that experienced a nuclear devastation on Mars and saw it being wiped out in one day. This would align with the evidence of there being elements existing only after atomic weapons have been detonated.

As you can see there is evidence not only for intelligence prior to modern man, but the possibility that nuclear devices have been active and used far back into the past within our solar system. There is a history of discussion that in the galaxy detonations of unknown origins have happened. Upon channeling the Pleiadians once, Barbara Marciniak referred to the Anunnaki using this technology themselves in Earth's great past. So we are aware that there is rich history of nuclear misuse in our galaxy but specifically our solar system.

The Pleiadians themselves underwent a great nuclear extinction that took much time to recover from which is why they look upon humanity so proudly knowing that we are ascending with more grace than they did. In various galactic historical records from Alex Collier and other extraterrestrial conduits, there are multiple accounts of issues related to nuclear fallout with DNA mutation and colonies having to start again. With our galaxy there is a great knowledge of this history and its consequences. It is known to all, not just earthlings. This crosses over into regressions when practitioners of this art have stumbled upon past lives with some earthly and others off planet involving death by blast or nuclear complications involving wastelands of various descriptions. Perhaps this is linked to the various UFO sightings near air force bases around the world and in the USA who have had encounters regarding missile silos resulting in arms of the nuclear variety being mysteriously disarmed without feasible explanation. Accounts that are in the public domain are easily found. The good ETs do not like nuclear weapons.

There is also consistency in the Maldek story. Various galactic and ancient astronaut historians have varying themes on the story being that a planet called Maldek was blown apart, creating what is now the asteroid belt that mysteriously sits in our solar system between Mars and Jupiter.

There are, of course, historical things that happen after Maldek, but many New-Agers often look closer to home to the next Earth civilization which grows spiritually involving the Pleiadians. Let us explore what the starseed legend says.

The majority of accounts within this field explore the idea that the Pleiadians selected Earth for seeding and this began some 200,000 years ago ending up in the Pacific Ocean on a large island mass which became known as Lemuria or Mu. The expression of these people was a feminine softer consciousness that began to kick off 50,000 years ago lasting 20,000 years. Lemuria soon became the first human civilization to evolve spiritually, and in some isolated ways technologically more so than the Earth we inhabit now.

Much is written about Lemuria and increasingly people are speaking about this ancient history around the world flooding the Internet with its legends. There are still Lemurian souls present on Earth who stayed all this time knowing that the golden age of Aquarius would arrive following the procession of the equinoxes. These are old souls cloaked with incarnation amnesia who are awakening on Earth at this time among many others.

Lemuria is said to have sunk into the ocean and there are various arguments on why this happened. It is said that the highest peaks of that lost island make up what is known as the isolated island of Hawaii. After Lemuria there was Atlantis. This was another civilization with a more masculine energy which sadly sunk into the seas, also. Some say this was around the time of the great flood 13,000 years ago. Regarding Atlantis, it is important to understand that there was more than one incarnation of this civilization with the same name and theories suggest maybe three. Which Atlantis do you hail from, or are you Lemurian? Some souls determine which one, but timelines have become blurred. A picture is unfolding that Earth's past is dogged with nuclear mismanagement, civilization meltdown, and man-made catastrophes with civilization attempting its sixth and final endeavor (Gaia in 2012).

It is important to grasp the historical issues for the next part. For some time in the galaxy, Earth has simply been bumbling along for thousands of years evolving very slowly. Gaia has been a very low vibrational entity with singular masculine energies regarding its inhabitants. It was stuck in the lower ranges of third dimensionality and countless battles with Anunnaki/Reptilian/Draconian controls in the background encompassing various bloodlines and behind-the-scenes dominance. Empires were lost and built again, and our galactic parents periodically stopped by to watch us fighting ourselves while looking on in horror, all the while knowing that if we passed the 2012 marker that we might become adult enough to join the galactic neighborhood, so to speak.

Meanwhile, we were self-contained in our little Gaia bubble. We were causing little harm to the rest of the solar system, and our seeders, the Pleiadians, looked on in horror as humans created war and battled generation after generation. Yet they looked from afar like parents waiting until the day we would grow up and stop fighting, which only through the laws of free will could be achieved seeing as Earth was the ultimate free will experiment. The Pleiadians adhered to the divine laws of noninterference as did others and watched painfully but lovingly on. Slowly humans evolved up until a turning point when various eyes far and wide, but especially our galaxy, sat up in their chairs, so to speak, and decided to begin taking a very keen interest in earthly activities. It is this time that UFO and ET sightings drastically rose and have continued ever since.

On 16 July 1945, in a remote desert location near Alamogordo, New Mexico, the first atomic bomb was successfully detonated; this was named the Trinity Test. There was a mushroom cloud 40,000 feet high, and the detonation was bigger than expected. Here was born the atomic age in modern times.

It is important to remember that the Earth is a conscious being herself and channelers are able to articulate her energy, which is of a feminine kind. Gaia had in fact been sending out an alarm call for some time, but due to an energetic matrix constructed around her put in place by outside factions, little came back in the way of outside help from the alliances nearby. Gaia had been calling out for aid, but upon the detonation of nuclear weapons the cry amplified and was finally heard.

This did not reside well with her consciousness, and her essence went into a deeper uneasiness. For some time Gaia was aware of the low vibrational energies that interfering factions had imposed but looked on patiently. This moment in modern history was to be the straw that broke the camel's back. In turn this sent ripples out into the universe that were heard especially by our neighbors; however, it was not the final nail in the coffin. It is said that intelligent life both physical and nonphysical, looked at Gaia in that moment and said, "Oh dear, the children of Earth have found the matches and they are playing with them."

This sentiment greatly climaxed when in 1945, on 6 August, an American B-29 bomber flew over the Japanese city of Hiroshima with the atomic bomb "Little Boy." The payload was dropped, detonating in the heart of the city, killing 80,000 people instantly with an end total of 120,000 deaths. To add insult to injury, in the same year on 9 August the USA dropped "Fat Man" on Nagasaki, killing 60,000 people with a total of 80,000 or more eventually dying as a result.

When observing the universal law of one, it states that there is conscious entanglement throughout the universe, and with this in mind you can imagine the ripple that was sent out for all to see. To have been there would be the equivalent of Obi-Wan Kenobi, sensing the destruction of Alderaan in the *Star Wars* movie. He famously said, "I felt a great disturbance in the force, as if millions of voices suddenly cried out in terror and were suddenly silenced. I fear something terrible has happened."

The bombs also created disturbances within various timelines and created issues multidimensionally that became time fractal issues felt in the future as well as the present, not to mention on a soul and Akashic level. The damage was far greater than earthly understanding could conceive and was felt throughout the cosmos.

Shortly after this Gaia's alarm bell began to chime throughout the universe and it began to be heard. It was hot news among our neighbors in the heavens. Gaia put out a call for help frequency that was heard far and wide, and beings in many places felt the distress signal when they became aware of what was going on. Gaia was in trouble and this would not be tolerated any further, especially with the historical events in past times regarding nuclear weapons. For what affects us in the now, affects others in all timelines in other places. Creator itself began to set in motion timelines to restore the jewel of the universe. There was a call to action. How could Earth's vibration be raised out of war like 3D mentalities without violating free will and the divine laws of noninterference? Perhaps there was a back doorway, one that would be hidden or very hard to prove upon its inception? There was a meeting of minds within the most prominent ET races in our immediate galaxy. The sentiment of some of the ET races was "If they can't help themselves, why should we help them?" However after a vote, a final outcome was achieved that Earth was too important to dismiss and that it, along with its current inhabitance, was to be saved and the great experiment of free will and living library would continue, but on a new trajectory.

There are races of beings that we have already discussed that one day might be recognized in a wider part of our culture. These beings who have personal attachments and interests in our planet such as the Sirians, Adromedans, Pleiadians, Arcturians, and more, began to volunteer souls of high frequency to come to Earth and take human vessels. This was in order to raise the light quota of the planet so that upon 2012 a high enough collective of light would meet the target needed to tip the dark/light balance back into a light quota changing Gaia timelines and where humanity would head to in terms of spiritual, physical, and technological advancement.

There are of course old souls from all of these races that have also been here for a very long time in the lead up to 2012, but more were needed. A lot more. So they began coming in the three great waves and thus the first wave, the baby boomers, began rushing to Earth and incarnating into bodies with a mission to stop further actions of this kind and create a better existence. This is the basis upon which the coming to Earth for starseeds works. Fantastical it may sound; however, when we look at the work of Dolores Cannon, we begin to see a strange and uncanny resemblance to this story that comes to light in a grounding way.

We will discuss the different types of souls shortly, but let us take a moment to place this information into a human reality that is more believable, starting with Dolores Cannon, who put the three waves into public consciousness through a scientific practice that is often used in day-to-day life. Born in St. Louis, Missouri, USA, in 1931, she traveled around the world with her husband, who was in the navy. Being a navy wife, she followed wherever he was posted.

Dolores and her husband were from all accounts normal people with no previous exposure to the world of esoterica, spirituality, or ETs and the belief systems that surround them. She worked as a hypnotist helping people with disorders such as smoking. Dolores had worked in this field for some time until 1968 when she was asked to help a patient on the military base who had an eating issue. Dolores took the patient into her professional care and began to help her with some very interesting and unexpected results.

Upon going into hypnosis, the patient began relaying past life stories while taking on a completely different vocal tone and personality to her own. Over time Dolores regressed her again and eventually five previous lifetimes and their accounts came to light which had been unknown to both parties. This was at a time when metaphysics was greatly unknown and there were few books on anything of the kind to be found. In time Dolores began to perfect her past life regressions while working a multitude of various disorder clients and over a forty-year period became one of the leading figures in the field.

It was the clients that began to give a very interesting insight into another world over a long time period. In eagerness Dolores took on many clients of different backgrounds, colors, and creeds, none of which necessarily had any knowledge into the world of metaphysics or the great beyond. Over a period she took into account the various past lives and accounts that seemed to bubble up from the clients and began to research the various descriptions and stories of events and places. Dolores was able to match them with accurate historical detail, verifying the accounts that her clients were detailing while under hypnosis. It is also important to understand that at this point the clients themselves had no prior understanding of these details either and became quite interested in the stories they had unknowingly detailed under hypnosis.

After becoming very adept, Dolores crafted the technique into a fine skill, naming it the Quantum Healing Hypnosis Technique (QHHT). This is the art of communicating with the subconscious/higher self and also source energy. In time she became a reincarnation practitioner and would often have messages from beings coming through including Nostradamus. Via various sessions with clients of all kinds and backgrounds a bigger picture began to unfold which was quite unexpected. This included the great shift (ascension), the collapse of the Soviet Union, the pope, hidden information of importance to mankind buried in the desert in the Middle East, the *Columbia* space shuttle disaster, and visitations by extraterrestrial races.

Increasingly she encountered clients who had no previous attachment to ETs who upon hypnosis would account stories of being on craft expressing the concept of having earthly family connections but also family from the stars and connections of other kinds that are unseen. In many cases the veil of amnesia was lifted, allowing for details of soul contracts, agreements with others, and plans made prior to being in a human vehicle at this time. Accounts without scientific, religious, or media-tainted dogma perspectives began to unfold and paint a picture that were consistent through many of her thousands of clients over a forty-year period. It began to unearth a story that was current through people across the world that were identifying events and mysterious things that they would have been unlikely to have been exposed to. A picture of alternative realities, ancient history, Earth mysteries, parallel universes, and lost civilizations began to unfold and a history unwritten began to escape into the world through Dolores.

More interestingly were the clients who instead of having various lives, had only one, this being their first time. Clients were expressing that this was their first time on Earth and had come from "source energy" as a volunteer to be on Earth at this time to raise the vibration and help humanity. They expressed that some of them had been nonphysicals before and others came from source energy or were part of other off-world families and parts of the galaxy. Many expressed deep desires to return home, suggesting that Earth, to these beautiful souls, was a heavy dense chaotic place that was often a struggle to understand or live in. Many of these souls through hypnotic states unraveled a story of "hearing" the call from Earth/Gaia and answering by coming as volunteers to help from all areas of the galaxy including ones we have discussed previously.

These are the starseeds, and by way of expressing where they came from is to understand what kind of soul they have, be it Arcturian, Andromedan, or many of the other races. Hybrids also have come to light who have a mix of various genetics, some of whom walk the streets in cities of Earth and have more ET DNA within their blood than human. Some actually express themselves as angelic beings and connect to the celestial realms. As Dolores continued her work, a picture began to unfold as to how this operation was happening and she began with every patient to paint a larger picture with waves of souls coming at different times. The starseeds began coming in via three waves, all with various distinguishing attributes that lend a hand in explaining who they are. A terminology has since developed which exists now in popular culture and we will explore a little about this to help paint a bigger picture.

Indigo Children

Before we begin with the type of souls flooding to Earth at this time, it is important to give an honorable mention to a lady who was very important in not only helping add to the concept of starseeds, but giving it credibility and even color coding the concept, turning it into a color diagnosis that has worked for people still to this day. Nancy Ann Tappe (1931–2012) has been referred to as a parapsychologist and therapist. She is one of the most acknowledged synesthetes (the condition of having synesthesia) who used this neurological ability in ways even she hadn't expected growing up. She would go on to spend over a decade working professionally with psychiatrists and color experts to format her teachings and philosophy to a global audience with various books, one most notably being *Understanding Your Life through Colour.*

Synesthesia is often seen as a perceptual phenomenon resulting in the stimulation of one sensory or cognitive pathway leading to automatic or sometimes involuntary experiences in a second sensory or cognitive pathway. The word synesthesia comes from two Greek words, syn, meaning *together*, and aisthesis, giving up, *perception*. Therefore, synesthesia literally means "joined perception."

People with this condition often see the world differently from most. For example, when you look at the ocean do you smell something sweet? When you listen to a particular instrument like a trumpet does it give you an involuntary spasm in your finger? Does a violin give you a twitch in your eye? Do you feel that the days of the week have unseen meaningful colors attached to them? Another example, Thursday always feels like an orange color whereas Friday is always a light blue color but you can't explain why? Perhaps the number ten always feels like a circular shape but as you count higher you feel the numbers turn more cubic in their nature. These are the everyday occurrences of synesthesia. No two synesthetes are exactly the same. Often within musicians who have this condition one might describe C Major as a fiery red color whereas the next synesthete will understand C Major as being magenta color or associate with other objects and things linked to the six senses that we use. While this goes for words and letters this also can expand out to greater fields within the daily lives of a synesthete.

In the case of Nancy Ann Tappe, she experienced sensory perceptions regarding shapes, tastes, and colors. She would eat potatoes and taste triangles. On a broader scale she would simulate personalities with color; however, she had an extrasensory ability to actually see that color around the people the minute they walked in a room, upon which she knew a lot about someone's personality and even physicality. She began to create a color system that when given to the person in question, would be met with astonishment and validation. There was a set of colors she saw that she worked with often and the more she worked with it, the more sophisticated the analysis became. It has been widely discussed how Nancy achieved this ability. Perhaps it was seeing someone's aura, or perhaps she was tapping into a person's electromagnetic field and neurologically coordinating their energies.

Here are the basics of her concept:

Physical Life Colors: *Magenta, Red, Pink, Lavender, Orange* Physical colors are action people. They use their bodies, usually doing first and then thinking. They are the best at "going with the flow." While this color was common in our grandparents' or great-grandparents' time, they are no longer being born since we have transitioned out of purely physical times.

Mental Life Colors: *Yellow, Tan, Green* Mental colors, think and plan. They express themselves with words. They observe, discriminate, and evaluate.

Spiritual Life Colors: *Blue, Violet* Those with spiritual colors express themselves idealistically. They are here to live and work creatively. They tend to judge and pass judgment.

Floaters: *Indigo, Crystal* Floaters do not have life lessons. Indigos are the bridge to the future. Crystals come in during times of transformation to assist others in their lessons.

In time Nancy turned this work into helping people around the world with a large client base in the USA and Switzerland.

Having built a solid foundation in her work, something very peculiar began to happen that was unexpected to not only Nancy but later the world. In the 1960s and especially later in the '80s she began to see a new color that was never there before, only appearing in young children and infants on a global scale. No matter where she went or where the clients came from this new color was present in the new generation and it was unexplainable. Upon spending time with young children, she was seeing an abundance of the color indigo around the children. It is said that others in the world of metaphysics and auric workers confirmed this, also validating the new indigo color that was surrounding the new souls coming in on the planet. This is how the phrase "indigo child" was created, which has stuck as a reference ever since. It has become the go-to phrase for souls who are on Earth raising its vibration. Those on both sides of the veil have explained these souls as being "cloaked with the violet flame." With this in mind we can now go back to the work of Dolores Cannon, who unearthed through her patients the waves of souls that were coming in via three stages.

First Wave: Indigos/Light Warriors

Dolores Cannon called these the "wayshowers." Sananda has been said to call them "the leap of faith." They have also been called the flower children as they were hippies and spiritual people of the 1960s. These souls began coming in around shortly after the detonation of the atomic bombs with large amounts arriving during the fifties. This was the baby boomer generation. A great influx of souls all coming to Earth by the hundreds of thousands. This first wave of souls generally had it the hardest. There were paradigms that were so entrenched into the world that many of these souls became leaders, known voices, and system busters working through the various experiences of Earth paving better ways while inventing and helping technologies and systems evolve. It was the job of these to set the foundations for the ones yet to come. Many of this wave struggled initially as there was little in the way of help or knowledge to lean on. Books and meditation videos and information regarding metaphysics were unknown, and it was a real push for these souls. In order to create a change these souls had to become activists in what they were doing, becoming more a light warrior than a lightworker in order to push through the very dense energy. It took actions to make things happen. Throughout all the starseed souls, there is a feeling of not being from Earth or feeling different and wanting to leave here but not knowing why.

Often people associate these souls with the great changes in culture and music. These souls were part of the flower power and hippy generation with their antiwar movements and similar philosophies. Others started businesses and began to work in new ways not seen before within various fields and markets. Around this time there was a creative explosion with music never heard before such as Elvis, the Beatles, and Jimi Hendrix, to name only a few. Fashion begins to explode and more light starts to emit from Earth. In the year 2012 many of these souls would be in their forties to sixties plus approximately. Upon coming in many made soul contracts that set paths for people they would help, work and live with, and things they would achieve. A lot of the first wave stayed in spiritual amnesia for a great while acting as "closet starseeds."

Ultimately these are the souls putting down the foundation for the ones that came after. They are the ones to seed the beginnings of new ideas in the way we work, live, and operate in the world including the technologies we use. They had it the hardest and had to lay the foundations in order for the next wave.

Second Wave: Indigos/Lightworkers

It is the second wavers born in the 1970s and '80s who are as of 2012 in their twenties and thirties that are the ones who really began to tip the scales into the light. The second wave has a different outlook on life working actively in the forefront like the first wave but also from behind the scenes. Many awaken at all different times, some with a bump, and others gradually without realizing it. It is the job of the second wave to anchor the work of the first wave in energy and continued work regards the way the world operates. Often second wavers still berate on how to be of service with wide-ranging ideas in activism. The Arcturians have the best advice for the second wave. They said: "Your work is not to drag the world kicking and screaming into a new awareness. Your job is simply to do your work sacredly, secretly, and silently, and those with eyes to see and ears to hear will respond."

The second wave is here to use subtle energies and build on what has come before. This wave has found it easier to come in than the first. They often are not activists but can be more passive with advice from the other side, suggesting that some souls in this category simply need to "just be." Being here is enough and often this category is spreading light without knowing it. They might be liked in school more; they are aware of and have positive effects and changes in other people's lives that often they don't see. Dolores Cannon, in *The Three Waves of Volunteers*, explained these souls as "Antennas that unconsciously channel energy onto the Earth. They do not have to do anything, they just have to be. Their energy affects everyone they come into contact with."

Often these souls have a feeling of wanting to get their job done and get out of here. These souls have a conscious feeling of "There's no way I'm coming back here in the next life, I'm getting out of here!" In turn this group is not prone to wanting children as much as the last generation or spreading karmic routes that make this life more complicated than it need be. These souls need to remember to stay grounded and ground to the Earth having a physical experience and less of an out-of-body experience. Grounding tools and practices are good for second wavers. Grounding themselves and their energy to Earth is where the waves of joy and expression of love will flow better. Stay in your body.

There is feedback from angelic realms from across the veil regarding the second wave and the old souls waking up of a similar age. It is understood that the "I'm never coming back here" sentiment is short-lived once the soul has left the body. Upon reaching the other side there is a greater awareness of how big the real picture is and "The Plan" with many souls yearning to come back as the party is just getting started. Many souls don't want to miss out on all the hard work that has been carried out which is coming into fruition. Often souls that have left their body early are said to be in "orderly queues" to come back down to Gaia and enjoy the new Earth. This sentiment of "never again" seems to pass as does the turnaround time that it is taking souls in order to reincarnate again, becoming much faster as time continues, but especially after 2012.

Second wavers are the light that is breaking up the dark. Slowly in the news you are seeing darkness being uncovered around the world and exposed, including in the military, the financial world, big pharma, and hidden child abuse. Darkness that has gone on forever that is covered up by the ruling elite. Light coming from the second wave is beginning to break all of this darkness down and uncover it. Increasingly you see more and more in the news about dark things that are coming into the light and being unearthed, usually because of the work of others or brave souls that came forward. Catholic priests and religious officials at the top of the church are being condemned for their abuse of power over children in the largest numbers ever seen. This is also reminiscent of discoveries and hidden truths in the ground and among our communities and social systems. The truth is coming out all around us about many things, including those who have hidden in dark places that are being illuminated now. This is why some great dark news stories have come to light. It is important for the second wavers not to go into fear and get caught up in the drama around them. This dark must come to the surface for it to be dissolved and second wavers must stay balanced as this happens.

Historically Indigos within the second wave didn't like school or agree with various systems or interfering governing bodies being involved in their lives. They are rebels and are the great question askers of "Why?" Why did I have to do this because society says I do? Why must I live this way because it happened in the past? Why can't I be me?! The first wave mostly had to slog through the heaviness that was making it harder, although there was one set of paradigms and less interpretation to get lost in. The second wave Indigoes have struggles the first wave didn't have. They are the great masters of duality fighting the dark while finding their way into the light and interpreting how to play in the new energies around the 2012 marker and onward. They are living in a world that is vastly expanding out of the foundations they were raised in. They are biased Akashically and can be confused by the great shift having spent the first half in the old energy. The shift can be very confusing for this category. However, when mastered, the results are excellent.

This group has a propensity for shying away from large crowds, people, and tight spaces that are suffocating. They feel free when alone and enjoy periods of time recharging in their own sanctuary, be it a change of scenery in a room or house with their comforts and hobbies. These souls often light up a room and aren't aware of the simple and subtle powers they have. Their job is to come into contact with people and share their light with the great irony being that often they find this greatly exhausting and spend larger resting periods at home or recharging without the noise of people or crowds.

Third Wave: Crystal, Rainbow, and Indigo Children

The Indigo souls continue to arrive, and mixed in with them is a new type of soul. These children are an explosion of light on Earth and will be the ones to tip us out of 4D into 5D and higher as a collective. They have a lot less light/dark duality to sail through if any. These are the souls coming in where there is no doubt now that the dark cannot survive with the light winning as a foregone conclusion. The angels are rejoicing in the heavens, and the star families are clapping their hands in eager anticipation as we leave junior school and graduate into cosmic adulthood with the wave of Crystal and Rainbow children.

These souls are said to be coming in with DNA that is beginning further up the twelve-strand DNA evolution and doesn't have to genetically evolve as much as the first and second wave. They come in at a much higher frequency, which can cause issues for mothers. With this wave the soul frequency can be a mismatch for the mother's body to cope. Often this can result in losing the baby in some form. Upon trying a second time the new soul's vibration is then a better match to the female body and the baby can be born, yet it is not a foregone conclusion that it will be straightforward, and a larger proportion of these children come into the world via C-section, but not always. C-sections have dramatically risen since the early 1990s. Perhaps there is a link? The Pleiadians working with Barbara Marciniak have also explained how on a soul level unborn babies feel EMFs. Mothers who are constantly on their phones, devices, sitting next to the Wi-Fi router, sleeping with the phone next to the stomach, or living next to a cell phone tower can sometimes cause the baby on a soul level to abort as the constant bombardment of EMFs is too much. If you thought 5G bad for humans, try large amounts for an unborn baby.

There is also a higher propensity for these children to be born with ADHD, ADD, or various levels of being on the "spectrum" like autism and Asperger's or things of this nature. It could be that they are dyslexic but highly attuned to the arts such as music or creativity, writing, or other expressive ventures like acting or dance. They have quirks that are often beautiful. These are the children that will invent the technologies of the future that will resolve a lot of the old paradigm issues, socially, ecologically, educationally, financially, and so on globally. There is a danger often with these children especially with symptoms of ADHD or ADD to be drugged and controlled by the pharmaceutical industry, which in turn hugely lowers their vibration. This is not what these children came here to do and there are often better ways to cope with a gifted child than drugging them. They come in with an energy that is often more balanced regards female and male and are able to transmute the two together in a more balanced expression. This can create a more androgynous personality, which by today's standards is widely accepted more and more.

The Crystal children are the enlightened new systems builders whereas the older generations were on Earth to take it down. There is discussion on exactly when these souls began coming in with various feelings settling around the '90s with an emphasis being closer to the mid- and late '90s. Archaic and controlling paradigms such as the educational system which these children find very frustrating will be a place they will reinvent. Newer crystal and Indigo children come in with a knowing but feel that they have to go through the system in order to get out of the other end. Often one of these children will look at a teacher during a lesson and think to themselves, "I could teach/understand this on a far higher level than you are able." There is a mighty field of old energy that the Crystal and Rainbow children need to make their way through and often they do, taking control of the old systems and often making them far better than before; that is, if the educational or pharmaceutical industries haven't done their best to slow or stop them entirely.

Often these children will have parents who are Indigo themselves whether they know it or not. Sometimes it is the case that they might not be, but there is a higher chance of Indigo parents. These children create a special bond with one or both of their parents and at an early age with the parents instinctively knowing what they need without having to discuss it. The parents will be tuned in and in many cases the mother will know on the exact day that they have indeed become pregnant intuitively.

Even if the parent hasn't awakened on a spiritual level, they will feel intuitively guided by the child in terms of what they need and when they need it most on a subconscious level, telepathic almost. This is why some of these children do not actively begin to speak until later stages than other children, sometimes three even four. There is nothing wrong with them. These children are very in tune with energies and can see and hear things others can't and perhaps have imaginary playmates or friends that exist at night. Losing these friends can be tough, like a divorce. So go easy on them.

In the same way a baby at a very young age looks at their guardian angels in a room at infancy, these children carry this on after many babies have lost that sense. They will feel their way with people and situations, often looking into a person's soul and understanding their being without the need for conversation to understand that person. They are often born with beautiful huge eyes that seem to look right into your soul. These children are very empathic and trying to pull the wool over their eyes won't work. If you are hiding something, they will intuitively know about it long before you have any idea. These children can't be deceived.

In turn they are very sensitive to environments and need plenty of love, often with hugs and assurance. They are compassionate beings and seem far beyond their years, with an inbuilt wisdom. They might have ideas that seem unrealistic, but it is important to take them seriously as these children will go forth and manifest these dreams and ideas. These young children across the world are already inventing devices and systems that you often see in the news, or more positive, less fear-driven media outlets. They are doing incredible things and really getting the attention of a few bigwigs. Often these children will be the ones in a family crisis to come up with the simplest idea that is the smartest resolution of the issue. It is important not to brush away their ideas as fantasy and imagination having grown up in a previous generation.

Crystal children find emotionally charged environments absolutely intolerable. It is deeply upsetting for them if there is a negative connotation. Following this they love to be in nature, out in the open with the Earth and the animals which they love very much. They are happy just being on their own and do not need the validation of social scenarios to make them happy. You can imagine walking through a woodland area with one of these children and watching them take in the world in a completely new way, almost as if there was something unseen beyond the normal viewable world.

These children have a brilliant high intelligence both in IQ and EQ (Emotional Quota). Often at school they have a high vibration and love learning via visual stimulus or while being active. They need creative breaks and need to be heard. Sometimes when the school report comes back and it states in true old paradigm terms the child hasn't achieved, it is not the case that the child isn't intelligent enough; more often it is the school that has methods that are archaic and far too linear limiting development. They need to have their true talents nurtured without the same old information being fired at them. Imagine going on a date and the man or woman talks at you for two hours and then leaves in ignorance, saying you didn't live up to the expectations. Crystal children need mutual interaction, not an authoritative personality squashing them. Outlets, bright colors, and imaginative environments are calming for them.

They have a sense of real independence. This might be with routine, it might be with food. They might eat in a certain way at certain times. They will know far better what their body needs than most because their vibration is far higher than normal and they are sensitive to the toxic world we live in. Processed foods, nicotine, caffeine, artificial sugars, and other toxic foods often will have a bad reaction. In turn they might have allergies or skin issues. The soul of these children comes from a pure place, and they need to be eating and living in the same way, which in turn will cure their and your own laments and issues. They are the blueprint for the next human being. Try it and see.

Often strange things might happen at home. The phone might ring and before you have had a chance to pick up, the child might quizzically say, "You don't need to answer that, it's that sales call from last week." Upon answering the call, it actually is. Another case is the child who was booked to go on a school trip. The parent is getting the child ready for the day out when suddenly he or she says, "Mum, I don't need to go in today now. Something has changed. The field trip is canceled," and sure enough upon inspection it is. These small moments need to be met with love and compassion.

Crystal children are the first breed of humans in aeons to finally come in with no fear. They find the concept of it incomprehensible and sometimes are able to transmute another's fear back at them so they are forced to look at it, which can be difficult even for an adult. This is why some fully grown adults can find these children a handful. These children are healers, mentally and physically.

There are times when we all get emotionally charged, frustrated, or even angry and use a computer or turn on a lightbulb to find it has either blown up or stopped working temporarily for no reason. High energies can have effects on the technologies we use and our devices. Crystals have this often. They emit high levels of frequency and can often get through various devices, machines, or something as simple as a watch that has stopped working. Be patient with them, they are still finding out how to handle their own energy and it could take a while, but when it does it will be so very beautiful for everyone around them.

The veil is really starting to thin now with the third wave and memories of things, places, people, past lives that might come back, and a sense of knowing who they really are or who they really should be can be present. Children are able to recall accounts of things that happened in places which upon being inspected are validated. We all have this ability; however, these are the first to really show it en masse.

It is argued that the establishment is aware of these children and would perhaps see them as too much of a handful in railroading their long-seeded plans for control and even domination in sectors of industry. Did you ever stop to think back to your parents, or even your grandparents when they lived in less hygienic times and yet lived healthy lives? They had one or two vaccinations at tops and cancer rates were low. Why is it then that the medical establishment is in a sense of practical desperation to vaccinate these children with hundreds of different jabs? These days the list is endless, and many children living in first world countries live in an environment where certain diseases have been wiped out completely. Why are the new generations pumped full of these vaccinations, and why is there such an outrage from the establishment when their actions are halted? So desperate are the people of the establishment that often they threaten to enforce mandatory vaccinations at a time when there is no threat at all. Our parents and grandparents lived well. What has changed? What is really in these vaccinations? Effectively you are meeting a stranger in a white coat and trusting them to put a needle in you and begin injecting something that you have no understanding of at all, nor how it was made or sourced, and all just because it's what we are used to? Why are these questions not commonplace? The truth is out there.

Rainbow children have similarities to the Crystal children yet there are some subtle differences and are more likely to have been born from the year 2000 onward. They can be born from Crystal children parents; however, it is also possible to be born of Indigo parents, depending on what the soul has chosen prior to coming to Gaia and the family they planned to come into. Often a Rainbow child soul will choose to incarnate into a family that is loving and stable knowing there is little or no karma so that they can be all they need to be without dysfunctionality in their home environment. They themselves have no karma at all and are able to work purely on their reason for coming to Earth at this time.

They are coming in more carefully in fewer numbers but slowly they are growing in all cultures, races, and creeds. Look for them in the new generations. They are a gift from God.

Whereas with the Indigo's mission is to show humanity how destructive, rigid, inflexible, and left brained people were, the Crystals were less about structure and systems but the human emotion and soul, showing how closed we have become. Now that the Crystal children have shown us that more compassion and heart is needed, unearthing this around the planet, it is the job of the Rainbow to show us how to fully live in our hearts again and begin to fully encompass the energies and ideas of fifth-dimensional living through leading and living it themselves.

Both Crystal children and Rainbows will look deep into your soul through their big eyes. While the Crystal might be looking back into the beholder with some sense of caution, the Rainbow is looking back at you with complete nonjudgmental unconditional love that is angelic almost. They are the perfect tag team. In much the same way the first wave had to break down systems so that the second could come in and anchor the energy by just being, so too is it the same for the Rainbows and Crystals to build on top of what was reconstructed. The Crystal is carrying out the work (often unknowing) so that the Rainbow children can anchor this firmly into pure unconditional love. The same as the second wave, the Rainbow just has to be, although be it on an entirely different level. The Crystal children have auras that are initially pure and clear but can change color. They have been called the aura chameleons. They are adaptable in color. The Rainbow child has an aura of bright multicolor all around them. This is felt in their lives as they adore bright colors in clothes and surroundings often using them in their art, drawings, or surroundings that they make for themselves.

This also matches their personality. They are fearless like the Crystals but will go to any animal or person without hesitation and often animals will feel very at ease with Crystal children but even more so with Rainbows. Whereas the Crystal children are said to be born after 2000 or slightly before, Rainbows will continue to arrive from 2000 to 2030, although it is yet to be seen.

Already there is a new soul arriving that has not been seen before coming in around the years 2020 onward known as the Diamond children, who are verging on ET hybrids.

There have been some similarities measured on a spiritual level between the vibration energy of a dolphin that is similar to a Rainbow child, with origins that go back even to Sirian energies. As we have discussed previously in this book, the Sirians are very psychic and telepathic, sensing all that is around them, especially in the cosmos.

Rainbows are beautiful angelic children sometimes referred to as virgin souls. Often this is their first time on Earth, and they are figuring things out on this planet as they go. This can mean that at school they should be extra careful of bullies as they have little in the way of defense initially and would still show compassion to one regardless. In time they of course will find their way.

We go back to the gender fluid term again. Perhaps they might be a girl but dress as a boy or the other way around. They aren't really bothered especially at a young age and will go forward and create their own way often almost completely on their own of any label or social conformity. It simply doesn't bother them. These children do have similarities to Crystal children in that they are compassionate but also have a rod of steel going through them. If you try to push something on them that they don't want, they will let you know! Perhaps it is a day out with the family, food, or clothes that is simply just out of their comfort zone. When these children do find what it is they want and love, they will run with it excelling at whatever it is. Perhaps leave a musical instrument lying around the house or crayons (in a safe environment) and see what they create. Perhaps they will paint a picture of someone that used to live in the house many years ago that has passed away as if they knew them personally without having prior knowledge. This wouldn't be frightening to a Rainbow or even a Crystal. They would do it intuitively. Crystal children and Rainbows are a step closer to their higher self, and the Rainbow child will think in algorithms that are far nonlinear like times of old. They live from their hearts and not from their heads. They are the true embodiment of the humans to come and experience little or no ascension symptoms. You could say they are almost like evolutionary hybrid children acting and looking like their far future Pleiadian brothers and sisters. Increasingly there are parents and especially mothers who are having and seeing children like this but are still in a box regarding things of this nature. Some are disinclined to begin looking for answers on why their child might be different albeit still beautiful. Many mothers and some fathers are increasingly googling from the closet about whether their child may be cut from this cloth but never speak of it. If that is the case, rest assured, dear one, you are not alone, and many other parents are all doing the same. Eventually you will unite. You are not going mad. It is far more likely, however, that in being categorized it will be the children themselves who will defer from any label, and that is very right and proper. Good for them, for labels are a thing of the past going forward.

It is important not to label, however, especially with the new souls as they are free beyond being "categorized." We use these terms as a guideline only.

The Old Soul

All souls are eternal. They always were, are, and always will be. You are older than time itself. Do you really think God sits at home wearing a timepiece clock watching? When you walk through a museum and see asteroid fragments in a glass case dated four billion years old or sit on a beach and feel the sand run through your fingers, try to understand that your soul is older than all of this.

When creator/God set out, it wanted to experience all that is, so it sent many parts of self into the universe to experience various things, sometimes taking on a physical body and internally developing a personality through genetic makeup or environmental conditioning. Your soul is part of creator God energy and therefore you are divine. God/creator is actually inside you. When you pray at night you are praying to the God that is inside you as you are part of God. Perhaps you have been around spiritual or mental wellness people and heard them greeting each other with the term "namaste"? *Namas* is Sanskrit for "bowing"; *te* is sanskrit for "to you." The Hindu religion has been using this for a very, very long time. Bowing is the old translation of this; however, in essence what they are saying is, "The God in me greets the God in you," or in other words, "Namaste." Ancient teaching has known this, but it has become lost in the modern world. That is why no matter where you are in your life, it's important to remember how important you are. You are a divine creation, arriving on Earth on purpose and in perfect timing.

When you hear people speak of new souls and old souls it is in reference to their experience on Earth. The three waves of souls especially the third wave are new souls. They haven't been here many times or it is their first. The old soul has been here for hundreds if not more likely thousands of years or longer, hence, old soul. They have been here the longest on Earth. We have discussed starseeds and their various traits and characteristics. Many souls coming in have forgotten who they are, but some come in with a knowing that this is their mission and this is why they are here. Very few, however, have contemplated that this is what they specialize in and they have gone to other places and raised the vibration there also in the same way that they are doing on Gaia now. They are specialist system busters raising vibration and this is not the first time. You have done it before, and Earth is yet the next adventure. More on this later.

In experiencing all that is, it means you have been females and males in previous lives in different countries and continents. This is why sometimes you might go somewhere on holiday and sense that you were there before or have an attachment that you simply cannot explain to a certain place. You are revising some form of previous experience. This can also cause some interesting and confusing situations. For example, there are old souls that have been in female bodies so many times that when it comes to trying a masculine physicality the soul still feels like it is a woman trapped in a man's body. Often this can make a man gay or want to love other men, which is natural and beautiful. This can also happen the other way around. This is not necessarily the case for new souls who are more gender fluid, however; it's more about the energy of the age they come in and increasingly Earth's energies, which are more gender balanced as the divine feminine energy is more equally matched with the divine masculine. We see this all the time in the modern world. Women are taking more ownership of their femininity, becoming more powerful, and the divide between masculine and feminine energies is balancing out year by year with women in all catagories coming back into their mastery and meeting men on equal terms in careers, money, and so on.

The soul is affected by where it has come from and the energy it is surrounded by. If we went back to Lemuria, you would find that women were the key stone and more important sex as they were the life givers with men taking a different role. In the coming Age of Aquarius there will be perfect harmony between both. People will look back at the James Brown song, "It's a Man's World," and say, gosh, that was such an old paradigm. Look how we have moved on!

In essence the old soul is someone who has an Akash filled to the brim with experiences, talents, skills, and wisdom collected over many lifetimes, but we are just talking about the ones on Earth to keep it simple. This soul is the most experienced on Earth when fully in their power. After lifetimes and lifetimes of trudging through old energy, they come in this lifetime in the new energy looking at the youngsters, wishing they were special, too, not knowing that they are some of the souls that can make the biggest impact on Earth right now. Old souls can be any age and they are the ones outside of the three waves who are awakening here, there, and everywhere and at different stages. The old soul has been here the longest with some of them claiming to be Atlantean and Lemurian and so on.

Often people wonder if they are an old soul and by the very asking of that question and by reading this book it is likely you are. The old soul has karma and Akashic issues to work through, but for the first time the energies will allow all karma to be completely dropped without having to come back in the next life. It can be done now in this lifetime. The payoff of all lifetimes on Gaia. The old soul carries self-worth issues, always asking, do I deserve to be here, is my life even meaningful, what's the point in being here? The old soul has always rolled the boulder uphill in the old energy with it pushing back in what has always felt like hard work. Like a great endless battle with little or no hope at the end of the tunnel no matter where the old soul turned. Finally now, the energy is on the side of the old soul since the early 2000s and mostly 2012 onward. There are so many lifetimes of dark energy lived through that by the time the old souls get back to Gaia they wonder why they bothered coming. The old soul's self-worth issue is very prevalent. The new souls come in and it's a party from the starting line. Very different. This soul may seem like a rock, but at home, alone, wrapped up in bed at night, the old soul really wonders what it's all about. Are you going to make it? Will you survive another minute being here? How much more can you take? What is my purpose? Please, someone tell me why I'm really here.

There is a tapestry of reasons why old souls came here with varying outcomes. No two stories are alike. Some have lived through battles, famines, wars; some were healers, spiritual people, and some lived on the edge of the town only being met by those in the town when something was wrong or when there was no one else to help. There are those who in old energies were burned at the stake or were sent away for having enlightened ideas, and every time you tried to be spiritual or enlightened you were removed from this planet, cast out, or gagged over and over and often by souls that were newer or younger than yours. Imagine Lemurian souls living during the Spanish Inquisition!

They can feel the change and want more and more of it. It's almost addictive. Old souls will go out and find information and read books on this kind of thing because for the first time there is something innately inside of them awakening without putting a finger on it like the newer souls can. That's because they have stage fright. Performance anxiety. Fear of enlightenment. They are awakening to something new and don't know what to do with it, having experienced quite the opposite for such a long time. Many are like rabbits in the headlights wanting to know more, but afraid that they might be laughed at or be discriminated against just like they did in the past throughout history. On some level there is an Akashic trigger saying, "you came out of your shell before, remember what happened last time?" This can put some old souls into a state of inaction or fear regarding really letting it all hang out.

Many old souls have played many parts in the Earth cycle. Some ran a blade through another's chest and took a life in a battle, and others were the ones who died. Old souls have lived through such a variety of soul contracts, sometimes just coming in for a short while and leaving again in order to facilitate an awakening for someone else. This is why the old souls come. They will ask, "Well, why did I have to go through all that stuff and be in battles and wars, sometimes on the winning side and sometimes on the losing side?" And it will be the old soul that gives the answer that the new souls can't, not with the same integrity—the old soul will come with a feeling of expression and say, NEVER AGAIN. No more wars, no more battles, that's old energy. That is why the old souls coming "online" and awakening at this time will be the first to dismantle any chance of there ever being a World War Three. It simply isn't going to happen, not anymore. Yes, there will be small localized battles in foreign countries, but even those will come to an end very soon. That is an experience that only this soul can give.

Old souls are having a remembrance. They are having déjà vu more often. Perhaps more than ever you will meet people, go for drinks, start a new job, or make new friends and you feel you have known them before and there is a link and familiarity that you just can't explain but it's there. This is partly due to soul groups who have been operating on the Earth plain for a long time and souls who are working together in the astral but are unaware upon waking up in the morning. Upon meeting these comrades in your daily reality there is a consciousness similar to your own, even though they might be older, younger, or not deemed as a correct social match, there's a connection and you just run with it. Having been here so long old souls are finding old friends, comrades, partners, and all kinds they have encountered in previous lives, and with the lowering of the veil this is becoming stronger. It is an Akashic intuitiveness the old soul feels through vast experience. This will only grow. Synchronicity is leading the way and old souls are having it more and more. Old souls can identify because it isn't the first time. You gained that experience. It's under the belt.

Old souls have a tendency in the new energy to feel lost, unlike the new souls. The new energy isn't responding the same way and the "feedback" isn't the same as the old energy. It doesn't act in the same way, and, boy, oh boy, it can be discombobulating, with old souls feeling like they don't know who they are anymore as an old energy identity slips away before the new one has seemingly anchored. When these souls begin to tune into the new radio frequency and draw on remembrance at a soul level and work through these issues, the results are incredible. Now you begin to see the soul matrix and how it all comes together, each with its own purpose, and the old soul is so very important and the light of an awakening soul is just as important as the new soul. Just different. All of this affects the magnetics on the planet, the grid systems, and the crystalline grid. More on this later. If you are an old soul, you're on purpose, and you're right on time, as they say.

The new soul will come in with a pineal gland that is much more active and able to function on a spiritual level that is intuitively more connected. For those of you unaware of this, it is a small pine-nut-sized gland in the front of the brain that allows for sight and feeling into the beyond. Often in adults this becomes calcified and hardens like a little rock over time due to pollutants in diet and the environment. In children it is still soft and malleable.

Going back to the old and new soul for a moment. The new soul will instinctually connect to the higher self, God, and the universe. If they need to pray or have a spiritual moment, they will have it when it is comfortable for them. They will connect to source or energies as a sovereign being in their own time and place. The old soul, however, is still indoctrinated by having to go to a building, sit in a room, and go and speak to a middleman or -woman in a funny hat, a long robe, and ask permission to connect to source or God. This is what the old energy has instilled in the old soul. The old energy indoctrination has said for aeons that you must sit in a cubicle and tell your sins to another person who will then in turn go back to the god who loves you, and then sort it at their end like some kind of religious middleman. The new soul will find this intolerable whereas the old soul knows better, but has forgotten. The new soul will find limiting religious constructs and their procedures exhausting, where the old soul is waking up to this idea.

Why go to someone else to connect to God when you can connect directly? God is alive and well in you at all times. No one can take that away, but they can give you the perception you are separate. This will change how religion will operate in the future. Everyone has the ability to connect at all times to the other side whenever they want without having to be told when, where, or how. This can be very conflicting for the old soul as the only trait that does pass through the veil of forgetfulness is spiritual knowing and acuity. The more you learn each time spiritually it collects in parts and begins to come through each time. It's Akashic.

The newer souls are having a harder time coming in regards to birth. The old soul has done it many times and it's a far easier transition. Children increasingly, but especially the old souls, will need less and less immediate parenting after birth including the new children coming in with more instinctive feelings on how to live. The old soul draws on this Akashically through experience and might start talking straight away. The new soul is just figuring it all out, and this is partly why a Rainbow or Crystal child might learn to speak later. It isn't intellect, they just arrived to a completely new planet and there are systems to learn from scratch.

Have you ever pondered why animals in the wild are born from their parents and often are walking and feeding themselves within days or even hours and yet humans are at the top of the food chain but we can't do this for ourselves in infancy? The parents must do everything in the beginning. Is this not strange for a species as evolved as us? Humans are top of the food chain and yet animals with much lower intellects can look after themselves at infancy. The change is coming. Have you not heard the old-timers saying in modern generations, "My god, they grow up fast these days, faster than our generation." Increasingly this will be the case as DNA and souls evolving in higher energies come in with knowledge regarding how to do things from the starting line. There will be a time in the future when the children pop out of the mother and have a full knowledge of who they were, getting on with things very quickly. That is some time in the distance, but we see the beginning of this already.

The old soul is especially well versed in what the new age calls a soul contract, with souls agreeing to come to Gaia and play a part or a role in a bigger story. Sometimes the grandparent will come back as the grandchild, and when those grandparents look into the grandchildren's eyes, they just know they are looking straight into someone they knew before and will bend over to do anything to look after them. It is quite possible they might just be looking at their own mum or their dad, because they are back!

Soul groups stick together. On a 3D level the genetics are seen visually. Other soul contracts differ. Often people in the new-age movement will be far too caught up on soul contracts. They will say, "Well, if I haven't carried out this or that then I haven't carried out my soul's purpose," concluding that they have failed spiritually. They might say, "Yes, I met this woman and we are romantically in love, but I know my purpose is to stay in this town, it's my calling." Another old soul might get stuck in a different way, and some more extreme people even believe that if you haven't carried out your spiritual work you are removed early. All of this is incorrect.

For souls new and old their contract or part in this experience is carried out in full just by being here and playing a part and the parameters change and adjust in a new energy. If that means moving to another town or changing a job for something better, then so be it. There is great variety in how consciousness is raised and there is no one 3D linear way. It's multidimensional and the potentials are being rewritten every single second so just go with the flow. This also begs the old soul to ask, "Well, why did I awaken to my truth in my twenties when my friend awakened to spirituality and enlightenment in their sixties?" It is about timing. There might be things that could affect those around you or yourself negatively should you come into your truth too early or too late. Everything is planned in divine accordance, and we are all where we are meant to be at the right time.

Timing is not the only factor that influences us. Karma combined with Akashic remembrance affects how we are driven, also, which is why in this case the new soul will have an easier time getting into new things. There is a drawback, however. Whereas the new soul has no karma and nothing to hold them back, the old soul has experience to draw from. In contrast this can make the new soul seem a little naive or even gullible. They will get there in the end, however. The old soul is not gullible. Old souls can know and feel things about people even if it is not believed at the time of explanation. What they say often will come to fruition in the end whether the younger souls end up listening or not. This is why the Rainbow children are more often born into stable loving families to create more of a buffer. It's karmic, or for the Rainbow children, their lack of. Another reason might be that the last time there was an awakening it was traumatic. You were persecuted for it, or perhaps it was just uncomfortable. This can be another factor that stops the old soul awakening in this lifetime. They just don't want the stress of it all again. Why go through all the stress of another painful and embarrassing awakening? People will think I'm nuts. No thanks.

It's important for the old soul to remember that what might not have worked in the past, especially in this lifetime, will be much more likely to work in the future. If things seemed like a slow slog in the past, try it again post-2012 and see how you do this time without the darkness clawing you back down. Whereas before the gas tank was a quarter empty and you were spiritually driving a small car, you are now in a sports car and the gas tank is full and waiting for you to transmute some energy. This time the manifestation will happen twice as fast with double the results.

∴ 93 ∴

You got to the top of the hill and it's leveled off. Some will feel like the bike has got boosters on it! Don't let the old energy be the record that plays for the future. This is especially important for the old soul. The plane is waiting to take off and all you have to do is just get on it and see what happens this time. The new souls don't need to worry about this. To move out of the past at the fastest rate is to drop karma, which they have little or none of. Forgive those who have hurt you, clear the past, and begin to pave the way for what's to come. It is harder to move into the light with baggage. You can't bring darkness into a light consciousness.

The years 2012–2020 are said to be the recalibration years. The years of assimilating the energies mentally and physically while removing the unnecessary bags. There will be many souls who have not let go early enough with 2019 being one of the final calibration years with everything happening all at once as the big push goes into 2020. The year 2019 for many will be a big year when the universe says to you, "I'm dragging you kicking and screaming to 2020 whether you like it or not and it's going to work out much better than you thought. Apologies for the painful push. It is said that the griffin is always born out of the ashes."

For the reader of this book who has gazed at these ideas for the first time you have done well to get this far. For the experienced esoteric practitioner this will all be fairly common sense. For those of you who are new to this, Alice is about to jump further into the rabbit hole so hold on tight as we begin to explore the very mystical concept of Enki's Gift.

We have explored the concept of being awakened and that this is happening in tandem with DNA activation. The two are entwined, but which comes first? The answer is they happen at the same time. Let us travel back to ET and starseed folklore. We have explored the Anunnaki and their interference with the human race, be it in the shadows that isn't immediately obvious. Enki is part of the Anunnaki family and a DNA specialist of sorts. He has a love of kinds for humanity unlike the rest of his family and saw the limitations of a human race regarding DNA that was switched off partly by other members of his family. While infighting and karmic issues began to dog the Anunnaki, Enki decided to give humanity a compassionate contribution known as Enki's Gift. A time-coded DNA instruction to help souls come online and awaken and raise consciousness without the inconvenient logistics of having to be present himself. If at the right time the cosmic energies were correct, light energy from the center of the galaxy (the center sun), and our own sun, would intern active human DNA coding, giving rise to its percentage quota becoming more active. This also adds to the driving force for souls coming into their light at this time. Earth has a great deal of help; however, we are just reaping the benefits and the smallest grass roots which are beginning to shoot up out of the dirt. This is confirmed by Barbara Marciniak, who famously channels the Pleiadians. This is how latent souls are awakening, also.

Extraterrestrial and Soul Origins

There is a great clamor among individuals in these times who wish to explore and express their star origins. Many starseeds and people who are simply curious are all with their ear to the wall and finger in the wind to measure and gauge who they are in terms of their star heritage. In doing so starseeds are wanting to equate an identity of sorts to themselves in a further understanding of who they are before arriving on Gaia. This might result in concluding that you identify as an Arcturian/Andromedan soul, for example. There is great desire among the community and the greater awakening world related to the finding of this connection and experiences off planet away from earthly experiences.

We came to this planet to have an earthly experience and focus on being grounded to Gaia, with the irony being that upon becoming interested within the topic of starseeds one begins to try to have more of an off-world out-of-body experience. ETs and the angelic realms have done well to often remind us that there is more importance in finding your Earth place than your star origin and to focus on that regards helping vibrations at this time. A further irony will be that upon stumbling across much of the information in this book, the very first thing starseeds often race to do is find out the origins of their star family. The equivalent of this could be explained as shopping, for example.

Being multidimensional means there can be multiple facets of us, especially when we are from the stars. Everyone on Earth is from the stars. It is undeniable even if you can only comprehend this on a chemical level. The material that makes up our bodies and the Earth came from space; there is no getting away from this. However, prior to coming to Earth there was an existence either in the future or the great past whereby we were someone, somewhere else, and part of one of the many great civilizations that are in the constellations all around us. The souls that flooded to Earth after the alarm bell was rung all came from a variation of places. So there is a great feeling especially among awakened starseeds (or people having a spiritual moment at this time) that they have or were having a consciousness experience prior to Earth.

Very often just on the principle that you seek these answers, there is a high chance you might have lived off-planet at some point. Earth was only just getting started (on Earth timelines) 4.5 billion years ago. There were no souls here at all. With that in consideration there must be outside visitation or traffic of souls in order for Earth to work with conscious souls living on it. Earth was not created with people on it; they came later. Where did they come from? In various religions the soul is explained as being eternal. It always was and always will be. So where did the souls come from to inhabit Earth?

There are many ways to explore this idea but the best advice that can be given is to go within. There you can find all the answers which were always there. When you go within you tap into your intuitiveness and your cosmic intuition, which is never wrong. You have to feel your way to the answers, observing whether it resonates to your tone or not. Discernment is crucial. Starseeds in the modern age often turn to books and the Internet in search of their star origins. There is a plethora of information out there and some of it can be confusing with different results each time leading to more confusion and frustration. Finding your origin is something to be savored over time like a beautiful relationship or a rare vintage wine. It is not something to rush into while making uneducated predictions. Take the time to collate all the information and experiences that are unfolding into your life, and the answer truly will come as it does to the majority of the seeds on Earth.

There are a great number of character traits that the Internet has to offer regards the different ET races all with their own flavor and taste. Do not be too hasty to assign yourself a label without properly reviewing all the details and giving them the time they need to cognize within the brain but more importantly your heart. Initially there are people one can visit who are adept in the world of the stars. Professional Akashic readers can help open up hidden worlds as much as some psychic mediums can. There is undoubtedly a connection to birth charts that have coherence in the worlds of astrology and astronomy with certain starseeds being born at ties with suns while having conjunctions with star systems rising and disappearing in the eastern and western sky. There is credence in planetary connections and moons passing through constellations at the time of birth and all of this has its place which a professional in any of these fields will be able to divulge should you cross their palms with silver. Past life regressions have a potential to unearth off-world experiences as well as many other practitioners that play and work in the magical world that is the esoteric. At your disposal is a great wealth of help that even a hundred years ago was at a limited supply. However, failing all of this there are other ways to satisfy an answer that will prove correct with a little self-work should you feel bold enough to take on the mantle for oneself intuitively. There are various forms of self-help that garner the same results.

It is said that by looking at the stars at night people have felt drawn to a specific constellation in which a fascination grew. Sometimes this is a path to understanding where you have derived from. Even looking at pictures of constellations and intuitively "feeling" the picture has led to revolutions for starseeds on a quest. Others have looked at sculptures or pictures of ETs and instantaneously felt drawn to them pushing aside the other ones. There is credence in synchronicity by putting the message out in the universe via thought or spoken word, which in turn can be powered further by the catalyst that is meditation. Just simply sit back and watch the synchronicities pour back to you in your everyday life after putting the message out there.

For example, you are watching a channeled message from the Andromedans, and they explain that they have been in receivership for years of all the broadcasts that are emanating from the entertainment industry via radio and satellites in outer space. Perhaps these ETs have been listening to the noise we have been broadcasting and they have viewed a TV series such as *I Love Lucy* from the early 1950s. You might listen to this story and inconceivably the next day turn on your TV and hey, presto, the first thing that comes on is an old episode of *I Love Lucy*. See how it works? There are signs about us all the time which are more receivable when we have a calm brain, and when we have a calm mind we can partially slip out of linearity for just long enough for events and things to happen.

Channeling is another one. You will see a multitude of women and men across the world channel entities, angels, and ETs. Providing they are authentic at their craft, you might find yourself resonating with one channeled being and not another. The very words and expressions flowing might tickle you in a certain way each time. You might hear the Pleiadians speaking and no matter who the vehicle channeling is, you feel deep inside that that is your tribe. Perhaps this might be the same as the Arcturians. The universe is like a menu waiting for you to resonate with a connection that you feel close to and there are plenty more we haven't even touched on.

Stranger still is the birthmark concept, that people have various moles or freckles, perhaps birthmarks or shapes that seem to exactly match a constellation. Perhaps that was a preconceived failsafe built into the experience prior to arrival. Dreams also play a large part in deciphering an origin. Some people often dream they are in other constellations being active at whatever they are doing. This is true of the daydreamer, too. Imagine you are in class, in the office, driving, or even making love with someone beautiful, and suddenly you get a vision of a place, a planet, or a face that comes to mind. The message will come often not as you expect it, but there is great joy once there is a clear symbiosis of all the collated information.

Birds of a feather flock together. You might feel that you get on well with starseeds of a certain origin better than others. There is such a great arena in which to find your cosmic or celestial place in the universe. Simply keep your eyes and ears open, don't jump to conclusions, and remember to feel your way through using your heart and not your head, and under no circumstances allow yourself to slip into fear. Fear will greatly stop energies you might have that are knocking on your ethereal door!

You might even be an angel; stranger things have happened. Often there can be more than one origin. Many starseeds will feel strongly to one or two, perhaps addressing themselves as a Sirian/ Orion hybrid. Others will have other hybrid attributes but with aspects of other timelines and dimensionality. For example, Jeff next door is an Arcturian Pleiadian hybrid with lesser Reptilian aspects built in. Breeds can mix and races on Earth can and so on. That is why it is important to take a leisurely pace at the conclusion until you have a mix that you feel truly resonates with yourself and the existence you live. As the author of this book, I am an Arcturian/Andromedan second-wave Indigo starseed with elements of Regulas (Lion Being) and my first incarnation into this universe was a feline Lyran ET. These are the traits that I feel and resonate strongest with.

These are all aspects one can find within the present. Blood tells a very interesting story of the past. One of the great discussions ongoing is the mysterious case of Rh negative and its interesting attributes. It is one of the rarest and unusual types especially being that it doesn't allow for cloning of itself unlike all the others. It can't be replicated, which in turn also does not allow it to interact with other blood types unless there is careful or planned medical intervention. Generally, blood comes in four types. A, B, AB, and O. Within this there are both negative and positive factors that create further different types of blood. This is based on the rhesus factor, which measures the rhesus-based antigens in the blood and whether they are present or not. This was born from scientific studies with monkeys called the rhesus macaque specifically within the field of blood transfusions and how blood is received or rejected in the recipient-donor relationship. It is also known as Rh. Studies of this kind showed that the rhesus factor allowed for both positive and negative results. The majority of humans on Earth show a positive rhesus at about 80–85 percent of the population, allowing for the vast majority of modern humans to receive blood from both positive and negative donors. In essence this correlates with evolutionary ideas that Hominids (caveman) came from or had evolutionary history that is shared with the monkey (rhesus macaque) and their blood. There were two forms of these cavemen called Homo Habilis and Homo Erectus. Logic would tell us that as humans have evolved so has our biology in order to thrive in nature. However, this is not the case with Rh negative as an Rh negative receiving any kind of Rh-positive blood triggers a strong immune attack trying to destroy the foreign antigens that are seemingly alien.

This is interesting because all species that are known in the present day can reproduce with the same despite size or color, in the same way that humans can reproduce interracially as long as it is with another human that is the same species. In effect the Rh-negative blood will react as if it were another species or not human and do its best to remove anything that it sees as being lesser. There are similarities to this in nature when species too far removed like donkeys and horses bred with failed results.

This has interesting results regarding humans trying for children. A woman with a negative Rh type mating with a positive rhesus factor male will encounter dangers as the two blood types refuse to work with the end result of the mother's own body doing everything in its power to reject her own baby as if it were alien. Medical intervention must happen in order to ease this issue. However, when an Rh-positive mother receives DNA from an Rh-negative father, the body allows for the baby to be easily born. So what you have here is a blood that has traits of an entirely different species that will only allow for forward evolution and not backward while killing off any monkey rhesus factors that are positive. Rarely in nature do you see this, and it gets more interesting still. Rh negative in effect can be seen as having no distinct earthly origin or link to monkeys, hence it will behave in alien ways. The question is, where does this blood type come from then?

Generally, it is understood that the first humans came from Africa spreading out all over the world. However, all of the inhabitants from this part of the world were all Rh positive with no Rh negative. So the big question is how do we track its origin? Not only does it seem alien, but it behaves in an alien way regarding human blood. Scientists of today still have no definitive understanding of where this blood type comes from and find it almost impossible to logically equate where this suddenly hit the human evolution story.

That leads many scientists to believe that people with Rh-negative antigens have evolved from another species and if so, where did they come from, who are they, and do they still exist? Regardless of these facts it is possible that there could have been genetic manipulation; however, were human technologies in the great past advanced enough to interfere with genetics to this extent and if so, why to the possible detriment of human life? Evolution evolved to give us everything we needed to survive, not take it away from us. Could it be that there was an outside source of some kind that is still unseen or are we simply not being given the whole truth by the medical and historical societies?

It is understood that only 15 percent of the world's population have the Rh-negative blood type with a very high proportion all nestled around the Pyrenees both south in Spain and north in France. These people are known as the Basque. They have a spoken and written language that is completely unique to that part of the world and have the highest concentration of Rh negative anywhere on Earth with 35 percent of people from this region having this blood type, which is a large quantity in contrast to other global countries.

Anthropologists have been astounded by this area for many generations. The single most isolated spoken language in the world is Korean, and after that it is Basque. It became an isolated language in Europe, which is unique. Was there something that came outside of Earth to have such a great cultural, genetic, and sociological impact? People of this blood type are said to have higher than normal perceptual or psychic awareness and even traits that make them immune to HIV. Although there are very rare blood types such as Delta 32, which make the person immune to HIV, it is believed that this could be a mutation forward throw of some kind potentially linked to great plagues and diseases of the past. Yet there is still no answer for Rh negative, which seemingly did not come from the evolution story we have been sold regarding man developing from monkeys. Stranger still is the ongoing debate of where modern-day humans came in; again, could there have been "outside" interference? It is widely discussed still regarding finding the link between humans and the evolution of hominids (Neanderthal, Homo Erectus, Australopithecus), which is still up for debate. These descendants are able to claim evolutionary DNA and blood types to the monkeys; however, there is yet a strong case to promote the last leap into modern humanity and how it happened. What was the bridge and how was the gap crossed?

Rh negative does seem to have extraterrestrial qualities to it that are not of this world as do other very rare blood types that are immune to AIDS, for example. With these very rare blood types also come strange attributes. In recent times scientists conducted heat tests on these blood types specifically looking at the microbes that are present. The blood was heated up to 700 degrees and exposed to liquid nitrogen. Using a custom dark field microscope, it was seen that the microbes were still alive. The same was done for dust from an ancient mummy, which upon putting it in a solution that had a PH that of blood, the microbes became alive again! Below are some documented traits that are characteristic of these rare blood types, which seem to cross over into the starseed or DNA-activated individual also. Perhaps you have had an awakening in your life and you relate to these symptoms or abilities? Are we seeing the average Joe on the street rising in consciousness and evolving to a place where rare blood types are having similar characteristics?

1. Truth seekers

2. Empathetic talents and abilities

3. Empathy and compassion for humankind

4. An extra rib or vertebra, or extra teeth

5. Higher than average IQ

6. Affinity of space and science

7. More sensitive vision and other senses

8. Increased psychic/intuitive abilities

9. Extra sensitivity to heat and sunlight

10. Lower body temperature

11. Predominance of green or hazel eyes that change color

12. Cannot be cloned

13. Unexplained scars

14. Piercing eyes

15. A feeling of not belonging

16. Ability to disrupt electrical devices

17. Prone to alien encounters

18. Physic dreams and/or abilities

19. Extrasensory perception

Taking into account these forward throw attributes, it is possible to see the consciousness that is to come and is now happening on Earth with the children coming in. There are great similarities in the Rh negative traits and the new children being born of all blood types with heightened DNA.

Other significant arguments are related to understanding where these blood types originated. Increasingly among metaphysical researchers there is a large online debate that explores the idea that the Anunnaki injected part of their DNA into Homo Habilis creating what has been the missing link to the Homosapien, which is the modern-day human. Some say this is far-fetched. Once is a chance, twice is coincidence, and three times is beyond reasonable doubt. If so, then why so much noise at this present time on the Internet?

As you can see, there are a great deal of ways to find oneself, soul connections, and star family. The work is one that must be centered flexing the intuitive muscle, which upon practicing will strengthen. Don't forget to read your own emotions, ask yourself how you feel, self-diagnose and think how and what connects and what doesn't. Being in tune with yourself from the inside out will help all the reflections of the outer self and world you're creating and living in.

Before meeting the ETs, here is a channeled message from the Arcturians to get their compassionate view upon the starseeds and the perspective upon which they are working their magic on Earth at this important time:

Dear Starseeds,

We want to offer you a narrative that even some of the most experienced of you might be new to. A lot of you (in some way) spent your life being outsiders and wondering why this is happening to you and why it seems to persist.

It's like some kind of bad dream that never ends. Every now and then your light is so bright that you have experiences that outshine everyone, and then you fall from grace with those around you failing to see what you see, the light you have shone and how it affected others in magnificent ways. We want to bring this to your attention. You came to Earth to raise its vibration. Do you think this is the first time you have done this? A lot of you have done this over and over and over again. You are the special forces of the ascension army going to planets and raising the vibration over and over. It's difficult work. That's why there are so many beings on the other side who have your support because only you were bravest to come and what is beneficial for your kind helps those you cannot see as all are one.

That's why they wash your feet and are huddled around you when you are sad. It's difficult for you when you are upset, and you can't see that we are holding your light right beside you.

When you cross over, regardless of how much of a nightmare you may or may not have been in this life, there is a celebration on the other side when you get there. There is no judgment. Religion has mis sold this to you, starseeds. Whatever name you want to buy, you are the new leaders of the spiritual world at this time on Gaia. This isn't your first time. So many of you need this message. The light and dark balance during the years 2020–2024 is climatic and so is the dark astral response as all the changes are set forth in both the inner and outer realities of your evolving world. Anxiety has been prevalent even for the strongest of you as you look beyond the changing you for what is arriving next and how it will land when it arrives.

Before the new Lemuria, the dark wants to stop you. We need you to get a message into your corporeal human brains. You have done this before, going to a planet to assist ascension in many efforts. Many times before. You are professionals. It's why when you have a reading the spirits say, "We love you, we support you, we are behind you. You are dearly loved."

You might be an outcast of your family, class system, culture. You are special forces coming to Gaia at this time, a part of creator, nonetheless to resolve some galactic imbalances. You are looked upon by ET, angels, and other beings as a savior, and yet you think of yourself as a lesser being, or someone who is not worthy. Someone who can't have the things that new souls or less developed souls have or have achieved.

A lot of you are old souls. You came here early in preparation. That's why some of you have given up. "I've done it over, and over, and guess what? I'm done."

We are talking to the akashically advanced souls now, the old souls. You just turned up to the party and you don't even know it but the organization is all about inducting you into the hall of fame. The biggest irony is that you feel that you're the one most unworthy. The irony is so bittersweet. How do we know all of this? We are you. The only difference, dear family, is that we came into our light long before you.

Very soon all of you will be on the page and talking to friends and family like this with the knowledge of the star mothers. And you know why? It's built into your Akash. You are a lightworker. You are the brave that go out and do this time and time again, and yet the new souls in older times have taken all the credit. Credit, where credit is due, is about to be paid out, starseeds.

Things are going to feel like they are falling into place more and more. You are more than the disbelievers around you. Soul growth is what you are undertaking making you leaders in this new time. You are the black sheep. You were the odd ones out. You never fitted in. Starseed, you're about to become the go-to person in the years to come. It might even be confusing, but get used to it now, before the collective dictates it to you. This is a message to you about your future. There is a plan, and it is one of love.

You are about to become the leaders, the outsiders. The ones that never fitted in. It's already in action.

You will be the hero on the hero's journey. Your family will start listening to you, your old friends will even turn around. You're about to become someone important lightworker. Suddenly the new energy is going to support you in a way you thought was never possible.

You are looked upon by beings you can't comprehend fully at this time and loved so dearly just for being here. All boots are on the ground now and practice time is over. We thank you greatly.

In service to Humanity

The Arcturians

(Channeled, Alexander Quinn)

3
ET, Phone Home

This chapter can be used conceptually to help investigate thoughts about what advanced civilizations might look like and where we might be in thousands or even millions of years' time regards evolution. Understand also that the beings in the following pages are real and have been active physically and nonphysically on Earth for a very long time. There are plenty of people who express their experience increasingly around the globe and who encounter beings. Their chronicles are all over the Internet and increasing many folds in a way never seen before—try googling it for yourself.

As of late, the starseed and spiritual worlds are booming with ET discussions, quietly simmering away since the early 2000s but especially since the dawning of 2012. Many now are branching out to have conversations on different types of media including Facebook, where large groups and forums exhibit hot activity. We are living in a world where humans look up into the sky seeing UFOs or light phenomena, and identify the objects in terms of an ET race due to their attributes. This phenomenon is boiling away in its pot and the steam is getting harder to ignore. People edge in just a little closer than ever before when you have something to say on the matter instead of disregarding it. In the last ten years or so, large groups of all kinds of people are having awakenings and epiphanies which are only now just on the cusp of becoming culturally acceptable. However, the higher end spectrum items for discussion that seem fantastical to most are still scrutinized behind closed doors with some of the most intellectual thinkers suffering from gelotophobia, the fear of being laughed at.

You will be greatly surprised at the scope and variety of individuals wishing to discuss the following, including some music artists such as Kanye West, who claimed to be a starseed, diagnosing himself as "An alien on a mission to help the Earth." As ever, one must use their own discernment, but is he really just another in a long line of characters that distinguish themselves as such in recent times?

Various beings of physicality and nonphysicality exist in the universe. You have heard or seen of apparitions, and everyone around the world knows of spirits or people that have a ghostly or unexplained story. Those, in particular, are the spirits of the Earth, but what about off-world beings like extraterrestrials in our galaxy who are said to directly impact Earth by helping at this time with what is called ascension? This chapter serves to give an idea of who they are and how they potentially operate.

There is strong evidence that these beings exist, given the direct experiences by people on Earth, and the secret government bodies that have been aware of the following information for a very long time. Various leaks have helped build this picture as well as some of the more spiritual people on Earth at this time, who confirm the whereabouts and activities of such beings. There have been CIA and other secret state employees from the United States, Europe, and further who have, in fear of their life, confirmed and accounted for the following information. As a rule of denomination one account could be isolated, two accounts it could be coincidence, but with three or more accounts as a rule of thumb, it's possible that there is more than a coincidence and a closer look should be given. Likewise, it is known that hundreds of thousands of people around the world have reported lights in the sky over many years. Are they all mad?

Many celebrities have also seen UFOs and speak about it in popular culture. Has everybody simply gone mad or is there some basis to spark all this derangement, and why are the experiences all around the globe following a similar tale? You even find UFOs in ancient cave paintings around the world, including religious and biblical depictions such as the fourteenth-century fresco of the *Madonna and Child*, where a strange saucer-shaped object hovers in the sky. Coins and sculptures peppered throughout our history continuously until modern times, offer hints that we are not alone. Films have been made about it, with popular culture often depicting ETs in comical ways, such as the famous poster of the 1990s, saying, "Take Me to Your Leader!" Why then, for the last millennia, is there a continual heartbeat or pulse reverberating around this field that keeps coming to the fore?

Believers and nonbelievers have asked why there is no disclosure, why have governments not discussed ETs more and if someone does, when will it come? Unfortunately, it is unlikely that it will come from governments or world leaders as this will be used for a reference point of control and further political gain. What the general public forgets is that WE ARE the disclosure. The masses, not the few. If all the starseeds were to take off their skin suits, you would have nonphysical ET souls walking all around the place.

If the public decides that we are not alone in the universe, the narrative that is sold by the ruling 1 percent becomes less relevant. That is why in general we must all stand together and not allow man-made constructs like religion, politics, and dogma to divide us all. United we are strong. Divided we are weak and controllable. It will be the people, the contactees' and the experiencers, who will tell the government what is real, instead of relying for handouts and programming to frame the official narrative. Fortunately to some degree, disclosure has happened. It was blacked out and has been suppressed by large parts of the media.

Paul Hellyer, Canada's former minister of national defense and longest serving member of the Privy Council of Canada, testified at the Citizen Hearing on Disclosure (CHD) in Washington, DC, in 2013. In essence he described that during his service in military office, he had come across conclusive evidence that we are not alone, and he could not keep it classified anymore. He addressed a panel of representatives explaining that in the same way a child grows up eventually coming to terms that the tooth fairy doesn't exist, the American taxpayer could handle the truth with it being about time! He explained how large corporations, the industrial military complex, and the petro-oil industrial complex, which make up the cabal, have kept this knowledge hidden and it was time to end the secrecy. For the attention of anyone who might be interested, this video still exists on YouTube and can be found in various lengths, some longer than others. He wears a yellow tie in the video. Give it a go.

In the following pages, we also explore how tribes around the globe have come into unexplainable knowledge and how these people might have been in contact one way or another. Is there some grounding evidence in the effects these beings have had on Earth as well as the heritage they have left?

In essence we have been programmed early on in life to believe that there only exists what we can see and touch. We have become conditioned to think and work within strict parameters that adhere to a 3D world, in turn becoming criticized for believing anything else. It seems there is a world of energies and beings thriving both on- and off-world with some taking form and others not that exist outside of our purview.

All around us are energies that we interact with but don't see and yet feel comfortable with because science has given it credence or made it "culturally acceptable," and therefore we do not have to think for ourselves as the onus and responsibility for having such thoughts has been taken away. Imagine a world where our own intuitive ability was so strong that we were able to identify and feel whether something had gravity or integrity without the involvement of third parties and we began to manage what we believed ourselves without culture or government interference like the Crystal and Rainbow children exist. We would be able to "self-manage" ourselves and our thoughts alone.

In light of all of this we are building a picture whereby throughout history and in various guises there are mysteries and forms of life that are behind them. These mysterious off-world and on-world entities have been behind much speculation for thousands of years and are currently at the forefront of the spiritual and starseed revelation. Even throughout the Bible there are passages of people living abnormally long lives and seemingly having supernatural powers. Our history is rampant with the fabric of this information and on YouTube we see more accounts being created, speaking of such things with epidemics of people sharing messages in the art that is called channeling. "Channeling" entities is becoming a norm and the otherworldly beings are coming through thick and fast these days. How on earth have we come to this juncture and what has created it and why now? UFO sightings within the last twenty-five years are at their highest numbers than ever before. Outside of ETs, people are experiencing synchronistic events in their lives like never before, as if the universe were leading the way on some new transitory flight onto a path far greater for their highest good. People are having incredible dreams and finding out the next day that in fact what they dreamed DID transpire in their waking day, be it only a song on the radio or some other element that became reality.

Modern thinking became very skewed, with humans who were terrified to speak anything outside of the norm even though the norm itself is laden with fantastical and absurd ideas more delusional than life in the universe. For example,

"Do you believe in God?"
"Yes."
"Can you see God?"
"No."
"Can you prove God exists?"
"No."
"Do you believe in extraterrestrials or the possibility of other life?"
"No."

There seems to be no logical explanation to the illogical beliefs we are programmed to regard as truth. In the Bible we are taught to believe that Moses parted the Red Sea and that Jesus could walk on water. This is read in schools around the world, and yet the thought of humans *not* being the only life in a universe that is larger than comprehension is passed off as insanity?

Humanity has sunk so far that if you are not reading off the script that has been designated and enforced then surely you are not living in the real world. Further still, modern thinking has become so entrenched in the allowed histories that upon suggesting there is anything else one is met with sharp exasperation. What is it in the hearts of people that could make them feel such immediate emotions at the thought of more? Perhaps if there was a reality outside of the narration that has been permitted, that would be a travesty of the greatest kind. People would wake up to the idea that society has been living a lie this whole time. Governments enforce climate change and environmental taxes when they and large corps have had free energy and other technologies all along that would solve these issues.

Take into consideration the SR-71 "Blackbird," which, as far as the public has been told, was and still is the fastest plane in military operation ever. This piece of engineering saw its first flight on 22 December 1964 when the Beatles were singing "I feel fine" and "Baby Love" was a hit for The Supremes. When you take that into context, what do you think they have now that they are not telling us about. Full disclosure was not realized until 1982. Taking into account how fast we have grown technologically it could be said we are at least 100–200 years behind in terms of the technologies that are not being shared with the public.

What this book endeavors to explore before anything else, are the attributes of being from other places and the way these beings are, because through them it will help paint a larger picture of dimensionality and the universe, and begin to unlock theoretical ideas. These beings have names, and they don't seem to be going away anytime soon, nor do the incredible number of growing audiences around the world who attend conferences that speak of them. The concept that there is more outside of the peripheral world that we live in has never been so explored and wanted than now. Are we entering a golden age, the golden age of Aquarius as the Mayans predicted?

If we have neighbors in the galaxy, then where did they themselves come from? This information has even reached mainstream media channels and bestselling programs such as ancient aliens on SKY HD. Let's see what the noise is all about while we play with a little galactic folk law before discussing topics that are more grounded. This part might seem fictional, and yet why are people waking up around the world at this present time all communicating this same story?

Knowledge is wonderful, but timing is critical. The right knowledge at the wrong time is deadly, which is partly to do with human consciousness and cultural conditioning. Telling someone even just two hundred years ago that all light would be electrical would have been a step too far and yet here we sit. In fact, it is likely you are reading these pages by electrical light now or on a device that has a similar nature be it a screen or something you are holding in your hand.

Given the right platform and the right time, a well-dressed lady called Lucy (for example) might be seeing a friend for dinner and suddenly drop that she is aware of beings called the Arcturians having heard about them in the news. Upon relating this revelation, she is shocked to find out that her dinner date Jessica knew all about them but had regarded it as old news and, in turn, had decided not to discuss it in general life. This is the undertone that seems to be simmering in modern society currently. There is yearning and aching to speak of such things, but finding space culturally or socially is yet something that is underway. Humans have always feared what they do not know or understand. Being not of Earth is very taboo, but gestation is over and the baby already seems to be on its way. Timing is key so let us explore what this taboo world is by looking in some detail and diving right into the deep end. Understanding parts of these beings will help on a conceptual level to understand not only how these forms of life might live in higher dimensionality, but where we as the human race are already going.

Note that the details of the constellations and their attributes within space and the stars are real and can be found in any trusted text or book. To understand where much of our ET heritage has come from is to understand its early beginnings as far back in this universe as it is possible to connect. So how did it all start?

The founders as they are sometimes called were a race

of beings who lived in the constellation of Lyra, hence the name Lyrans when speaking of these beings. They were the precursor and blueprint for so many beings and humans within the Milky Way system that we have today. While the Lyrans were the blueprint for many humanoids and beings in our area of the galaxy, it is believed that the very first physical beings were Reptilian beings, and some say some Alpha Draconis. Some of those bloodlines are the oldest and purest in the universe, and you see this mentality play on regards the blue bloods on Earth interbreeding and the royals selecting those who enter their royal bloodlines regarding this mentality.

Prior to the Reptilians there were creator beings who were nonphysical and the Elohim are said to be one of the most ancient of beings in this universe. We start with the Lyrans as this lineage corresponds to how much of the Milky Way came to be inhabited.

The Lyrans were advanced geneticists and had an appearance of humanoid and feline features, some would say cat-like. This is also why you can have cat-like Pleiadian beings who still carry the Lyran lineage in their bloodlines.

The Lyrans also developed another species, which found their origins in the Vega star system of Lyra, who ate a strict diet of raw vegetables which became known as the vagan diet, which in today's world has translated into the vegan word we know. These were beings of light developing peaceful worlds. The Reptilians being some of the first and oldest beings in this universe were great explorers and took the view that this was their universe upon which they must explore and conquer fully as this is how it was delivered to them by a bird carrion race who came from another universe who are said to have seeded Draconians.

While traversing the galaxies to create colonies they came across a relatively well hidden and quiet part of the universe discovering the Lyrans and discussions began regarding creation. The Reptilians wished to live, work, cocreate their value with Lyran beings and there was a difference in perspectives with remedies that could not be found. Talks turned to war, in turn destroying three planets and millions of inhabitants. This began a process whereby colonization to other star systems in search of safe and peaceful civilizations began, concluding in some of the beings we know and understand now that we shall discuss shortly. The history of the Milky Way galaxy is the story of this development and the rise of new genetically engineered beings, both dark and light, and how they began to cocreate and exist not only in our Milky Way galaxy but farther out.

This is a small glimpse into the existence of those beings and their attributes. The particulars you are about to read are a mixture of leaked information from deep state governments, psychics, ET contactees, and channeled information. Your governments at the highest levels are aware of these beings and much more for they have dealt with them personally throughout the dawning of modern man, but especially since the turn of the last century. Leaders of many countries were and are aware of these beings especially American presidents as many of them throughout history have been personally approached by these beings at important junctures of human history.

The Arcturians

A highly evolved and spiritual race of very loving beings come from the Bootes constellation, from a blue planet yet to be discovered by modern scientists, circling the brightest star called Arcturus and is the fourth brightest star in the night sky. It has a reddish tinge. It's relatively close at 36.7 light-years from the sun. Arcturus is a red giant around 7.1 billion years old shining 110 times brighter than the sun. That makes the Arcturians some of our closest neighbors and in the past also protectors of our planet and solar system.

Arcturians often exist in a spiritual plane and ascend through the various dimensions ranging from fourth to ninth and higher. They are some of the most evolved ETs in the galaxy, expressing some of the highest consciousness in the universe with many not residing in physical bodies at all but in energetic spirit form. When in physicality they stand from three to four feet in height and have a skin tone that is bluish green with large eyes and a large cranium, seeing mostly with their telepathic nature as their main organ of perception. It is important to understand that a very high consciousness changes the laws of physics as we know it on Earth. These beings have the abilities to change from etheric to physical at will depending on the situation, something completely alien to humans at this moment in time. When in physicality they have three fingers, they often use telekinesis and mental abilities to move physical objects. Their source of nourishment is said to be an effervescent liquid that is vitalizing to their entire being, but they are also able to survive purely on positive light energy sleeping for up to a few hours a week in which they perform important soul and astral travel activities.

Arcturians have high levels of spiritual knowledge and are dedicated to the service of healing love, and peace including nonjudgmental/unconditional loving, and have mastered these techniques beyond the point that the linear human mind can comprehend at this time. They are the great healers of the galaxy and are carrying out many specific operations regarding healing humanity's DNA and soul issues derived from the large amount of trauma accumulated on Earth over such a long period of time.

Spiritual development is taught at a very early age with life experience roles being tailored by that person's own personal spiritual journey. Professions (in human terms) are sorted by that individual's vibrational frequency and the colors in the aura. For example, it is said that only souls with a violet color as the predominant frequency are allocated care and teaching of young Arcturians as only the wisest souls are allowed to associate with the young and their development.

Their developed spiritual and cellular nature has allowed them to avoid the aging process since they have the ability to transcend time and space much like other ETs we cover and in turn do not suffer sickness or ill health in their physical form as illness was eradicated long ago. They have a collective consciousness that allows them to live in a state of oneness. One of their most important philosophies is that of healing and compassion for the universe. They are governed by what they call the elders, some of the most spiritually advanced souls in the universe, and are revered by the Arcturian people for their wisdom, knowledge, and extremely high vibrational frequencies.

The same is true for those that give birth within the culture who are said to be screened and tested, in terms of their auric and vibrational frequencies, so that when chosen by the elders to give birth to an Arcturian child they go through a process involving no physical contact whatsoever. The two individuals create a mind link where the female and male essence is perfectly balanced coming together to raise their vibrations for a seventh or higher frequency vibration in order for the birthing process to ensure they are bringing in the most highly evolved souls. This frequency, which is an electron force of sorts, also creates other beings which are a replica of the link of a similar vibration to a descended master (in human terms). Jesus was a descended master. The birthing process is considered something to be revered and one of the most important and highly sought-after practices.

In Arcturian society there is no sense of competition or winner-takes-all mentality as they have transcended the ego part of the consciousness and lower fear-based self. Success is measured in terms of light frequency and vibration. They have ways of checking their personal frequencies so that each individual is manifesting correctly, and if an Arcturian is not meeting their own goals for evolution, then the elders do not waste time in sending teachers to help that individual. Their core values are those of love, light, and compassion—fundamental qualities of the fifth dimension, which we will cover in a later chapter about the dimensions and densities. Negativity, fear, and guilt are erased from their culture and they are able to digest information on an energy level many, many times faster than humans.

They are currently helping to activate various nodes and noles of the Earth which have been lying dormant in wait for the great ascension of humankind at the right time. They are said to have bases on Earth as do other ETs helping with ascension at this time and are under water and inside mountains such as Mount Shasta. Arcturians have made attempts with governments such as the US to free humanity from entrapment and slavery to aiding us into a higher consciousness and state of awareness but with little effect. Sadly, governments and the industrial military complex have refused offers as they are only interested in weaponizing potential technology exchanges which were part of an old 3D mentality.

These Earth groups are ego and materialistically programmed and for these reasons Arcturians have had great difficulty discussing issues for the greater good of humanity in the long run, as opposed to short-term gain, for small elite groups and cabals have been operating in old Earth energies pre-2012, before ascension, and only now are just beginning to have the seeds for a different future.

The Arcturians have long worked with the ascended masters known as the Brotherhood of the All and have served as guardians of Earth protecting us from other civilizations with advanced technological development. This is partly due to their starships being some of the most advanced in the universe, which is partly why Earth has not been attacked by negative warlike extraterrestrials, although some still have managed to get to Earth in smaller numbers and create damage, but more on that later. World governments know who these beings are and keep files at a secret level far higher than nuclear bombs/devices—so top secret that often they have no markings at all.

Arcturians greatly promote the power of meditation in order to slow the mind down and clear it of non-useful clutter. They are advocates of going within oneself in order to find the answers, without having to find answers externally through the trappings of instant gratification and validation from the material world and other external stimuli. Such things are enjoyed after enlightenment and not before. They practice an almost constant state of meditation and often go within to find the answers for the questions they seek, as expressed in the following Arcturian message.

One can use the Internet to find the answers they seek on many issues, but when you learn to quiet the mind and connect with the inner web, then you will truly begin to seek the answers you are looking for and the light which will illuminate the path ahead.

Innerstanding will lead you to better outer knowing. Lower density has your reality dictated upon you from your external world often not by choice. Operating within a higher dimensionality nurtures you to manipulate your external world from within creating more aptitude for free will and allowance of true self and expression of self—making you a creator of realities.

(Channeled, Alexander Quinn)

For more information on the Arcturians, see Edgar Cayce. He was one of the most renowned psychics for many generations and was chosen by the Arcturians to share their sacred information. He was very ahead of his time, sharing information and giving readings to thousands of people in his lifetime, from 1877 to 1945, and if you believe in reincarnation, look upon the works of David Wilcock, whom some regard as the reincarnated addition of Edgar Cayce, whose soul has come back in modern times.

The Arcturians were in fact the very first race ever to visit Earth before the Pleiadians seeded humanoids, and before the Reptilians.

The Arcturians travel the universe in their crafts, which use technologies beyond human consciousness and anything the 3D brain can imagine. The *Athena* is said to be a huge mothership that is revered across the galaxy. Their civilization has evolved past the need for computerization, and they have interfaced their own consciousness with the ships themselves; in other words, you think it and the craft does it.

Information on these technologies has leaked and accounts have come from whistle-blowers such as Bob Lazar, a former engineer at Area 51. It is said that the Arcturians' ships are powered by crystals from a part of the Milky Way that is as yet undiscovered. They are currently working with Earth in order to help raise the planet's vibrations into the fifth and higher dimensions and expand our spiritual understanding. They have communicated with humans on Earth for many years through dream state, telepathy, and channeling, using the subconscious mind. Some people, such as Daniel Scranton, channel the Arcturians almost exclusively. If you like listening to only Arcturian channeled messages, you might have this essence of star inheritance within you. Explore it!

The Pleiadians

As you look up at the night sky to the constellation in the Taurus system, the Pleiades is the star system that is the eye of the bull. To the right of the Orion system are the Pleiades, which are thought to have formed 100 million years ago, which in galactic terms is new. Scientists have often wondered how a civilization might have evolved there and have found the timelines too constraining due to the newness of a civilization evolving in such a short time period. Of course, science has a flaw in which it bases knowledge only on what has happened on Earth, not taking into account that physics and evolution might work differently in other parts of the galaxy. In time, this will become more apparent. The Pleiadians were at one point the new kids on the block, so to speak. They went through their own ascension process and were the newest in galactic terms—that was, until humans on Earth showed up. Humans on Gaia are now the new kids on the block.

However, the beings that live here are known as the Pleiadians and are of humanoid form, looking similar to humans and standing slightly taller in height and stature. Pleiadians have advancements of approximately one million years ahead of us in terms of spiritual understanding. This area of the night sky is also known as the seven sisters and the brightest stars that shine are the seven residing closely together: Sterope, Merope, Electra, Maia, Taygeta, Celaeno, and Alcyone. The Pleiadians are key players in the ascension of the human race at this time and have had permission from a collective of beings called the Galactic Federation, who play a role in Gaia's vibration elevation at this time. This assistance helps humans make the necessary changes to become part of the galactic neighborhood and join the rest of the family.

It is said around 250,000 years ago the Pleiadians came

to Earth and have worked much with the Earth's inhabitants, appearing in legends and tales across religions and cultures throughout the world. They also aided in the development of ancient civilizations, Lemuria being the first and then in a lesser way Atlantis, which came later in various forms and different stages.

Some say it was the Pleiadians who helped cavemen fast track the jump to human evolution through their insertion of DNA; however, there are also other contributing factors such as the Anunnaki that have a direct ancient link to rare blood types and genetics. The Pleiadians helped our DNA code become quantum and work at a much higher rate than it does now in other stages of humanity's story. We are their family spiritually and genetically, like a removed cousin. We look similar to them and have a part of them in us.

Pleiadians have the ability to use interstellar ships that can reach Earth in approximately a few hours covering 420 light years. Their ships are like a ball of pure white light and do not appear to have any obvious working parts externally like man-made objects. Could this account for all the mysterious UFOs and ships seen in the sky over the time duration humans have lived on Earth? The answer is yes, although many thousands of races have visited Earth over the years.

Pleiadians are descendants of a group called the Lyrans, who upon leaving eventually settled in the Pleiades among other places. Within our galaxy there is a trend where more advanced civilizations seed new ones, in much the same way the Arcturians helped seed the Pleiadians. One day it will be the turn of Earth, once it has gone through various evolutionary forms and reached a similar state as the Pleiadians whereby we are a danger neither to ourselves nor the rest of the universe. When the inhabitants of Earth eventually create technologies advanced enough to leave our solar system we will arrive in other planets' atmospheres and become the UFOs or ETs ourselves!

Pleiadians are so integral to us and us to them, as they are our distant family from the past and the future. They view us as their children who are about to become adults in the evolution process. They, along with other races, have been very concerned about the way we have treated our planet and they fear we might damage it irrevocably. They understand that free will is essential to Earth and try their best not to affect the Earth and humanity to the extent whereby their actions are responsible for humankind's timelines and outcomes. Instead, they gently hold our hand quietly from unseen places, making sure we are growing in the right direction and learning from our own mistakes or correcting them ourselves as we go along.

At this time, we are not spiritually advanced enough to handle the Pleiadians simply turning up in their crafts, as this would affect the psyche of the human too greatly. In light of all of this, Pleiadian ships arriving would cause panic and confusion, and others would feel a predisposition to worship them with governments falling. In turn, this could lead humankind to think of themselves as Earth citizens instead of part of a country with borders, for example. It would potentially cause immediate chaos. The Earth would never be the same as the knowledge they would bring about science, philosophy, and life could have a devastating effect on our social, economic, religious, and political structures. It would be a case of too much too soon, which could overwhelm our world. Imagine putting a caveman in the streets of London and watching his cognitive brain become damagingly overwhelmed. They will arrive at a time when human consciousness is ready to fully embrace their presence on a footing that is of equal and mutual standing. In much the same way a child grows looking up to their parents, upon which time they evolve into adulthood and begin a different relationship that is closer to friendship on a more equal footing. They do not wish to be worshipped by us as gods from the stars. In light of this, they give us small digestible pieces of information usually through telepathic or dream states to increasingly awaken individuals about Gaia. People channel their messages often and some, such as Pleiadian channeler Wendy Kennedy, can be found on YouTube.

When the time comes, they will be able to help us complete the cycle of extinguishing the separating issues associated with many different ideologies and social customs that have helped some but mostly slowed us down as a civilization. Looking at a civilization such as the Pleiadians would inspire us to reengineer the many dividing social concepts that humans constantly entertain such as financial systems.

There are many other races of beings and ETs in the galaxy that doubted our ability to ascend, feeling we should not be given the chance to do so after looking at the barbaric and bloodthirsty events we have played out in our past. The Pleiadians were there in the front row championing us from the start despite all the odds. They are increasingly open to contact with humans, but one must ask for contact. Meditation, intention with purity of heart, and love are the ways to contact them. Perhaps during a dream state or through benevolent means, they will come to you with a message directly or somehow let you know they are there. Those who channel the Pleiadians sometimes end their transmissions with, "We thank our vehicle for letting us channel this message, although remember, dear ones, you don't have to use this channel. Go inside yourself and ask permission to contact us and we shall answer your call."

Pleiadians are mostly beings of fifth-dimensional frequency and above. They are about love, compassion, wisdom, and peace. People who have had direct contact with these beings describe a calm feeling of love surrounding them.

These beings are telepathic and stand around six to ten foot tall, sometimes with white skin, blond and occasionally platinum hair although Pleiadians often get confused with the Nordics and other beings that are human looking such as tall whites, yet some say the Nordics are an entirely different race altogether! Many live on one of the planets called Erra. The surface gravity is slightly less than on Earth, and for this reason Pleiadians have a slightly different bone density as there is less physical structure needed to hold them up.

Estimates are that there are in fact hundreds of millions of Pleiadians living on Erra. They have had great profundity for managing their population and the resources used to cater for all. In respect to this, they live in less densely populated areas and in smaller numbers spread out over larger areas unlike the cities of Earth that are generally very polluted and overcrowded. Pleiadians on Erra live in a utopian world free of hunger, war, and disease thanks to advanced technology and spiritual awareness. All are catered for and homeless and hungry people are a concept that is unimaginable to them. Basic needs are a given right, not a privilege earned.

Earth systems are designed financially so that the few hold all the wealth, creating large imbalances regards how wealth is created and distributed. The Pleiadians work and acquire resources through a barter system. Due to there being no economics you do not see polarization of wealth and power and the issues that are associated with these ideas. Many services are provided and beyond that, further assets are appropriated regarding a system based on one's service and contribution to society.

Pleiadian culture does not exist upon the presumption of forced or dualistic elected governments that are often polarized regards the vote of that era or year. Many Pleiadians are self-governing beings free to live as they wish, seeking advice only from councils of elders who are the most experienced. On Earth we have been made to believe we must be governed at all times, creating subservience within society. Pleiadian culture is the opposite of this.

They also inhabit various Earth-like planets in the star system which helps avoid overpopulation on any of their planets where certain purposes are carried out specifically such as manufacturing or industry regards larger-scale creations.

A Pleiadian spends much time in the early years learning about the universe and their place within it, later going on to become a master in his or her specific field of talent. This process begins within the first hundred years or so it is thought. As a human becomes ready to die, the Pleiadian is just starting their physical journey into adulthood with life spans existing anywhere from five hundred to one thousand years approximately.

The Greek name "Pleiades" probably comes from a word meaning "to sail." In the ancient Mediterranean world, the day that the Pleiades cluster first appeared in the morning sky before sunrise denoted the opening of the navigation season. Cherokee legends say that they were in contact with the Pleiadian people and that some of the earliest of the natives themselves came from the stars, including tribes such as the Hopi. There is great hidden and secret knowledge within Native American tribes of people still coming from the stars and many think this connection was Pleiadian. These Native Americans were said to be able to communicate with the people that came from the stars. Starseeds around the world are remembering past lives as Pleiadians and call themselves Pleiadian starseeds due to the various characteristics of this race. This is the fascination of the various races we will discuss. The number-one question often burning on the mind of someone who is awakening to this kind of reality is, "Which race do I most assimilate to? Therefore I am a [blank] starseed."

Pleiadians, the Ps, as they are sometimes called, live a collective telepathic consciousness as one. Their DNA functions at a higher level and disease is not able to attach to their cellular makeup and frequency. This is also partly due to them being of a higher consciousness and living in the fourth but mostly fifth dimensionality upward. They mostly eat fruit and vegetable-like plants that are larger than those or Earth and far more nutritional. These beings do not eat any kind of meat.

The Reptilians

Popular culture, leaked sources, direct contact, ET messages, and ancient history allude to there being an ancient global cabal of shapeshifting multidimensional beings (though human in appearance) who have controlled humanity from the shadows. David Icke, a leading thinker in this area, has traveled the world discussing his thoughts on the matter. Interestingly there seems to be within the music industry reported links of this, with Billy Corgan, the lead singer of the Smashing Pumpkins, going public both in the press and on the Howard Stern show to discuss witnessing the transformation of a person in front of his very eyes. One minute they were human looking and the next they had the appearance of a reptile, he explains. Likewise, the late artist Prince also seems to know something we don't, due to his request to see David Icke upon hearing he was coming to one of his UK shows. When it was brought to Prince's attention that David Icke would be attending his concert, he automatically went out of his way to welcome Mr. Icke, even mentioning that not only had he read his books, but that he was a believer himself. Reptilian legend regularly makes an appearance throughout the entertainment industry and especially Hollywood. Also, Reptilian stories and depictions have made appearances within religions, carvings, and ancient stories for as long as recorded time goes back on Earth. So where is the basis in all of this?

Widespread speculation has chronicled that Reptilians have taken over Earth by using various forms of social structures such as politics, entertainment, and large corporations. This way, they control from the top of the food chain using positions of power across all industries so that no weak point in the structure can be left open. They have been on Earth for many thousands of years, and it is thought by David Icke that they first appeared as far back as 230,000 years ago.

These nonhuman entities are also able to operate in the unseen and dematerialize, working in an oscillation outside of the current human spectrum. They are potentially a predator race that when unmasked have a Reptilian form with grey-greenish skin and scales which varies to more monstrous-looking beings. It is said that some of the oldest bloodlines ruling are Reptilian in nature. The most influential of these Reptilian conspiracy influencers often agree that the most famous of all could be the queen of England. There are reports that when President Putin visited the queen in London, she mysteriously began to show visual signs of reptilian appearance in terms of physicality. It seems that Princess Diana, however, was the first to openly begin referencing the royal family as lizards.

We know this due to accounts from Christine Fitzgerald, a brilliant and gifted healer, who was a close friend and confidante of Diana for nine years. Christine had a very strong understanding of the esoteric and this afforded Princess Diana the abilities to share discussions that were very new age at the time. Christine recounted that Diana used nicknames for the Windsors such as

"The Lizards" and "The Reptiles." Accounts from this time are recorded of Diana saying, "They're not human."

On a more global scale there is great discussion about the outrageous number of missing children around the world that go unaccounted for and yet which the media do little to report. It is regarded within many circles that this is linked to the Luciferian Reptilian agenda, which in addition leads to ritualistic sacrifice. This is thought to be the real birth of Satanism. There is also a great common thread that suggests these beings feed off low or negative energies, which they prompt from humans, such as fear, doubt, hate, and anger. Reptilians are also known for feeding of human sexual energy, which in spiritual terms has been known as "loosh." Using all these tools, they amalgamate frequency energies and turn them into a source upon which they feed energetically. For example, a human might go to a music concert and feed off the positive energy while a Reptilian entity would feed off the suffering or fear of a crowd. It is an almost parasitic way of absorbing energy.

Actor Mel Gibson is famously known to have added to the concept of Reptilian Luciferian activities (for more information, see https://planetaryliberation.community/). Gibson appeared on the *Graham Norton Show* in 2017 and shocked guests backstage publicly discussing the true nature of Hollywood elite's dark deeds, saying, "Hollywood studios are drenched in the blood of innocent children, baby blood is so popular in Hollywood that it basically operates as a currency of its own."

He later added, "They are an epidemic of parasites who control Hollywood."

He continued with, "They are enemies of mankind continually acting contrary to our best interests" and "breaking every god given taboo known to man, including the sanctity of children."

He said, "Babies are their premium brand of high-grade caviar cocaine diamond steak."

He further went on to conclude this with, "Hollywood is an institutionalized pedophile ring, but for some children it is but a stepping stone to be drawn fully into Satanic covens where they are sacrificed. This is where many of the missing children have disappeared."

Could it be that Satanic and Reptilian origins are one and the same? Mr. Gibson concludes with, "These people have their own religious and spiritual teachings and their own social and moral frameworks. They have their sacred texts, they are sick, believe me, and they couldn't be more at odds with what America stands for."

Gibson sets out a very interesting debate here. Perhaps there is more to this than just Satanic child rings? There is undeniably a global issue with children vanishing worldwide. Increasingly, satanic ritual abuse survivors are appearing every year confirming these details and more.

The National Center for Missing and Exploited Children has officially stated that roughly 800,000 children are reported missing each year in the United States. That equates to nearly 2,000 a day. Inside of that the NCMEC also has documented 115 child stranger abduction cases each year, which means a child was taken by an unknown person. Here are other yearly figures from around the world from the National Center for Missing and Exploited Children. Their statistics are made from police reports and other children agencies and can be viewed from their web page: globalmissingkids.org/awareness/missing-children-statistics/.

- Australia, an estimated 20,000 children are reported missing every year
- Canada, an estimated 45,288 children are reported missing each year
- Germany, an estimated 100,000 children are reported missing each year
- India, an estimated 96,000 children go missing each year
- Jamaica, an estimated 1,984 children were reported missing in 2015
- Russia, an estimated 45,000 children were reported missing in 2015

- Spain, an estimated 20,000 children are reported missing every year
- United Kingdom, an estimated 112,853 children are reported missing every year

In 2015, 441,125 children simply vanished off the face of the Earth. These, however, are only the reported cases and the list doesn't include unreported cases in various other countries. It is thought that the real number might be closer to or double! That's double the amount of little people disappearing into thin air? Where are these children vanishing to, and why is mainstream media not reporting it?

Whistle-blowers and leaked sources have gone on to say there is a need for young children being that humans at an early stage have fewer impurities and diseases in their bodies with the flesh becoming tastier and softer to eat like a human would prefer lamb to mutton. In the same way they prefer young humans mentally because they are able to infuse fear faster and more heavily using the inexperience of a young mind to control the experience more easily.

Outside of being used for body parts, children's minds are more easily bent and used for other forms of abuse also led by dark players who sell to high bidders on various markets. In the most extreme cases, Luciferian and Reptilian worshippers use a drug called adrenochrome. This is a chemical compound with the molecular formula $C9H9NO3$ produced by the oxidation of adrenaline (epinephrine). This drug has come to light within popular culture such as in Hunter S. Thompson's works, including *Fear and Loathing in Las Vegas* whereby the user takes the substance causing a very euphoric state, but sometimes causing schizophrenic side effects that can lead to violence.

There is widespread rumor that the creators of a very disturbing and gruesome video known as razzledrip were carried out under the influence of adrenochrome. Accounts of Satanic rituals have documented a process taking the adrenaline directly from the victim's body while in a fear-induced state, which is then stored and used recreationally often during a Satanic ritual or later. It is coming to light that adrenochrome is a drug harvested en masse from many children around the world. Increasingly in the new-age community, people suspect children have been found in underground lock-ups and bases otherwise known as DUMBs (Deep Underground Military Bases). Many believe that during the Covid pandemic these bases were found with many children being freed from torturous conditions by special units and governmental bodies who wish to stay secret while working for the good guys or white hats as they are referred to. This is a large subject all on its own that can be searched for and is widely discussed by more than just fringe thinkers. Adrenochrome and children markets are vast subjects. In later years there have been many more survivors, and their stories are not for the faint hearted. These stories have finally begun to hatch out now that the world is beginning to change.

On YouTube you can find various accounts of Satanic and child abuse stories from real accounts of people who got involved but found it "too hot to handle." A prime example of this is Ronald Bernard, a money trader who became involved in high-level transactions and business on a darker level. As he climbed the ladder, he became more ingratiated into this world, increasingly becoming pushed to bend the reality of what he knew was wrong and right. Ronald explains that at the very height of his career he began to encounter individuals within the banking system and large corporations who would expose him to the most elite gatherings in Europe. It was at this point he began to encounter ritualistic child abuse, child pedophilia, and sacrifice, upon which time he backed out. He has since spoken out, after being in hiding for many years, and has released his stories to the threat of his own life. These videos can be found on YouTube to the effect of Satanic Child Sacrifice ex Illuminati Banker Testimony—Ronald Bernard.

It is understood that the Reptilians have also put part of their own DNA into the human mix, which lies dormant until activated by ritualistic activities controlled by the Illuminati. These are often held at private locations, various castles, and stately homes across Europe, which have been used for evil and dark purposes. In Belgium there exists the Chateau des Amerois, aka Mothers of Darkness Castle, and it is said to be home to some of the Illuminati's darkest rituals, blackmail parties, and more.

The Reptilian effort also works to control not only the mind but also parts of the human brain. Within the healing and spiritual world, it is understood that the pineal gland within the human brain is the part of us that is divine. This small nut-shaped piece of the brain where the third eye is centered just behind the forehead, is the part of humanity that when stimulated allows for divine connection and for receiving types of metaphysical information. It is the interface system to the other side, or, in other terms, psychic ability and knowing one's true self.

People who have taken ayahuasca within the Amazon or shamanic environments around the world have expressed a pressure in the third eye area after taking the substance and feeling this part of the brain being awakened. The majority of people have discussed a clarity of thought after taking the drug. It has been proven that the fluoride and sodium fluoride in the tap water we drink have a calcifying effect on this part of the brain making the small nut-shaped tissue hard, effectively shutting this part of our brain down. Conspiracy theorists worldwide have advocated that the big industrialists linked to old family hierarchical and Luciferian agendas have been poisoning the masses with forced fluoridated water for years, while claiming that it's actually in our best interests, specifically for our teeth. If it was the case that this was good for teeth, then why would the amount in toothpaste not be enough, why then would there be an extra forced amount within the tap water people drink and why do more people not explore the value in voluntary fluoridated water instead of forced? Furthermore, is there a depopulation agenda at play here? Evidence seems to exist as seen on the Georgia Guidestones, which have inscribed on them their apparent advocacy of population control and eugenics. Cancer rates are also higher than ever, but why?

There is further speculation from the occult and black magic community that unlucky victims with certain bloodlines are more open to possession than others. This is partly why the Illuminati and various Reptilian pedophilia rings are so obsessed with knowing the bloodline of an individual. Within ritual sacrifice or Satanic abuse, the practitioner will often seek a victim from a certain bloodline or heritage. This in turn makes the victim more susceptible to the dark magic and ritualistic potency required for the desired effects of invoking entities or appeasing astral or demonic parties present that require either sacrifice or ritualistic rape. Psychics within the dark magic world are often recruited to find children of this nature and hunt them down. They offer their findings to the highest bidder within the highest parts of certain religious institutions, or to the elite of hierarchical structures like large corporations and families with ancient bloodlines.

Some of these organizations have genealogical databases with vast information of DNA data banks, designed to identify those desired bloodlines, and tabs are kept on these specified people. In times gone by, high-level witches have been used in the modern world employed by the "Club of Rome" to actively seek very high vibrational souls entering Gaia so that they can either use that soul essence before it is ingratiated into the body or begin to enslave or torture it from birth and beyond.

Rituals often happen in circumstances such as the Eyes Wide Shut party as seen in the film *Eyes Wide Shut*. It is understood the powers that be weren't happy that the public was given an insight into that world as depicted by the film. Is it a coincidence that the director suffered a very untimely death immediately upon finishing the making of the film? We will never know. Things that go on in castles and very old stately homes were never meant to be for the consumption of the public it would seem and are kept very secret although many celebrities who will remain nameless have openly spoken about such atrocities as child hunting parties on private estates.

The Reptilians themselves are said to be some of the oldest races in the known universe and have been present long before the universe was as densely populated as it is today. Legend has it that a race known as the Carians, a warrior race with bird-like qualities to their heads, came from another universe to ours and with them, their creation—the Reptilians.

Within starseed and ancient astronaut mythology, the

Reptilians were created and then left in the Alpha Draconi star system where to this day many still exist and are known as the Alpha Draconians. They are considered the royalty of Reptilians, the forefathers of Reptilians that came after. The Carians are said to have given the Reptilians ideas and philosophies in which to thrive and exist. These included domination, warrior-like mentality, and the belief systems that everything was theirs in the universe to take and own and that this universe was theirs by right.

If you were to look at Alpha Draconian Reptilians, they would appear more dinosaur-like than later Reptilians, some liken them to a very large raptor with attributes such as long tails, standing anywhere from eight to eighteen feet tall. Some species even have wings making them higher within the social structures. They have a large liver and two beating hearts roughly in the same place as humans. They are incredibly strong. Their appearance alone strikes fear into the eyes of the beholder, something they desire, as they can feed from the fear created like a tangible source of food. Intel sources say to kill these beings is difficult because they are often mentally ahead of the human soldier by many steps. A double tap shot to the heart is said to be the best way to eliminate one of these beings should you ever be faced with defending yourself!

They have had interstellar space travel for a long time and have conquered and spread to many star systems, often with force or using manipulation. One of the most densely populated areas of Reptilian descendants is in the Orion constellation, which is considered a place best avoided should one have the capability to even go there as a human; this race generally has a hostile, negative, and aggressive disposition toward races that they see as inferior. These beings have been said to see humans likened to a herd of cattle, and they would wish to enslave us. The truth is, they see humans more like insects that can be stepped on, but this is not to be confused with the many good Reptilian races that exist within our Milky Way Galaxy.

Throughout history in the galaxy there is a story written into our Akashic DNA including the Orion wars that even today are being healed without our DNA. Beings and races have fought the Reptilians in this area of the galaxy for aeons, at the cost of many lives. While acquiring large parts of the universe, Reptilians would leave other beings there to govern, including a type of malevolent Grey aliens. Certain malevolent Greys are said to have been created by the Reptilians, though it can't be proven as of yet. Effectively the Greys were a slave race, carrying out the Alpha Draconian agendas, which explains why on Earth fear-based systems and restrictive hierarchies were created—because they find humans to be an inferior species.

Reptilians, believing that Earth/Gaia is rightfully theirs, have been visiting our solar system for millions of years, and some have even made bases on Earth. These beings that came to Earth have slit eyes, scaly skin, and come in a variety of colors, green and greyish being predominant but other colors such as white and black. Gaia has been referred to as the Living Library by the Pleiadians with many animals existing that are present in ET form. The dinosaurs were part of this construct from a Draconian perspective which later died out.

The purest bloodline Reptilian children are taught early on that fear rules and that love is a weak emotion. It is said the mother shortly after birth abandons her offspring so that they must fend for themselves, with those surviving joining a warrior class. Due to this, many Reptilians are stuck in a survival state and resonate mostly in the third and fourth dimensionality. Many are not able to transcend themselves into the fifth dimensionality, which represents pureness of heart and love. Draconian education promotes fear of other races, distrust, and paranoia of any that are not Reptilian. Many have been indoctrinated to believe that humanoids invaded the universe and came here to steal their resources. Reptilian children are taught that they are superior to all other beings and that they must be perceived as a type of royalty. Their mission on Earth has been to thrive and feed off human suffering, creating conflict while infiltrating deep into our governments and other ruling structures, financial and educational systems, and play a crucial part in many wars on Earth and its previous destructions and creations thereof.

We see elements of the Reptilian force in the film *The Exorcist*, said to be one of the scariest films ever made. At the start of the movie there is a depiction of a Reptilian stone statue known as Pazuzu, the main antagonist who enslaves a young girl spiritually. In folk law, the Anunnaki and Reptilian entities were said to have had a presence in Iranian history, where the film is first set in its opening scenes. Did the creator William Peter Blatty have an understanding of ET mythology? It seems likely. It is said that the ancient Babylonian people knew of Reptilian and demonic entities through their history. Within the *Exorcist* film this reptilian entity is known as Pazuzu, a king of demons that originates from Assyrian and Babylonian mythology. Throughout history you find entities like this that can be linked back to either Anunnaki or Reptilian origins. More on the Anunnaki later.

It is important to understand that there are increasingly growing groups of good Reptilians who have moved away from the ancient teaching and cultural beliefs ingrained into them at such an early age. More frequently there are Reptilian souls coming to Earth as hybrids and working to help raise Earth's energy for good. Some have also defected and broken away in order to carry out good and work with other races. Many Reptilians wish to explore an existence outside of the warrior and survival state and live harmonious lives in high-dimensional realities. There are ET contacts in many countries who claim to have contact with fifth-dimensional beings called the Fajan, a fifth-dimensional race from the Andromedan galaxy with a Reptilian appearance.

Throughout this book, we will explain the concept of ascension and the raising of human light and consciousness, sometimes alluding to the battle of light and dark. For those around the planet, this is a concept that is understandable for all, and many who believe in the duality of evil have heard bedtime stories of its presence within human history. There is indeed a duality in the light/dark "battle" at this present time, and to truly understand the starseed ascension phenomenon that is expedient, is to also understand why some might want it stopped! The Greys, archonic entities, and the Reptilians have a similarity in common. They must survive using parasitic means of living, taking from others' life forces and energies to one degree or another in order to feed their own. This is because they themselves have lost the divine connection with creator/source/God energy and must manipulate it from others. This is why humans have been so easily manipulated in the past by these energies. Sadly, no parties were meant to last forever, and the ultimate hangover of all time is now hitting these players.

Reptilians have a sense of addiction regarding the physical reality we live in, which had been very dense, where they are able to control without being "seen." Within the ascension debate, the ultimate sentence to describe the conceptual basis of the battle of light and dark is "the desire to keep the reins on humanity." Why let humanity blossom from an energetically heavy physical prison that is controllable into free thinking spiritual beings living a life of divinity? You see this in the way that social structures are changing, where people are taking back more power and control today. The few at the top are finding it harder to keep hold of the reins and indoctrinate the many. This is an essential concept to understanding the mechanics of the light/dark battle in what is known as ascension. We will cover this shortly using real science.

To truly understand the Reptilian infiltration and see it work in the daily lives of humans is to ascertain the lie every human being on Earth has lived for all these years, never understanding the atrocities that have been bestowed upon them via the indoctrination keeping them in a state of poisoned codependency. For this reason, full disclosure must not happen all in one go, because to completely unleash the symphony of dark truths that entwine through the fabric of every human existence on Earth at this moment in time would be catastrophic. Disclosure must happen in stages, because unleashing all truths and the darkness in totality would drastically decrease the light on Earth that is so needed as many humans would go into shock and potentially more fear. It will be generations before the full exposure of the indoctrination can be lifted along with other events and their truths that have been mis-sold to the public such as events and deaths of people who tragically lost their lives before their time was completed.

These realities exist around us in every moment although humanity for a long time chose not to see them due to the codependent state they have been conditioned to live in like an abusive relationship that they keep returning to.

Much like other ETs and beings in the solar system, we are designed to live many hundreds of years younger than we have been made to believe and aging is a cruel process that has been genetically and environmentally enforced upon us without grace. Aging in the way we do is an artificial abomination that we must put right including the systems speeding up our deaths. Historically when you return to times in the Bible and Atlantis you read of people living double and triple the lifetimes we do now, and this is because our genetics were designed this way.

Satanic agendas often have similar notions as the Reptilian cabal. They wish to keep the minds of the masses weak, while doing all they can to shorten human life using technologies and sciences such as aging accelerators, soft metals, and sedatives within the food and water we drink.

Chemtrails and other nefarious agendas pollute the very air we breathe with governments telling us that these trails in the sky that are full of toxic metals are nothing but aviation afterburn.

The same is said for the pharmaceutical companies often owned by ruling elite families, some of whom have been involved in the highest levels of political office who knowingly introduce soft metals into the pills humanity consumes. The result of this is that some people lose their minds early in the form of dementia and Alzheimer's along with other additives that during trial stages killed people once reaching the brain. Big pharmaceutical companies promise to find new cures and then profit from vending further poisons that worsen the issues they created in the first place often via more pills as addictive as heroin which have swept across the United States, causing unparalleled devastation such as Oxycontin, a pill often handed out for the most mundane of issues.

The agenda has always been to confuse and propagate the masses to use chemical poisons absorbed orally or via the skin that create internal damage and blood poisoning via the promise of eternal youth enforced by large cosmetic companies and endorsed by celebrities, some who are controlled by handlers or mind programs such as MK Ultra.

All of this is known to the cabal who understand the full consequences these poisons have on the physical and reproductive body so that mothers give birth to more disabled or mentally impaired children who will become reliant on further medical and pharmaceutical substances that will fill the pockets of those companies even more. This is the Reptilian Satanic ethos at play. Keep humanity suffering in illness while profits are reaped.

The cabal has conditioned us to believe these poisons are actually good for us with a variety of advertisements, cartoons, and positive masking with marketing and advertising often targeting the most vulnerable, the young and the elderly. We live in a world where the infant is heavily injected with a huge variety of never seen before so-called vaccinations that our parents never had which are injected by the dozens. Today when your children don't have these vaccines these organizations call you night and day asking why your child has not been injected in an almost frantic state of control.

Dentistry in the past also used fillings in people's teeth with toxic metals that numb the senses and robbed you of your intelligence through metal poisoning. The end game, however, is to keep humanity weak, depressed, reliant, docile, and obese so that when we seek medical help via big pharmaceutical companies so they can pump us with even more poisons, reducing life expectancy, further keeping our life force minimalized and our mental abilities beyond the six senses dulled.

Energetically the idea has always been to keep humanity enslaved in a low consciousness of material fear stopping one from connecting to their innerself but instead money and material possession first; the result is that those that "had it all" felt even emptier, a kind of material torture and the spiral continues as there is a total dependency on the external world only. This plays out in all different kinds of ways making people believe that money will destroy the soul but never understanding why. This then feeds an idea that paper or numbers in a digital system that have no consciousness are evil and in return people never achieve their own personal abundance because they have been conditioned to have ideas about money that keep them poor. Money and financial teaching are never taught at schools as a result of this. Why empower everyone with regards to ownership and tools on how to manage currency and create wealth and freedom from a system that needs you locked within it?

The iniquitous goal of separation from self has been further amplified by external pleasures such as pornography and video games that steal vast amounts of time keeping those that use in a total state of pleasurable dependency. These technologies also keep souls in lower brain frequencies that are far more controllable and susceptible to conditioning from the already controlled outside world.

Another one of the great weapons the Reptilian cabal has established in order to command is the controlled design of divide and rule by establishing governments of different polarities that force people to become divided within their own families and communities while the elite rule both sides enforcing controlled agendas and regulations through both. This you see in some religions also. They create ideas that we are all separate in terms of race and creed allowing this as a narrative for more wars and organizations that create further anger and hate that are funded by the same people who make more profit from the violence it creates and the headlines it generates. This, in turn, adds up to more distractions in the world that remove us from ourselves and create even more fear. These are the same people who claim they wish to live in a multicultural world full of diversity and yet never mix their bloodlines or ethnicity with others, keeping their bloodlines as pure as possible.

All of this they portray as doing lovingly for our own wealth, health, and safety while undermining all of these attributes in other ways that make our lives controlled, subversively brainwashing us into a false sense of gratitude for those that are slowly killing us—the rulers at the top of the game.

Those that get too close to the truth or shine too much light are mocked, discredited, or murdered. You see this in all markets like the energy sector and the music industry. This of course depends on the outcome that suits the plan in action and if a truth is too close to being explored or exposed and sudden deaths are all written off as suicides when the individuals' lives were balanced. You see this increasingly in social media sites regarding the fact-checker age that now exists enforcing narratives that have been scripted by those that rule and own big tech: Motto: Do as we say, do not talk about this narrative, or face being eliminated. Community guidelines are indoctrinated with fear and threats but sold within the narrative of keeping the world a safer place for your own good, the very opposite idea of freedom of speech and democracy upon which most democratic nations are built.

In all of this the truth will always be kept hidden at great expense to human life and even the environment so that there are no holes in the grand game of illusionary control. A prime example of this is the fossil-fuel generation who have been made to feel guilty, who are punished and taxed through climate change regulations when oil companies and governments held free energy technologies and answers to environmental issues for generations. These have been kept in vaults and secret rooms with their inventors often gagged or worse to progress the age of trillion-dollar oil and petroleum industries and to keep the divide between the rich and the poor widening ever still.

The plan is executed by drip feeding slowly, slowly as not to raise alarm while tricking the world into governing and financial laws that offer the illusion of freedoms while actually stealing them away, keeping generations in entrapment legally and financially constantly running on the hamster wheel rat race. This system will never allow you to escape unless you wish to forfeit your house and other possessions that people have been made to believe only represent their true light in terms of material wealth. All of this is designed to keep humanity permanently distracted and confused as to who they really are or from connecting to their own soul becoming the powerful beings they are while at at home with their microwave meals and other poisons that are imbued into the food via cooking in carcinogenic plastics that the establishment say are safe to be super heated within ovens.

Owning all advertising and media outlets including the news is their way to consistently sell fear porn keeping people in fear dependency while coming back for more in a codependent need for solutions and updates that is constantly fueled day and night. This in turn has humanity in the palm of their hands allowing free will to be abused as humanity blindly follows into any direction that is handed out to them questioning no part of it while believing that it must be for their greatest good.

So programmed are those in the fear matrix that they will lash out at others trying to shine light on it because in a lower density there is no unity consciousness so the ego creates self-governing identities for the individual with self-serving truths that must be defended within the egoic state of perpetual survival. Even though these souls know deep down something doesn't feel right, they do everything to attempt to keep the docile reality they are used to, accomplishing a never-ending cycle of never having to think for themselves and allowing their free will to be abused by leaders who think for them.

In an age of lies, truth has become a conspiracy theory with everything made into inverted realities going backward to stop forward thinking or consciousness evolution. When we all stand up together, the game ends instantly. They are doing everything they can to defend their prison from the awakening of the inmates. However, they cannot stop ascension and the inmates are awakening on a global scale each day. This has the elites running scared with the end result being that as more light and truth is created, more fear must be manufactured like a bully in a playground holding onto the last bastions of power before the teacher arrives.

The Andromedans

These beings come from a system outside of the Milky Way in a galaxy called Andromeda. This is approximately just over 2.5 million light years away from Earth, which, in human terms, is considerably farther away than say the Arcturians, who dwell in the Bootes constellation at 36 light years.

They have been on Earth coming and going for a very long time much like the Pleiadians and other beings that are in the galaxy. There are beings from an area called Zenetae, whom Alex Collier is famously known to have spoken to on many occasions, and he has been collecting data that is still in circulation regards these beings (for more information, see Collier's website, https:// www.alexcollier.org/). These ETs are the typical Andromedans that are known in popular culture. However, it is important to understand that this galaxy is a very large place and there are many varieties within it such as plant, animal, insect, and etheric and plasmic conscious. Regards the Zenetae, they are said to be three forms of sex with male and female and one being completely androgynous.

Zenetae beings are typically more humanoid and are anywhere from five to ten feet depending on age and have bluish skin with delicate arms and legs, slightly larger than human eyes, and are said to only sleep two hours a day. They are fifth-dimensional and higher beings with a telepathic and loving benevolent nature about them who have Earth's best interests at heart. They are leading masters in the fields of all things scientific and are the great innovators of science and holographic technologies.

The Andromedans are known for being somewhat of a police force with their own and other galaxies at maintaining peace, especially from the Reptilians and Alpha Draconians who enslaved so many throughout time. In regard to this, they are also proficient in terms of the crop circles we see in fields, which are a sign of inspiration to humanity and a warning to malevolent beings to stay clear. There are examples of benevolent beings leaving "positive vibrational" messages such as the famous alien head with binary code crop circle August 2002 in Hampshire, England. This face has features that are more generic and its origins are still up for debate. There is a large ring next to the face with binary code within the circle which was translated into English. When decoded it said, "Beware the bearers of false gifts and their broken promises. Much pain, but still time. Believe. There is good out there. We oppose deception. Conduit closing."

The Andromedans, via the Andromedan Council, were inducted into the Galactic Federation of light approximately three million years ago in Earth time. The Andromedan Council are important ambassadors for these beings often coming forward to speak to or be freely channeled by people on Earth at this time. This council is an interstellar governing body made up of many planets and beings both etheric (soul only, intelligence without a body) and physical beings with a presence in both the Milky Way and the Andromeda galaxies. They are said to have a direct interest in Earth regarding their own future which is directly intertwined. Alex Collier asked the Andromedans when in contact with them for information regarding this and this was their response.

In Collier's words:

What they have been recently discussing is the tyranny in our future, 357 years from now, because that affects everybody. Apparently what they have done, through time travel, is that they have been able to figure out where the significant shift in energy occurred that causes the tyranny 357 years in our future. They have traced it back to our solar system, and they have been able to further track it down to Earth, Earth's moon and Mars. Those three places. The very first meeting the Andromedan Council had was to decide whether or not to directly intervene with what was going on here.

According to Moraney, there were only 78 systems that met this first time. Of those 78, just short of half decided that they wanted nothing to do with us at all, regardless of the problems. I think it is really important that you know why they wanted nothing to do with us. We are talking about star systems that are hundreds of millions of light years away from us. Even some who have never met us. They just knew the vibration of the planet reflected those on it. The reason why they wanted nothing to do with us is that from their perspective, Earth humans don't respect themselves, each other or the planet. What possibly can be the value of Earth humans?

Fortunately, the majority of the council gave the opinion that because Earth has been manipulated for over 5,700 years, that we deserved an opportunity to prove ourselves and at least have a shot at proving the other part of the council wrong.

The Andromedan council which are a governing body are also aware of interfering factions and responsible for the process of helping remove all Reptilian, grey and malevolent races that are said to make up the vast account of traumatic abduction experiences and some of the quota which is part of the missing child pandemic. It is said these malevolent beings have made bases on Earth, the Moon and Mars and in Earth's underground systems, which incorporate many tunnel systems and places inhabited by these beings which the Andromedans are helping destroy using very advanced technologies said to be using sound and laser waves. These bases were situated over many parts of the world with the USA having the highest proportion of these beings who went into hiding after the 2012 human and Earthly ascension began. It has become public knowledge that the USA has human tunnel systems operated by military personnel spanning most of the country by which you can drive great lengths from city to city deep underground. This is partly where some malevolent beings have been found working with the government and others in cave systems of which are natural and others which are non-human made.

As ever, Hollywood often uses subtle ways to give small doses of information to the public in contextual ways that seem feasible without being too outlandish such as the 1996 movie *Independence Day*. The film *Us* (2019) states, "Across the U.S., there are thousands of miles of underground tunnels that have been long forgotten." The film says they "include abandoned subway tunnels, unused sewers or old mine shafts and many have no clear purpose at all." "No purpose at all" is of course an understatement of yet another Hollywood film trickling out information.

Alex Collier continues to say, "Warnings from the Andromedans are said to have been given out to these malevolent beings to evacuate Earth or be destroyed. Some did leave but others hid and their numbers are very small now. In time their presence will be destroyed as will some of the engineered constructs that they created in order to keep humans dumbed down, isolated and kept in fear/stress limited conscious mental constructs."

There is an array of many excellent videos on learning how to channel on YouTube and though some people are trying it, most are frightened to attempt it. Those who have or are connected with these beings report amazing and wonderful experiences. Interactions with Andromedans are not how you would envisage. At first, they might show you that you have connected with them by using wonderful and interesting ways of synchronicity in your life in order to begin the connection slowly, without creating fear.

Andromedan ships can vary from motherships being twenty-five miles wide, to smaller ships, known as command ships, being a mile across hovering lower in the Earth's atmosphere. There are even smaller scout ships. Often these ships are in higher dimensions/densities and are out of our spectrum of vision. These ships can dematerialize and materialize any time they want, in order to be seen. This explains some of the large bank of military classified UFO sightings and encounters with objects that met with advanced fighter jets, which seemingly appeared out of nowhere. There is a theory that can offer some basic concepts and thought processes about the ability of an object that can appear or disappear. Let's explain a little how this might work. Everything is science and the Andromedans have physics with an attitude!

Anders Jonas Angström (13 August 1814–21 June 1874) was a Swedish physicist and one of the founders of the science of spectroscopy. He created what is known now as the Angström Unit, which in very basic terms measures a length of light in waves. Today it is used extensively in crystallography, solid-state physics, and chemistry as a unit for d-spacings, otherwise known as the distance between atomic planes in a crystal. It also has uses, cell parameters, interatomic distances, and x-ray wavelengths. As light waves or Angström Units increase, we cease to be able to visually find appearance in something with our human eyes.

If you can imagine the vibration of an object, or conceptually an Andromedan vehicle, it begins to disappear from human visual sight as the vibrational components of the matter (the ship or vehicle) rise and rise until you cannot see it anymore. We are taught in school that such technologies simply do not exist, and we are programmed to jest at the thought of such advancements. However, examples of objects seemingly dematerializing can be found about homes across the world. Take the humble fan as a basic example. We use a fan with rotary blades on a hot day to keep ourselves cool. Prior to switching the fan on, we see the blades at a standstill. They still look physical; however, as you turn on the fan, the blades energy increases dramatically until they cross an event horizon whereby they seem to disappear and you begin to see through them when they are spinning, and yet you are aware they are still there. This is the basic concept with ET ships such as Andromedan vehicles which simply vanish without movement as they slip in and out of dimensionality.

Dr. Steven Greer, who used to be a renowned traumatologist within the American medical community, became very involved within the UFO and technological environment of the ET world and has since held exposés and briefed American presidents on such technologies. He has been personally invited on occasions by joint chiefs of staff to discuss such matters, and there are e-mails and CIA-headed written letters to prove it. Greer has made a strong case that the industrial military complex has for a very long time had technologies of this kind and have kept it hidden from the public, which in turn has kept humanity potentially a hundred or so years behind where we should be in terms of technological advancement. In very recent years, the US government has come out to say that they possess antigravity technologies, although the media have done a great deal to "hush" such potentially harming statements.

There have also been other definitive moments regarding crafts of this nature. Ben Rich was an American engineer and the second director of Lockheed's Skunk Works from 1975 to 1991, which is still a multibillion-dollar company today. Lockheed Martin Corporation (part of Skunk Works) is an American global aerospace, defense, security, and advanced technology company with worldwide interests. Ben Rich himself is famously known for saying, "There are two types of UFOs, the ones we build, and the ones they build . . . I am a believer in both categories." The following are all different sayings Rich has said that appear on many websites globally.

"The U.S. Air Force has just given us a contract to take E.T. back home."

"We also know how to travel to the stars."

"Anything you can imagine we already know how to do."

"If you've seen it in *Star Trek* or *Star Wars*, we've been there and done that."

"We have things in the Nevada desert that are alien to your way of thinking far beyond anything you see on *Star Trek*."

As you can see, an Andromedan craft is not so far from the realities of a normal tax-paying citizen. Ben Rich made no attempt to cover up these statements or revoke them while he was alive. To the naked eye, an Andromedan craft will either look etheric without moving parts or sometimes like a huge glowing ball of etheric light pulsating.

As a general rule, it is easier to distinguish extraterrestrial ships from back engineered manmade flying crafts, because man-made Earth manufactured ships are often much smaller, comprised of earthly materials and moving parts that are of a 3D nature, while Andromedan or other alien ships are dream-like ethereal and light constructed craft with quantum energies that earthly engineers haven't yet mastered. More on this later. Take the TR-B3, for example, a military made antigravity craft that is presently in use. When viewed, it does not have the etheric and ET-looking traits that allow for it to be transdimensional as it looks solid with potential moving parts.

Within starseed folklore and channeled messages around the world, there is continuity regarding the Andromedans, who were originally from another part of the universe called Lyra.

Many of the cultures on various planets within the Andromedan system have an abundance of water. Some of these planets are completely covered in water. These beings are known for living both on the surface and under the surface on the ocean floor in cocooned cities with protective barriers. Some of the ships the military keep quiet about are Andromedan, which can sit deep down on the ocean floor.

In general, Andromedans are said to live up to or between 1,000 to 5,000 years and like many fifth-dimensional beings perceive the past, present, and future all as one. In the time that it takes for Earth/Gaia to travel one rotation around the sun, it is understood that an Andromedans' cellular composition is completely renewed and regenerated. In human bodies this is closer to seven years, which is the cellular schedule the human body honors. Much like many other extraterrestrials, the Andromedans' way of quantifying time is done on a far larger scale. A human's experience of time is only based upon one sun and a solar system we can't travel out of yet (or so we are told). We base time on our planet Earth rotating around our nearest sun. Many beings, including the Andromedans, work on a larger scale of what is known as Revs, which is short for revolution. This equates to the time taken for a solar or star system to rotate around the center of the galaxy. As all star systems rotate at the same speed around the center of the galaxy, it can be quantified as rotations or "Revs." For example, it is said that since humans have been on Earth, we have only achieved a quarter of one Rev. The Pleiadians have achieved approximately one or slightly more than one Rev. There are still much older civilizations who have achieved many Revs.

It is said there are also Andromedan ETs, who are here among us at this time, who have come in physical form that look more human as many other races have done also. It is understood they have an Asian and sometimes Mediterranean appearance with tanned olive skin and stunning blue eyes. Perhaps if you are sitting in a cafe one day and a being of this description begins to speak to you telepathically, you might be encountering an Andromedan. In this instance, you have nothing to fear, as they have a frequency signature that would allow you to feel warm, safe, and loved. Humans can pick up on energy signatures easily. Have you ever been to an old house or a room in a building that felt negative or villainous? It is your psychic self, picking up on negative energies, and this is partly to do with the crystalline grid, but more on that in the following chapter.

Meeting an Andromedan, for example, would feel quite the opposite, although popular culture would leave you to believe they are dangerous, such as films like *Independence Day* with actor Will Smith. These older perceptions, however, are slowly dying out. It is thought that out of all the starseeds on Earth at this time, the Andromedan quota is one of the smallest regarding the main ET races. Often these starseeds have the characteristic of being completely unaware of their Andromedan spiritual origin and operate unbeknown to themselves as a being of light raising the Earth frequency while simply going about their normal day-to-day lives.

There are many well-known people who channel or are in direct contact with the Andromedans such as Alex Collier, whom we have mentioned, and Elaine J. Thompson, who is a natural clairvoyant medium. Below is an original channeled message from Elaine J. Thompson that helps understand the multidimensionality that not only the Andromedans have, but many other dimensional beings have. It opens the mind to seeing how humans have been prepared to live in survival mode for a long time without allowing our full potential to shine.

Mankind's duality is represented in the two halves of the brain. In truth the logical functioning of the brain is necessary only in lower dimensions. What seems logical is what appears in the reality in front of you, the reality you have created. It is logical that one brick sits on top of the next brick, but if you remove the logic, you see only the energy, and you will see no actual separation between the bricks. When you realise there is no need for a third dimensional physicality, you will release the need for logic. That does not happen automatically, it comes

ET, Phone Home

with understanding. When you begin to understand, you will know the following things.

Firstly, that you can change shape, or travel somewhere else in an instant, that you can fly and send and receive telepathy. When this is fully recognised, the left logical side of the brain becomes unnecessary and more of a stumbling block rather than a helping tool.

For you, there is no logic in being able to fly. If I asked you now, can you fly? you would say, no, I am too heavy and the force of gravity is too strong. If you left your physical body then you could astral travel freely, but as you are still within your body and you relate to being that body, then your logical mind dictates that some things are impossible. Your logical mind dictates that you cannot pass your hand through a wall. In reality with manipulation of molecular frequency all things are possible. As a species, you are shifting from logical to spatial thinking. Whole brain thinking is the middle path and not the ultimate goal. Within the right hemisphere of the brain, all your latent abilities are held. To access this fully it means not trying to logically understand, but knowing and feeling and staying connected without words. If you can forsake your logic for just a while, you will begin to realise the many stages and levels of development that can be reached within the right brain.

You are a technological society, and for third dimensional functioning, you need, or have needed in your past, the greater function of logic and understanding. You plant a seed and it grows. This is logical, but these are just basic elementary facts. What you are missing is that when you plant the seed for growing, it is a fact, that without the energy of the creator (god) the energy of all that is, that flows through everything, the seed would never grow. You have all been in Earth kindergarten learning the basics, and now it's time to graduate into high school. You have the ability to change from one thing to another, to change your cellular structure, your energetic body.

The front of the brain above the third eye and all around the area where the pituitary gland is located, becomes connected underneath to the back part of the brain. This black area of the brain known as the Substantia Nigra, is an area that your doctors and scientists know very little about. Within this dark area of the brain lies the capabilities of molecular change and total restructuring of the body. This does not mean that you will be totally illogical and unable to function. What it means is that all the things that you cannot see with your eyes or understand with your logical mind will become apparent to you.

This is when the beauty of silence arrives, simply because in silence, the only language is telepathy and telepathic language, the language of feeling. It is how you feel, it is right brained. The energy of telepathy knows no boundaries. Telepathy can span a universe and take you from one place to another so that your whole essence is or can be present in another dimension.

In 1954, blue Andromedans landed in Florida and began talks with President Eisenhower. He was strongly urged not to trust the "Greys" at the time and that the consequences would not be good for humanity. This advice was ignored and instead the government at the time decided to work with the Grey race in turn for some of their technologies; this technology, such as antigravity, has since been hidden from the public and kept in underground bases and complexes.

The Hopi natives in the US spoke long ago of blue-skinned light warriors from the stars and have been in contact with them for a very long time. Are these the Andromedans or perhaps another race altogether?

The Sirians

Sirius is one of the brightest stars in the night sky, nestling in the Canis Major constellation, with Sirius being twice as large as Earth's sun and up to twenty-five times brighter. Its sister sun, Sirius B, is a white dwarf that neighbors the giant star, being just a fraction of the size. The inhabitants of this system are multidimensional ranging from beings of fourth density and higher with etheric nonphysicals and beings inhabiting physical bodies.

The Sirians mostly are benevolent and are playing a part in Gaia's ascension. These are from Sirius A. However, it is feared there are some that have had negative intentions toward Earth and interfere for personal gain and corruption stemming from Reptilian ideas. These beings are mostly from Sirius B where the smaller star is. The Sirius system is incredibly diverse with aquatic and even some Reptilian-looking beings. Others come in all shapes and sizes with various colors and skin types. The famous aquatic beings often encountered are called Mommas, and they live on a planet that is mostly warm and covered in water where they incorporate very advanced skills in sound and acoustics. They look like merman/mermaids crossed with a streamlined body. These are the accounts that are relayed often when an Earth being has astral traveled or has had interaction. Some Sirians have webbed feet and fingers, and the ones we are aware of have two arms and two legs with humanoid features. Whales and dolphins are often associated with having the spirit essence soul of the Sirian beings.

The native people of various lands knew of these star systems and the beings that lived there in Sirius before modern man arrived. The Dogon are an ethnic group living in the central plateau region of Mali, in West Africa, south of the Niger bend, near the city of Bandiagara. Their population numbers between 400,000 and 800,000, and they have been in existence for a few thousand years with their own systems of astronomy and calendrical measurements. In their teachings and scriptures, they described beings who visited in great ships with an aquatic appearance capable of walking on land called the Mommas. Their skin was primarily green, but like a chameleon, it sometimes changed colors. Dogon elders range in various accounts which explain appearances where beings were changeable with all the colors of the rainbow manifesting depending on their state of being.

Most interesting is the description of their world to the Dogon tribe and the recountings of the Sirius cluster and their watery worlds. It wasn't until 1930 when French anthropologists colonizing the area began to hear great legends from the tribal priests about the advanced information these beings had passed on regarding the Sirius star system. Upon further investigation, it became clear that the Dogon tribe had precise knowledge of cosmological facts that were still unknown by developing modern astronomy. The French colonists were fascinated to learn various facts such as Sirius being part of a binary star system, whose second star, Sirius B, was a white dwarf taking fifty years to complete its orbital paths. The existence of Sirius B had only been examined through mathematical calculations undertaken by Friedrich Bessel in 1844. To this day, it is still the greatest mystery of how a relatively isolated tribe knew so much about the cosmos.

Dogon artifacts dating back hundreds of years depict the orbits of Sirius A and B. Many years later in 1970 astronomers finally had telescopes that were powerful enough to reach in to the Sirius constellation upon which they found and photographed Sirius B, concluding that everything the Dogon tribe had said was correct. Stranger still is the identification of the exact number of moons around Jupiter and the rings around Saturn centuries before telescopes had been invented. Various scientific sources increasingly found it hard to explain the knowledge the tribe was sitting on as it has far predated the advent of modern cosmology. These aquatic beings have also appeared in Babylonian, Arcadian, and Sumerian texts and legends and have passed down information about the cosmos in these areas, too.

It is also known from other UFO experiencers who have channeled information, that other beings who are more humanoid in appearance have a luminous bright blue skin due to ultraviolet light from the sun of Sirius A. Some ancient astronaut scientists believe that the African race has its genetic origins going back 100,000 years or more to the Sirian races to some degree.

The benevolent beings in the Sirian constellation are very spiritually evolved and resonate at a very high frequency of unconditional love and compassion. Many resemble humanoid beings larger than us, with larger developed brains and separate additional lobes much like the brain structure of a dolphin or whale. This allows for stereoscopic vision. As a result, Sirians are able to see into matter itself, understanding the atomic structure, visualizing it internally and externally.

Ancient Egypt was heavily influenced by Sirian spirituality, and it is said Sirians descended on this part of the world in ancient times helping build the great empire while offering great technologies and spiritual teachings. The Sirians are some of the greatest teachers in our galaxy with great schools within this part of the galaxy that other beings far and wide travel to in order to learn and seek more knowledge about the cosmos and more. They, like the Arcturians, are also capable of great healing. This correlates with the great Egyptian god Isis, who was advocated as the greatest healer of that time, and who, according to legend, restored Cyrus's body and brought him back to life after he had been murdered by Seth. The Sirians are also considered great warriors, a skill which was passed to the men of ancient northeastern Africa. Along with the Arcturians, the Sirians are some of the first beings to visit Earth around four to five million years ago, having influences on the South American regions also.

Here is a channeled message from the Sirian High Council spoken in their own words:

Many light beings are now focused upon Earth's transition in consciousness from the Pleiades and Andromeda, joining with us to help raise the vibration. However desperate they may seem to you, the current events playing out in your world are part of the process of your awakening. Pay attention but observe with detachment what goes around you. Be centered stilling the lower emotions. Be wary and look carefully about you, turning your focus away from the horror and toward beauty, love, and the miracles that surround you in every moment of your lives.

The Anunnaki

The Anunnaki have played a major role in the evolution and history of Earth, but mostly from a self-serving perspective to aid their own personal agendas that have created more problems and karmic issues than they envisaged for both humankind and themselves.

Some of these beings have lost their connection to the God source and are utilizing human and other soul types as an energetic food source to live many thousands of years. Some of these beings can live up to 500,000 years or so, and their leaders even longer. This is partly due to the very high frequency at which their energy resonates. The higher the frequency a being is resonating at, the faster their timeline is manifesting in comparison to beings of a lower density such as Earth. These beings are also the masters of genetic engineering and this helps them live longer also. What may be 1,000 years in terms of human years is to the Anunnaki only days. Time is relative to different vibrations. These beings work on multidimensional terms as other ETs do but on much longer periods of time; however, with this comes issues regarding their pinpointing moments in the time continuum. On Earth we only have the now, otherwise known as the present. For multidimensional beings, time is not linear, it is the future, present, and past at the same time. For this reason, and taking into account the long period in which these beings live, they find it much harder than some multidimensional beings to find Earth's now/present with far more time navigation needed in order to pinpoint and access Earth events and their processes.

They are etheric beings who can genetically create and host any body they wish to for that given purpose. They have historically taken on the form of beings of melanin attributes with dark or black beards; other depictions exist in carved-out stone structures portraying mesopotamian Persians but other people who have detailed them have experienced them as etheric dragon-like beings when not in physical vessels. Being genetic and DNA engineer super masters, they are able to manipulate and tailor DNA in a way that is far beyond many races. They do not have emotions like humans have but are highly intelligent as they are working on mind principles. They look at our wide range of emotions with great fascination and trepidation. While they understand the motivation that emotion can bring to creating, they also see humans as unbalanced regards the also wide range of negative emotions that can be processed and have in the past used this to their advantage in the early days of their visits to Earth.

The Anunnaki have been manipulating the human world through genetic and mind-control techniques for thousands of years for their own purposes. Lesser forms have been created by the CIA such as MK Ultra, a technique the CIA claim isn't used anymore, having been warned of its human rights infringement, but which is in fact still being used. Mind control offers a large realm of entertainment with YouTube providing a cacophony of what is known as mind-control glitches. These cannot be proven, but they are open to speculation and are very mysterious.

1. Al Roker is an American broadcaster who mysteriously froze live on air after the words "holy ghost" were uttered; a trigger word perhaps?
2. Wendy Williams, Halloween special where she freezes live on air.
3. Draymond Green, at a press conference, completely freezes.

It is often speculated that the Anunnaki orchestrated various political and religious systems including other social structures in order to keep humans divided, segregated, and in turn weaker so that the masses have little power. Some say they are the original creators of the class systems and various bloodlines that are the ruling elite, otherwise known as the Illuminati. In the Bible they are known as the fallen angels and the Sumerian gods. Anunnaki, the word itself, means "those who came down from heaven." In biblical terms they have been referenced as the Nephilim, who are the Anunnaki in human form often depicted as giants in the Bible.

The Nephilim were seen as an abomination. Folklore says that when the Anunnaki came to Earth residing in their space port which is now known as the Middle East, they eventually began to reproduce with humans and create a race of giants known as the Nephilim, who are said in the Bible to have lived a very long time.

There is perhaps credence in this story as huge skeletons of giants have been found around various parts of the Earth and are increasingly being uncovered and dug up. Pictures can now be found in mainstream media and images acquired on Google. Stranger still are ruling elites and government hierarchies which have gagged archaeological communities globally regarding finding these remains and continue to discredit and deny all claims of these very large human-like skeletons that increasingly are being found. Many of these skeletons that were found are destroyed or kept out of public view. Is this another history kept hidden?

Starseed folklore seems to have a common thread regarding the Anunnaki. It is said that they came to Earth when they demanded from the Sirians that their races have a place to evolve on the Earth as equal placement to human beings because they did not have the ability to evolve with the source creator. This was a hidden deception as they were not interested in equality or evolution on the Earth, but interested more in resources such as mining for gold and minerals, as well as making humans a manipulated race to serve the Reptilian genetic based races and their projects and agendas.

When the Anunnaki created the Nephilim it was seen by the higher factions of the Lyran-Elohim council as a violation to tamper with human genetics. In turn the Lyran-Elohim council, including some Sirians, disallowed the Anunnaki to continue on Earth. They considered it a violation, which angered the Anunnaki because other extraterrestrial races were being allowed to introduce genetic material into the Earth, as the "grand experiment." This created a conflict and another war broke out. A war with the Anunnaki and other Anunnaki sympathizers such as the Dracs and Sirian Anunnaki hybrids began. In turn the Galactic Federation supported this movement in a bid to assist the ascension timeline for Gaia, thus taking back sovereignty of Earth for its higher and greater good again.

There have been vast abuses of technology on Earth coming from these beings with inside military sources hemorrhaging news of trading advanced technology related to mass mind control and AI systems that have made their way to the military industrial complex over many years which have been used by super soldiers and other modified military personnel. It is said within some classified military circles that these technologies are their greatest hardware, and adopted for the super soldier, a huge discussion that is very public and can be looked up. This is also an example of MK Ultra. Max Spiers is a whistle-blower who was part of the super soldier program who managed to break out and spoke much on the "super soldier program" before his mysterious death in Poland. Max's videos can be easily found on the Internet.

The media and entertainment industries play a great part in this, too. This is part of the great plan to control and imprison the masses in a place where the many never see the walls in which they are imprisoned. This not only has worked on a physical level but also on the nonphysical and astral planes, too, where the enemy is hidden. Some have claimed that the Anunnaki set up a soul matrix in order to recycle Earth souls into a permanent repeated Earth incantation whereby no Earth soul upon death was able to escape and would return in a vicious cycle forever empowering the Anunnaki end game on Earth constantly being reborn as physicals in a human body.

Since the ascension timeline began, various factions, benevolent ETs, and light organizations have put an end to this soul matrix, allowing the soul to choose where it wishes to travel to next rather than be forced back to Earth in the recalling process, often leading to false and negative soul contracts. The spiritual community and those that call themselves starseeds have also widely discussed the existence of those called the Archons. It is believed in certain circles that these are astral beings who have worked in part with the Anunnaki. The Archons are often described as fourth-density beings that feed off fear and other negative human traits.

There is speculation regarding their agenda with some suggesting that they are part of the Anunnaki team otherwise known as the "Watchers" and are an astral force in place to keep both light and darkness balanced within the engineered matrix. Some more extreme views lean toward the Archons being lower dimensional beings who facilitate feeding off the energies of humans in a parasitic modality and that this helps the Anunnaki agenda. Archon starseeds are believed to exist although they are very rare and as the author of this book I have only met one Archon starseed, or in other words, a being of this description incarnated into human form.

As we delve deeper into the starseed ET experience, it is important to understand that as the Bible explains, the soul truly is eternal. The soul is all that ever was and all that ever will be and is a part of God, or what ETs and entities call Creator. There truly is no sting in death. Upon leaving your human body you leave Earth and visit the astral and nonphysical realms where you rejoin family members both from the stars and from earthly or family connections, sometimes even animals that you loved. This can also include councils that are part of the original discussion prior to visiting Earth.

The soul journey matrix is complex and something we shall touch on later. For this reason, you hear increasingly of people who have had past lives and remember in incredible detail who they were with various past life elements still present in current incarnations. This is now increasing as the veil is becoming thinner between earthly and other dimensional planes through the ascension process. In a nutshell, it means we have more ability to remember who we are, to connect with our higher self or over soul, and to be closer to our "guardian angels" and the unconditional love of God and creator.

The Anunnaki have a great bloodline and family history

within Akkadian, Babylonian, Assyrian, and most importantly Sumerian texts and artwork. They have even been described in such books as the *Necronomicon*, a part-fictional grimoire (textbook of magic) appearing in stories by the horror writer H. P. Lovecraft. Upon searching by Google we find those who even entertain the concept of the Anunnaki associating images of Sumerian stonework carvings.

Other accounts tell of them coming to Earth about 450,000 years ago as tall beings about three meters high. This civilization has also made many appearances within our Bible with members playing different roles. There is a family tree that is expressed within mythologies including religious texts that go back hundreds and thousands of years keeping a consistent thread throughout. It is easiest to describe the shape of this family tree by starting with Anu. He is also known as the Great Father of the Sky, lord of all the other gods. He maintains this position as the Sumerian tale unfolds, until passing it to Enlil and then in Babylonian lore to Marduk. Barbara Marciniak, a Pleiadian channeler, has entertained the idea that Anu has had not only great influence in human culture but languages also putting himself firmly in many words so that there is a remembrance that we are not always consciously aware of. Within the English language you can find many traces of Anu: alph<u>anu</u>merical, m<u>anu</u>facturer, gr<u>anu</u>lation, m<u>anu</u>scripts, cle<u>anu</u>ps, m<u>anu</u>ally, tet<u>anu</u>s, pe<u>anu</u>ts, J<u>anu</u>ary, <u>Anu</u>nnaki.

His parents are two primordial gods, Anshar and Kishar. Some have seen these figures as the titans who preceded the ancient Greek gods. After Anu's two consorts are Antu, known as the Great Mother of the Sky, and Ki, the Earth Mother. Both gave him children. Ki gave birth to Enlil, lord of the air and guardian of the Tablet of Destinies, and Nin-hursag, Lady of the Mountain. Anu's other consort was Nammu, who gave birth to Enki, lord of the waters, who has also been referred to as Poseidon in legend. Different accounts vary from religions and texts; however, there is some level of grounding throughout. In similar ancient times we begin to see the scriptures of the first gods and goddesses being recorded, including Gaia, which is a Greek word meaning

Earth. In Greek mythology Gaia was the mother goddess who presided over the Earth, and in galactic terms Gaia (later called Earth) was originally known as Agartha, which many still use as a term to explore the possibility of a civilization and their domain from Atlantis who are believed to be existing inside Gaia/Earth even now. Let us continue back with the Anunnaki.

Enlil and Enki are half-brothers. Following Enlil's birth, he and Ki took command of the Earth, while Anu continued to reign in heaven, or from an off-planet perspective. Enki then has a son called Marduk, who in time becomes the supreme ruler of Earth. Where matters complicate is with Marduk, who only shows up in the Babylonian version of the myth, while in the Sumerian version, Enlil beats Tiamat and reigns supreme. The Anunnaki family tree and timelines are complex but can be found and read about as common knowledge. As we have stated previously, many starseeds at this time have had or are having the dream of the great flood and the waters that engulfed the Earth 13,000 years ago, which is also part of the Noah and the Ark stories. Have you woken up one night dreaming of a great tidal wave engulfing all of the Earth? Perhaps you are older than you think, on a soul level. If you are having or have had this dream, it is a milestone to exclaim that you are remembering and coming online again. It should not be taken as a prophecy inducing panic in which you sell up, move to higher ground, and get ready for the world to sink again, because it is not happening. Rest assured.

In other texts Yahweh was getting fed up with the sins of humankind. More specifically, he was upset about the corruption of mankind by beings referred to as the Nephilim, which can be translated as the abomination of ETs reproducing with humans. This is even referred to within the Bible from the Book of Jubilees, 7:21–25:

> For owing to these three things came the flood upon the Earth, namely, owing to the fornication wherein the Watchers against the law of their ordinances went a whoring after the daughters of men, and took themselves

wives of all which they chose: and they made the beginning of uncleanness. And they begat sons the Naphidim, and they were all unlike, and they devoured one another: and the Giants slew the Naphil, and the Naphil slew the Eljo, and the Eljo mankind, and one man another.

And every one sold himself to work iniquity and to shed much blood, and the earth was filled with iniquity. And after this they sinned against the beasts and birds, and all that moves and walks on the earth: and much blood was shed on the earth, and every imagination and desire of men imagined vanity and evil continually. And the Lord destroyed everything from off the face of the earth; because of the wickedness of their deeds, and because of the blood which they had shed in the midst of the earth He destroyed everything.

We find that Anu, Enlil, Enki, and Nin-hursag have created the "Nephilim" and that a major destructive flood is on its way with little in the way to protect humankind. Enki, who shows compassion to humanity and decides he will warn a leader of the people and consequently the Ark is built. In starseed folklore (usually more ET heavy), there are discussions that the Pleiadians turned up in huge galactic ships and demanded to speak to Anu. Anu says, "Hey, okay, I'll surrender control of Earth, but I'm taking all my creation with me." Other myths explain that Enlil becomes tired of maintaining humanity and uses great floods to achieve this. As the god of weather, this is feasible.

There are thought to be three planets that the Anunnaki call home, with the most important being Nibiru. This is a red planet ten times bigger than Earth returning every 3,600 years in a huge elliptical orbit. It is said their royalty are born only on this planet, which of course is where Anu the great god comes from. Other names for Nibiru include Planet X, Nemesis, Wormwood, Blackstar, Kachina, Terral, and the Planet of the Crossing. This is not to be confused with the black sun or the black star in High Masonry organizations with reference to Saturn the planet. The two are different. Other theories suggest that due to the huge mass of something coming so close to Earth there would be tectonic plate movement and other gravitational issues such as tidal waves or earthquake disasters. Theories have arisen to not only the great flood 13,000 years ago but also of the extinction of the dinosaurs becoming possible regarding the consequences of such a large cosmic body entering the solar system on a route close to Earth.

Here is where the strange part comes in. In very recent times both astrologers and scientists have indeed identified a large red planet that is approximately ten times larger than the Earth and that has an elongated elliptical orbit that swings into our solar system calculated at approximately 3.5 thousand years or so. Headline news has called it Planet 9 and Planet X with some large broadcasters covering this news, such as the BBC. NASA has made statements on its website that there is no hiding the evidence of this huge mass and there are entire books written on the subject both scientific and some on the side of conspiracy ideas regarding the subject. Many legends predicted that the Anunnaki would come back to Earth around the year of 2012 to settle old scores and put their house back in order, or maybe even to hand it back over to humans. Of course, only time will tell. Perhaps it is strange timing that the powers that be have begun to elude a large red planet with a large elliptical orbit as of late?

The Greys and Zeta Reticulans

It is important to understand that the "evil" Grey aliens that are depicted in movies, popular culture, abduction, and government experimentations are separate to the "Zetas" and the way they operate. However, both have origins from the Zeta Reticuli binary star system and couldn't be more different. In basic terms the Zetas are more benevolent while some Greys have proven to be more malevolent. This is due to manipulation from other ETs. There are said to be many different types of Grey- and Zeta-looking beings with huge differences in genetic and physical makeup. For the sake of introducing the ideas of these beings we will simplify their differences for now.

The Zetas are three to four feet tall and have large heads. Skin color can vary from being very white to more grey with large dark eyes, a very small nose, and a tiny mouth. The Greys can be said to have similar features, but some have darker grey skin with a harsher texture that is less smooth standing taller. Facially some of the Greys appearance is not as pleasant to look at as the Zetas, who have a more neutral facial structure and would be seen as more inviting upon encountering them. The Zetas generally resemble more humanoid characteristics whereas some of the Greys have faces less like humans, such as only holes where a nose would be and no nose structure. The eyes also are more slanted and not friendly looking at all in some cases and some of these larger Greys have been genetically bred by Reptilian beings for control.

The Zetas originate in the Reticuli A system, whereas it is thought that the Greys were a renegade group genetically enhanced for control and darker purposes by Orion and potentially Reptilian groups that originated from the B system. These grey aliens came to break away from their neutral benevolent origins of the Zeta in Reticuli A and became exiles in the Reticuli B area. These twin stars exist in the reticulum system thirty-nine light years away from Earth, which by galactic terms would make them our direct neighbors. Both Zeta 1 and Zeta 2 have an average age of between six and eight billion years. This makes them from one to three billion years older than our sun and suggests that any life on planets associated with them could be much further along in its evolutionary process than we are. These two stars are similar in many ways to our own sun and can be seen more easily from the southern hemisphere. If you were to look deep into the darkness of the night sky you would be able to just make out two dots. Both beings have ships that are able to reach our solar system with the Zetas being more technologically and spiritually advanced.

Let us start with the Zetas, who are among the many beings helping ascension on Gaia at this time. They are four feet tall, have very long fingers with four on each hand, and are generally slender and thin looking with no hair on their body wearing tight body suits. Some beings in this category wear no clothes at all, they like to go nude! They have small human-looking noses and a chin that is humanoid. From past experiences both individual and governmental, it has been confirmed they wear the jumpsuit. These beings are generally thought to be more physical than nonphysical living in their bodies most of the time. They are known to be incredibly scientifically and technologically advanced, perhaps even in the region of one million Earth years in our future. Zetas have home planets that make up different atmospheric mixtures of air which would kill a human. Leaks have hinted that they breathe high quantities of nitrogen and helium. Government sources have explained how a ship with these beings was shot down while keeping a Zeta alive with a self-contained room in which a special gas mixture for their breathing was created in order to sustain life.

Zetas are extensive travelers. Many of them spend much, if not all their time on their ships and explore the galaxies and universe using time travel and star gates. Star gates have also been on Earth for thousands of years with some of them being linked to pyramid structures around the world years ago in Asia, Egypt, and South America. These structures have also been found in Antarctica by scientists and military personnel. They have been known about for quite some time while their true nature is still under discussion. Stonehenge in Wiltshire, England, also seemed to have served as a potential portal at some time in the past.

The Zetas have taken their technologies to a place of great heightened levels. In much the same way that the Arcturians can interface with their technologies in a symbiotic and telepathic way, the Zetas also have managed this, although relying more heavily on the technological side. If a person were to go on a Zeta ship, it would be perceived that their technologies were being managed through the power of thought with very little physical work needed with what humans might call computerized hardware. Their ships have been built with a type of consciousness of its own, which is how they travel through space. The Zetas do have somewhat of a technological dependence but have managed to balance their spirituality in tandem.

These beings can integrate with the consciousness of

anything of material or living organic matter including the consciousness of other beings and humans. They have high level mental abilities like telepathy and telekinetic talents. They do not express emotion as humans do but express feelings more with the mind in telepathy instead of facial expression. They are able to understand human emotion but register other beings and experiences more as frequencies. Their facial expressions are usually fairly static but sometimes become expressive.

Zetas have the ability to clone their own bodies and even perform walk-in soul abilities. A walk-in is when a soul enters another body intentionally becoming part of that being's consciousness or soul expression. The Zetas have worked with other galactic groups in a bid to mix human and Zeta DNA, creating human Zeta hybrids facilitating a speeding up of human evolution requirements for DNA and spiritual evolution during ascension. This is known as the hybridization program, which is under great speculation at this time regards the dark activities humans are involved with versus the light and dark agendas of ET activities within this field. This coincides with women around the world who report becoming pregnant but whose baby mysteriously disappears at two to three months without traces or scarring. Reported cases revolve around females dreaming that the baby would be taken and waking to explore that the dream might have been a reality. These cases are still very taboo but have increased in numbers in times of late and there are very few support groups for mothers who are part of soul contracts who agree to the hybridization program prior to entering Earth and taking human form. Often the man in the relationship is not brought into the discussion and these events are less spoken about than abductions. Often these children will grow up on ships from afar and sometimes the mother or even father of these hybrid children will meet them momentarily if it is safe to do so, but these are rare events.

There are also other Zeta hybrids that are somewhat closer in appearance and genetic makeup to the Greys. It is these two other factions of Reticuli that have been involved in the abduction of various humans and the bad experiences told by humans. If you were to come across some Greys, however, you would feel just by their presence and physicality that some were not good and there are thought to be many different species with different agendas. Many humans/starseeds on Earth at this time have, however, had encounters with Zetas and explained the overwhelming sense of unconditional love and calmness they felt in their presence.

As humans are increasingly having contact, it is a good time for us to discern energies and begin to ask ourselves from our heart chakras, does this feel good, do I feel safe, is this frequency harmful to me? As we grow in ascension, we will move from using the logical brain to the heart and new deeper perceptions about people, and other beings and frequencies around us will become clearer than ever without the logical brain getting in the way.

A type of Grey also has a narrative that is closer to home from an alternate reality of Earth that is distantly linked to humans.

These Greys were once human-like. Due to mismanagement of nuclear weaponry they managed to create a situation on Earth whereby billions lost their lives and those that managed to survive began a long and painful process of mutation via radiation interference left within the atmosphere and environment. In turn this affected their ability to reproduce, lowering numbers even more, which presented a new issue—how to sustain their civilization. This created a complex solution in needing to discover and arrive in alternate Earth timeline realities before their self-created catastrophe had begun. This was in an aid to find viable human DNA in order to create hybrid variants of themselves with a type of biology that could reproduce and cultivate a new sustainable culture. Some call these new hybrids the Essassarni, a cousin of the Greys, who are a human Zeta mix. In order to speed up the healing process and evolutionary time scale upon which this huge undertaking was needed, some of the Greys needed to change the unity consciousness to that of a hive mind and approached the Mantis beings, who began to help oversee this huge operation. This is partly why Grey-like beings are often seen with Mantis beings both in physicality and etherically as factions of Greys work very closely with the

Mantoids, who resemble the Praying Mantis beings on Earth. In this you begin to see why the Pleiadians call Earth the living library as huge amounts of the living cosmos and its genetic material which are relational to other beings in the universe are stored here on Gaia. Many creatures within the animal kingdom resemble ETs that exist within the universe although the majority living in close proximity to Earth look very humanoid.

It is important to understand that in dimensionality there are various timelines happening simultaneously that can be harnessed, influenced, and changed with enough collective intent and even on a personal level. In effect what we see here is a previous Earth timeline that many beings in our galaxy have done a great deal to avoid, as it also has repercussions for other races and beings because we are all interconnected. For example, the Pleiadians, who look very like us, are the future version of us, so if there is a catastrophe, it could materialize in harmful ways in their realities in the future, also. This balance is always trying to be kept. This is why many beings have done their best to avoid what happened to the Greys in this instance, which was a nuclear Armageddon climaxing sometime near or around in the 2000 period or prior in the Cold War era that ends in a Holocaust causing the Earth humans to mutate and become a race of Grey like beings. It is in the best interests of various beings that this didn't happen as the universe is greatly more interconnected than thought. What affects one, can affect them all.

The Greys have various hybrids. Some mixed with benevolent DNA and others with malevolent DNA. There is a slave under race of Greys supporting a larger and more intelligent kind that are clones with a lower IQ created for work. These Greys have a consciousness that has been implanted into their being/neural/brain system that is preprogrammed. These usually serve the larger Greys who have been interfering with Earth since around the time of the great world wars 1930+. It is these beings that are much to blame for the phenomenon of the various worldwide abductions. It is also important to understand at this juncture, that with increasing technological ability, the military industrial complex composed of various groups, have also hoaxed groups/people with fake abductions that are very sophisticated making the believer think it was in fact the Greys themselves. The two are not to be confused although they can appear similar in nature to the experiencer with the advanced technologies the military secret state possesses. With that said, some visitations that are "good" can sometimes be seen as traumatic or bad when it was not the case. This can be for a variety of reasons, one being that the brain in lower densities can't compute events accurately and recall can be disturbing to the untrained mind as they are unable to understand what it is they are being faced with. Usually the human will enter into a state of fear regarding the unknown concept that seems beyond earthly comprehension. Other reasons for recall of positive encounters being perceived incoherently is because of the toxins, preservatives, and various pharma drugs we take together with antibiotics that we ingest from various meats that have been given to the animal when it was alive. These poisons in the food we eat lower our perception of reality and especially sub- and super-conscious events upon recall.

These Grey beings have been on Earth for some time and have worked in mostly underground bases similar to that of Groom Lake at Area 51 where various unregistered black collaborations have taken place for years. Some of the bases that house these beings are deep underground with advanced tunnel systems. Often in our galaxy the Greys and Reptilians have worked together with the Greys being manipulated as a form of mercenaries carrying out various agendas. Some of these beings are known as the Orion Greys, who have themselves become a slave race and have been part of the Grey Orion wars that once happened in our skies.

The Greys' agenda is explained well by Alex Collier, the Andromedan contact who worked closely with two Andromedan beings over a period of years who gave him information. There are various details of his accounts that can be traced to other portrayals, giving us a good idea of just how far ahead the Nazis really were in their mad race to rule the world. Since then these ideas have even become commonplace in the Hollywood belief systems with films such as *Indiana Jones and the Kingdom of the*

Crystal Skull.

The following is Alex Collier's transcript in which he met directly with Andromedans to give their perspective on the Greys.

The Greys made contact with a world governmental body for the first time in 1933 in Germany. However, they were turned away by the German government because it had already committed itself to involvement with the Giza intelligence. A renegade group of human extraterrestrials that were headquartered under the Giza plateau in Egypt. They were predominantly renegade Pleiadians. They were on their own, doing their own thing. Ashtar, Command and even Jehovah were a part of the group, for some time. They came down here and played God with us. People worshipped them because they had technology which they used as their power, big time.

During the 1930s, the Germans were building rockets and starting a space program due to their contacts with the extra-terrestrials of the Giza intelligence. The technology developed however and was used to create weapons because the German governmental body involved were concerned that there was going to be an alien invasion. The Giza intelligence had told them that the Greys were here to invade, but this actually did not occur. Plans for weapons such as sound devices, lasers, neutron bombs, particle beam weapons, etc. were designed. Although many of these weapons were not created until much later in history, a lot of other technology was shared with the Germans, by the Giza Intelligence, like how to do anti-gravity, free energy, etc.

The United States was the first to open its doors to the alien race known as the Greys. I have been told of only one contact in 1934, where the Greys made their presence known to the U.S. government, in the state of Washington. I don't know the particular details but somehow the government knew that the Greys were there. It wasn't until 1947, that actual contact occurred with the Greys and United States officials.

The first face to face contact was due to the shooting down of an alien craft, namely the Roswell incident. This pressed the Greys into a contact earlier than they had actually anticipated doing themselves. After the crash in Roswell, the United States, the Soviet Union, and the British, at the very highest levels, became blood brothers. By the way, none of these governments knew what Germany was really up to. The Germans were very, very secretive about their contact with the Giza Intelligence.

The Roswell incident created more of an urgency to develop a true space program to defend the Earth. The United States and the Soviet governments thought that this alien presence could be a threat, because these aliens were so technologically advanced. But the Greys in their own fashion, really backdoored these governments through deceit. The true space program, this underground program that we are just now beginning to hear about, was originally financed by members of the Club of Rome. Now, you'll need to do some homework, to find out who those members are. And don't be surprised at who you see. We will talk more about that later, when we discuss the moon.

Prior to this, in the 1850s to the 1950s, a hundred years, there had been some utilisation of cattle and humans in experiments by the Greys. The NSA, which was created in the 1950's, learned that the Greys were responsible. In 1952, the U.S. government prepared itself for the realisation of ongoing alien contact when our military radar system started to down their craft. The Greys knew that in order to perform their experiments on such a large scale, to save their race, they would need the cooperation of a high political body. In other words, they had to come to terms. A select politically structured body, created secretly within the United States Government, was designed to be the liaison between the Greys, the

ET, Phone Home

technological gods, and the Earth humans. The military was very enthusiastic for communication with the aliens, in hopes of exchanging technology for raw materials. This liaison group, this political structure, was the NSA, the super secret National Security Agency.

For contact and study of the aliens was its original purpose. In May of 1954, at Holloman Air Force Base, the United States Government made a formal agreement with the Grey race. Some of the terms of this agreement were the exchange of technology, of anti-gravity, metals, alloys, and environmental technologies to assist the Earth with free energy and medical application regarding the human body. All the Greys asked for in return, was to be allowed to study human development, both in the emotional consciousness makeup, and to reside here on Earth. This single act of signing a contract with an extraterrestrial race was the most significant act in human history because it launched us in a direction we were never intended to go in the first place, and it thrust us into a role that we were not prepared for either. Being hosts to an alien race.

Essentially, what this contract has also done, has handcuffed the Andromedan council and those benevolent extraterrestrial races from being able to take a more active role in the Earth's evolution. It has placed the burdens squarely on the shoulders of humanity to enlighten itself of the facts, and to consciously create ascension on an individual basis. This is partly down to Earth being a free will planet that other races must respect. Because this particular treaty was agreed upon between the aliens and the "ULTRA" units in the NSA, which actually is a government unto itself, they in effect turned away help from outside benevolent races that we could have obtained before.

Now pay close attention, because this is the first time I've ever mentioned this. The particular document and original exchange material may be found today in the NSA facility, called Blue Moon, under Kirtland Air Force Base in New Mexico. It's exact entrance is in the Monzoni Mountains. This location houses the private department of energy technological labs. Currently, the building of free energy devices for use in space and on the Moon and Mars is ongoing, in this particular area.

Much of the alien technology has been reconstructed and sent via a connecting tunnel to Los Alamos and an area located underneath the cliff sides of Los Alamos canyon, where huge vaults are built into the Earth. This facility is twenty-nine thousand square feet in size. There are also laboratories equipped to study light, thought and pure energy there. This facility is also used as a jail for aliens captured by the black (secret) government.

Corporations that are currently assisting the aliens and the black government are large companies involved in oil, aerospace, defence, arms, security, and advanced technologies including mining, communications and numerous more big corporate outfits. The NSA is exempt from all laws in the United States unless the NSA itself is specifically mentioned in any creation of law.

This is due to its interaction with aliens and it's sometimes necessary infringements of civil rights and constitutional rights of the American people. In other words, to make it exempt from breaking any laws and hurting anybody here, they made it completely separate, and it is completely separate, even though your tax dollars pay for the running of it. There was also a great deal of private money used by the NSA to build alien technology and to keep humanity under control keeping the status quo secure. Even the CIA doesn't know much about the Ultra or Blue Moon units of the NSA. These are the two highest units the NSA has that deals directly with alien technology and information.

Now realise that the Greys are genetic engineers, though not the only ones. Most of the aliens from off planet are genetic engineers because they value life forms as opposed to gold and silver. Genetic life forms and things of that nature are their wealth. A lot of the genetic engineering and experimentation is going on here on Earth and on Mars and its moon Phobos by the Greys.

They are using this opportunity to try to satisfy their own agenda, which is to create DNA and genetic stock that is clean enough to foster new physical life forms that are capable of regeneration and birth for their race. As of right now, the Greys are most interested in female genetic stock because all family lineages follow the female rather than the male. Why? Because you always know who your mother is, you may not always know who your father is.

Many new races have been created this way throughout our galaxy. It's not something that's new going on here. This has been going on for a very long time. Few races today have actually remained as pure genetic stock, with the exception of two races that the Andromedans say are really genetically clean. That is the Reptilians from Alpha Draconis, and the other is what we call, or know as the Elohim, which are a very ancient race that survived Lyra. All other races are a varied degree of hybrid or mixture of races of different genetic stock.

Another point is that the Greys themselves would like to be free from the Orion empire. They will have no chance of survival themselves if they do not create or match their body type or genetics with ours. You see, time is quickly running out for them and we as a race are also evolving at a tremendous rate. On a spiritual conscious level, we are evolving dramatically, making our genetics harder to use while they are dying out like there's no tomorrow and they are very aware of this fact. So, even though what they're doing is wrong, they really are caught in a very tough position themselves. Because what they're doing to us has been done to them. I'm just trying to draw parallels. I'm not justifying it in any way. By the way, when any of the aliens give birth to a child, they take that child outside of the Earth's atmosphere so the child is born fully aware of its reincarnation history, so it realises who it is, and it doesn't carry the veil. Why is this? Apparently, there is some kind of agreement, if you're born within the Earth's atmosphere, you've got to be veiled. It's just part of what comes with being born here.

The Grey masters' assigned agenda is to create a slave race which is currently in full swing, for the purposes of control, physical services, labour and sexual energy. Now I will explain this. The acts of feeding war, anger, psychic energy, genetic experiments, hybrids as a food source, genetic and biological materials. The Greys and their masters feed off this, our energy. As examples:

If two people are fighting, they create a lot of emotional negative energy and this is why you will find that whenever there are wars going on, there's a lot of UFO activity. Negative energy! They just feed off it. It's like when you are making love to your man or to your wife, and you reach that moment where you are both at the same place at the same time, in a loving benevolent way. That's how it feels for them regarding negative energy release. The energy of fear, that rush of adrenaline, young teens on a battlefield running around scared, this is what they crave, all of the negative emotional aspects.

By creating a space of love, the Greys, the Draconians, and the Orions won't be able to handle the vibration. They have got to leave, or we're going to have to ask for some serious intervention here. You see, the Greys are currently monitoring the brain waves of those they have implanted. They have done this for the better part of a hundred years on Earth. So generations of family members have had implants. The cloning of human beings, of life forms and the art of subversion was taught by the Greys to the NSA. On the two highest levels of human interaction with the Greys within the NSA, there exist cloned human beings and humans so

⁘ 176 ⁘

heavily implanted, that according to the Andromedans, they do not consider them human beings anymore. They have joined the group Mind of the Greys. They have lost free will. They are clone robots. Their soul is trapped and they are no longer considered compassionate human beings.

The Greys clone their own race into a cast of slaves, just like ants. They all basically think the same things at the same time. Their minds are like radios. If there are no radio waves, they don't do anything. They have computers which transmit radio-like waves, telling them what their jobs are, their functions that they must carry out. If the computers, their group mind, were shut down, the Greys would no longer know what to do for themselves. They do not possess individual intelligence like us, although they would very much like to create us to be like them.

The Greys also consider what we call God, a mind, like we think of our own mind. They have completely detached themselves from their spiritual essence, so long ago, that their physical existence and personality has become pure ego. The Draconians are pure ego, as well. Many other races genetically altered by the Draconians, are also experiencing the separation from their own essence too.

Now, I don't understand the process or exactly how it works, but the Greys no longer believe themselves to be spirit, to be in essence. They're trapped mentally, emotionally, physically in a physical existence, therefore, that's all they see. They literally disown and fractionalise themselves away from their spiritual essence. It's no longer a part of them. Human beings have also been known to do that themselves, as well. You know we can fractionalise ourselves into many different personalities. The Greys are pure ego!

They are very sophisticated in mathematics and energy sciences. It has been said that our military at the time of the Holloman Air Force meeting, that there was an exchange of personnel. Our military gave the Greys sixteen military personnel that were supposed to be taken to the Greys' point of origin and that they left us one or two guys or something of theirs along those same lines. Well, according to the Andromedans, it was really a hundred and nine human beings that were taken at that particular exchange. They have not returned. As a matter of fact, they did not go to the Greys' point of origin, which was Zeta Reticuli 2, rather they went to the motherships and Phobos where they were experimented on.

The Greys gave virus technology to the NSA, which then was handed on to lower levels within our military complex. In Africa, we find the testing ground for the AIDS virus. There's a reason for this. This virus technology was given by the Greys to the biological unit in Ultra within the NSA. One of NSA's underground facilities is underneath Fort Meade in Maryland. At that location there are nineteen acres of underground caverns, with some of the most highly technological and sophisticated supercomputers in the world, that were built and designed inside the facility. They have never seen the light of day. This area, and the one in Mt. Hood, Oregon are engaged in massive surveillance of the world's telephones, telegraph, telex, fax, radio, television, microwave communication, NORAD and also space radio waves. The complex in Mt. Hood is where our military is cloning human beings and aliens. I don't know what alien races.

Jumping back in history a bit. In the late 1950's, the Greys also approached the Russians regarding the signing of treaties and mutual exchange. The Russians, however, already at the time, were included in the proceedings of the NSA, chose not to sign this independent treaty because they knew full well that the Greys would try to pit the United States against the Soviet Union. It is in fact the Soviet Union that informed JFK of Grey's presence, during the Cuban missile crisis. The Andromedans have stated that the Russians were trying to blackmail the U.S. into sharing alien technology, thus the Bay of Pigs. That's when they put the missiles they pointed at the United States. The Russians became increasingly aware that the NSA and the CIA were developing incredible technology and were not sharing it, as was their agreement, shortly after the Holliman agreement.

Apparently, JFK asked the CIA three times if the Russian allegations were true. The CIA lied twice to the president, even though nuclear weapons were only eighteen minutes away from striking the U.S. They just flat out lied to him and said, "No. They're nuts." This prompted JFK to want to scatter the CIA to the winds. This is one of the more important reasons the "black" government found JFK as a threat and had him make a physical transition prematurely.

It was JFK's desire that some of this technology would reach the common people and be used for the betterment of mankind and that it be made known to the American people that the alien presence was upon us. This is one of the reasons why he successfully launched a civilian space program so that all Americans and people of the world could share in the discovery.

Many operations have been created by the Greys over the past five hundred years for the purposes of manipulation and control of our religious belief systems. I don't want to offend anybody, but I'm going to tell you just the way it's been presented to me. All you have to do is listen. If it doesn't feel right for you, then dismiss it. If it does feel right, and you get the chills, then maybe you should start paying attention to it.

To have us morally and spiritually compromise our free will to a saviour like image, the Greys by allowing us to compromise ourselves under these false pretences, they are absolved from the creation of any Karma for themselves. Instead, they let us create Karma for ourselves. It really is such a set up. The power of belief systems can be used as fuel for the game of seducing people into believing that certain things are true. By the power created by conscious thoughts, we can literally make these things occur and come true, whether they benefit us or not. These are real spiritual dynamics at work here and they're being used against us. Our physical matter (physical body) is the embodiment of ideas or belief systems. Our Universe consists of ideas and thought systems, condensed and turned towards itself, inwards. We turn it towards ourselves to create and originate spirit and energy. Now if I need to say it again I will. This is our definition again, word for word. Our physical matter is the embodiment of ideas (belief systems). Our universe consists of ideas and thought, condensed and turned towards itself, inwards. To create and originate spirit and energy. In other words, we really are gods/creators. We really can do anything we want to do.

We, of Earth, have evolved only in technical and material sciences. Our spiritual evolution, for the most part, has been suppressed from us by a group of extraterrestrials, and now the black government and its plan for a New World Order. Because upon learning these spiritual truths, the NSA and the black world government, realised that everything that they have been trying to do can be swept away. According to the Andromedans, their exact words were, "Could be swept away in a day, should humanity become enlightened."

If a billion people come to the realisation and a decision that we no longer want this reality, it can literally change with the setting and the rising of the sun. But, they stress, we need to be clear of what we want, which is part of the decision, and our responsibility factors. That is ours. In other words, if we're going to create it, we take responsibility for it. In the 1950's the so-called meetings of the Jason society were triggered by information given to the Ultra unit in the NSA by the Greys about the world's situation regarding pollution and population. It was at this particular time that the Greys offered little assistance or sharing of technology regarding environmental issues. This has persisted even today. The Pleiadians have in fact, offered more solutions than any other group to date, but they were turned away by the NSA. This prompted the first of three alternatives that have been discussed in UFO circles already.

These alternatives are in fact, and were in fact, a reality. That's alternative one, two, three and four. The New World Order/Illuminati is in a major predicament. The Greys are twenty-five hundred years ahead of us technologically. The black government is afraid to tell us the truth concerning this reality because they fear a revolution, overthrow, and desire self-preservation from the people who will want their scalps.

Two large motherships are on the planet right now, hiding in the oceans. One is in the Pacific Ocean, below the equator and the other one is in the Atlantic. I don't know where. I don't know who they are, but they're here. My sense is that they're benevolent because the government has actually talked about implementing alternative four which was creating a controlled pole shift. The Andromedans have said no way would they allow this to happen. So my sense is that there are benevolent ships that are anchoring the planet on its axis. That's my opinion. The military knows that this is why they're testing sound in the oceans, especially in the Pacific.

Bad ETs have been attacking us more openly in space. It started with the Russian Phobos probe when it was destroyed. The Mars observer was captured by Reptilians on Mars. It isn't going to come online. It's gone. Also, closer to home, in December 1993, a Landsat satellite disappeared in orbit, just vanished. In August of 1993, the European space agency lost two communications satellites, again, they literally just vanished from orbit. The Canadian TELSTAR was destroyed in our atmosphere on January 15, 1994. It was seen crashing to Earth. This was shot down by the Greys. Again, I don't know why. A NASA Satcom 3 communications satellite vanished in May of 1979. It was just taken. Two Soviet Millennia satellites were also taken. They just vanished from our orbit, from our atmosphere.

The Pleiadians are assisting the Andromedan Council in attempting to quarantine our solar system from invading forces, namely the Orion group and Alpha Draconis in a bid to remove all Greys and Reptilians. The quarantine line, the defence line, is between Uranus and Pluto and consists of a mixture of benevolent races, both physical and non-physical. There are Pleiadians, Andromedans, Arcturians, Syrians from Sirius A, Reticulin, Accordance and Umonians from Umo. This line of defence is really like a last resort. Apparently, two huge Grey motherships have already been turned back that were on their way to Earth and Mars. And apparently there were casualties on both sides in the exchange of turning them away.

Please realise that currently, there are fifteen thousand Greys underneath the United States. The Greys (Dows) are in fact, a renegade group of Reticulans. They are not from Reticuli and haven't been back there for hundreds and hundreds of thousands of years. They have been travelling through space in their arc's. Before they came to Earth, they were residing on Sirius B. That was their originating point before coming here. There are approximately eighteen hundred and thirty-three Reptilians living beneath the United States. Their habitat is from one hundred to two hundred miles beneath the surface of the Earth. They generally live in caverns and the ancient tunnel systems were created hundreds of thousands of years ago. They are not benevolent, and, every once in a while, they come up for a contact. They have been seen in New York City, Missouri, Chicago, and in the southwest United States. These areas happen to be the largest areas where missing children occur, numbering in the thousands. The Andromedans state that 13712 children have been taken by these Reptilians over the last twenty-five years. In Linda Molten-Howe's book, *Alien Harvest*, there is mention of human body parts seen in underground bases. The Andromedans confirm that we are being used for food. The Greys use our blood and it is the Reptilians that consume the live human flesh. Their favourite food is children because they lack nicotine, caffeine, and other environmental pollutants. Like we eat veal, they eat us.

The Greys are searching for walk-ins because they want to learn about spirit. I'm speaking about benevolence and not Satanic possession or that kind of stuff. Walk-ins are necessary at this particular time. (Walk-in's being when an entity or consciousness invades or attaches by agreement to a body or becomes part of another person's soul or being.) They are higher evolved souls. Many are on the planet right now and are a part of the Andromedan Council. Many more are coming in the next three years to balance the negativity that is being created. Because of the Council's laws of non-intervention, the Andromedan Council found it necessary to intervene in another way without violating its council directives. These walk-ins are also known as starseeds.

Thus, the walk-ins who are actually Earth human beings, are here to do that kind of work. It's a backdoor approach.

Keep these facts in mind. There are eighteen thousand Greys; fifteen thousand here on the Earth and three thousand on the Moon. The regular government which makes up the majority of Washington, D.C. doesn't have a clue as to what's really going on. The black government consists of various levels. At the top, they know everything, the lower levels only know small pieces, on a need to know basis, usually just one piece of the puzzle. The total picture is one outrageous secret based on deliberate deceit that creates the subversion of the public trust.

We can see from Alex Collier's account from the Andromedans as he begins to open up about the industrial military complex along with the various bases that exist on Earth. He mentions the walk-ins or beings that have come into Earth bodies, we will touch more on these as the book continues and the various waves that have come to Earth in raising its vibration. These people have become known as starseeds, lightworkers, Rainbow children, Indigo children, and so on.

Agartha (Inner Earth)

The word "Agartha" has deep Buddhist origins. It is thought to be symbolic of a subterranean world the Buddhists believe exists within the hollows of the Earth itself. The belief is that millions of inhabitants and many cities exist within the inner Earth with its subterranean world capital, Shamballah being at the top of its hierarchy. Other theories suggest that after the fall of Atlantis many traveled into the inner Earth and have been there ever since leading an existence that is of a higher spiritual experience.

In Agartha the ruler is known as the King of the World, who is believed to be in direct contact with the Dalai Lama of Tibet, who was and still remains his terrestrial representative. It is understood that contact is both telepathic and transmitted from dream-like messages. Legend has it that subterranean tunnel systems reach Tibet itself allowing for physical visits should further contact be necessary. These mysterious tunnels also honeycomb Brazil in the west and Tibet in the east. These two are strategic parts of the Earth.

The famous Russian artist, philosopher, and explorer, Nicholas Roerich, who traveled extensively in the Far East and who also earned several nominations for the Nobel Peace Prize longlist, was a believer in these ideas and traveled the Far East exploring them. Gandhi, a political and spiritual leader, spent time with Nicholas Roerich and says, "Roerich himself stays in my memory. He was a man with extensive knowledge and enormous experience, a man with a big heart, deeply influenced by all that he observed."

Roerich is one of many interesting sources that claim Lhasa, the capital of Tibet, was connected by a tunnel with Shamballah. He further went on to detail the significance of the entrance of this tunnel which was guarded by lamas who were sworn to keep its whereabouts a secret from the outside world, by decree of the Dalai Lama.

Other theories explore tunnels that are believed to exist connecting the Pyramid of Gizeh with Agartha by which some the ancient Atlanteans returned to the surface during the great time of ancient Egypt with these people and the Pharaohs establishing contact in this way. These are the potential links the Egyptians used to describe these encounters as interaction with the gods or supermen of the underworld. Ancient Egypt is part of starseed folklore regarding the people who hid in the inner Earth after the great flood of Earth 13,000 years ago. Some of the first major accounts of these people are of them appearing in Egypt.

There are various accounts in historical texts all over the world that these inner Earth people came to the surface to teach the human race and save it from further wars and self-induced destruction. The tunnel systems could also explain historically how the Incas managed to escape from the Spanish conquerors and the Inquisition, with entire armies entering them, carrying with them their gold and treasures on the backs of llamas, which they did when the Spanish conquerors first came.

This could potentially describe the mysterious disappearance of various tribes in our history who have entered these tunnel systems seeking refuge. It is claimed that these tunnels had a form of artificial lighting and were built by the race that had constructed Tiahuanaco, a perfectly constructed stone city long before the first Inca appeared in Peru.

As with other beings we have discussed we have looked into the beings themselves with some detail and it is understood that there is no old age in Agartha as we know it on the surface of

Earth. It is a society where one can live for many centuries and look young and vibrant. These beings have a cellular capability that is far ahead of human means and some of them are said to be giant like in their proportions.

Inner Earth consciousness has been said to look at surface dwellers and their lack of development due to being exposed to the harmful effects of solar radiation and the autointoxication of food from cross-contaminated sources within diets leading to shorter lives. Inner Earth beings live longer because of their genetic, biological, and environmental conditions and the habits they maintain, especially diet.

The scientific culture of these inner Earth people is the result of superior mental and spiritual development which is thought to be because of their fruit diet leading to endocrine systems that are balanced and harmonious in their functioning. This is seen in children who are not conditioned to "abnormal" activity by metabolic toxins, as produced by such foods as meat, dairy, eggs, and stimulants such as coffee, tobacco, and alcohol. Therefore by keeping their bloodstream free from toxins, the subterranean people are able to live in a better physiology also leading to superior brain power. This in turn could be what leads to superiority regarding quantum development and general intellect of the head and the heart's intuition.

It can be misconstrued that much of the inner Earth legend is nothing more than myth, that is until the documented case of Richard Evelyn Byrd Jr. (25 October 1888–11 March 1957), who was an American naval officer and explorer. Byrd was a recipient of the Medal of Honor, the highest honor for valor given by the United States, and was a pioneering American aviator, polar explorer, and organizer of polar logistics.

Admiral Byrd was the leader of aircraft flights in which he served as a navigator and expedition leader crossing the Atlantic Ocean, a segment of the Arctic Ocean, and a segment of the Antarctic Plateau. It was Byrd who claimed his expeditions had been the first to reach both the North Pole and the South Pole by air.

Toward the end of WW2 Admiral Byrd had gathered

intelligence that the Nazis had not only colonized and built bases in the Antarctic, but had been visiting the North Pole also on expeditions using antigravity technologies given to them by an unknown source. It was understood by the intelligence at the time that when exploration and Nazi military groups had arrived at the North Pole, they were met by a much more advanced antigravity craft and a battle had ensued with casualties on both sides. It is believed and later confirmed these were the people from inner Earth protecting themselves. This information has since become public; however, the public find this debatable at present time.

Admiral Richard E. Byrd was aware of these strange tales and quickly set out to visit both Poles in order to grasp the truth. He flew for 1,700 and 2,300 miles, respectively, across the North and South Poles, to the icy and snowbound lands that lie on the other side, whose geography is fairly well known; therefore, it was incomprehensible for him to make statements referring to this territory on the other side of the Poles as "the great unknown." Also, he would have no reason to use such a term as "Land of Everlasting Mystery." Byrd was not a poet, and what he described was what he observed from his airplane. Byrd explains how he saw lands of lush green and fruitful pastures. It is believed that in the Arctic there he saw an opening in the Earth, a hole-like structure somewhere around the North Pole. Many believe it can be entered and upon doing so reach the inner Earth people. Sometimes this has been described as a city in the sky. It is open to interpretation; however, many independent tales equate to similar experiences.

During his Arctic flight of 1,700 miles beyond the North Pole, Byrd reported by radio that he saw below him, not ice and snow, but land areas consisting of mountains, forests, green vegetation, lakes and rivers, and in the underbrush saw a strange animal resembling a mammoth found frozen in Arctic ice. Evidently, he had entered a warmer region than the icebound territory that extends from the Pole to Siberia. If Byrd had this region in mind, he would have no reason to call it the "Great Unknown," since it could be reached by flying across the Pole to the other side of the Arctic region.

These claims were first written about by an American writer, William Reed, in a book called *The Phantom of the Poles*, published in 1906 soon after a military man called Admiral Peary claimed to have discovered the North Pole. In 1920 another book was published, written by Marshall Gardner, called *A Journey to the Earth's Interior or Have the Poles Really Been Discovered?*, making the same claim. Strangely, Gardner had no knowledge of Reed's book and came to his conclusions independently.

Both Reed and Gardner claimed that the Earth was hollow, with openings at both Poles and that in its interior lives a vast population of inhabitants of an advanced civilization. Could this be the Great Unknown Admiral Byrd alluded to?

Around this time there was speculation in the American press regarding this topic, which was heavily suppressed by the government. Eventually the United States government feared that other countries may learn about Byrd's discovery. So the US government conducted similar flights, which explored these regions with far greater execution; however, their reports were never published. Twelve years later in 1959, Ray Palmer, editor of *Flying Saucers* magazine, gave publicity to Admiral Byrd's discovery after learning the details of the exploration. He was so inspired by the story that he published the information in his magazine, which was for sale on newsstands throughout the United States.

Then followed a series of strange incidents, indicating that secret forces were at work to prevent the information contained in the December issue of *Flying Saucers* magazine. It was at this time the secret government began to ramp up their anti-propaganda campaign against the accounts that had happened to Admiral Byrd.

Soon after in December, the 1959 issue of *Flying Saucers* was ready to mail to subscribers and placed on newsstands, where it was mysteriously removed from circulation—evidently by the same secret forces that suppressed the public release of this information since 1947. When the trucks arrived to deliver the magazines from the printer to the publisher, no magazines were found in the trucks. A phone call by the publisher (Mr. Palmer) to the printer resulted in his not finding any shipping receipt providing any shipment to have been made. Since the magazines had been paid for, the publisher asked that the printer return the plates to the press and run off the copies due. But, strangely, the plates were not available, and were so badly damaged that no reprint could be made.

Thousands of magazines that had been printed had mysteriously disappeared, and 5,000 subscribers who were to receive the magazine were left mysteriously empty handed. One distributor who received 750 copies to sell on his newsstand was reported missing, and 750 magazines disappeared with him. These magazines were sent to him with the request that they be returned if not delivered. They did not come back. Since the magazine disappeared completely, several months later it was republished and sent to subscribers. It was clear sabotage from the elite ruling black operations within the government and military organizations attempting to suppress information.

In recent years Admiral Byrd's personal diaries and log books have been made available. Here is an actual account of his personal log book as Admiral Byrd flew over the Arctic.

FLIGHT LOG – BASE CAMP ARCTIC – 2/19/1947

0600 Hours- All preparations are complete for our flight northward and we are airborne with full fuel tanks at 0610 Hours.

0620 Hours- fuel mixture on starboard engine seems too rich, adjustment made and Pratt Whitneys are running smoothly.

0730 Hours- Radio Check with base camp. All is well and radio reception is normal.

0740 Hours- Note slight oil leak in starboard engine, oil pressure indicator seems normal however.

0800 Hours- Slight turbulence noted from easterly direction at altitude of 2321 feet, correction to 1700 feet, no further turbulence, but tail wind increases, slight adjustment in throttle controls, aircraft performing very well now.

0815 Hours- Radio Check with base camp, situation normal.

0830 Hours- Turbulence encountered again, increase altitude to 2900 feet, smooth flight conditions again.

0910 Hours- Vast Ice and snow below, note coloration of yellowish nature, and disperse in a linear pattern. Altering course for a better examination of this colour pattern below, note reddish or purple colour also. Circled this area two full turns and return to assigned compass heading. Position check made again to base camp, and relay information concerning coronations in the Ice and snow below.

0910 Hours- Both Magnetic and Gyro compasses began to gyrate and wobble, we are unable to hold our heading by instrumentation. Take bearing with sun compass, yet all seems well. The controls are seemingly slow to respond and have sluggish quality, but there is no indication of Icing!

0915 Hours- In the distance is what appears to be mountains.

0949 Hours- 29 minutes elapsed flight time from the first sighting of the mountains, it is no illusion. They are mountains and consist of a small range that I have never seen before!

0955 Hours- Altitude change to 2950 feet, encountering strong turbulence again.

1000 Hours- We are crossing over the small mountain range and still proceeding northward as best as can be ascertained. Beyond the mountain range is what appears to be a valley with a small river or stream running through the center portion. There should be no green valley below! Something is definitely wrong and abnormal here! We should be over Ice and Snow! To the portside are great forests growing on the mountain slopes. Our navigation Instruments are still spinning, the gyroscope is oscillating back and forth!

1005 Hours- I alter altitude to 1400 feet and execute a sharp left turn to better examine the valley below. It is green with either moss or a type of tight knit grass. The Light here seems different. I cannot see the Sun anymore. We make another left turn and we spot what seems to be a large animal of some kind below us. It appears to be an elephant! NO!!! It looks more like a mammoth! This is incredible! Yet, there it is! Decrease altitude to 1000 feet and take binoculars to better examine the animal.

ET, Phone Home

It is confirmed—it is definitely a mammoth-like animal! Report this to base camp.

1030 Hours- Encountering more rolling green hills now. The external temperature indicator reads 74 degrees Fahrenheit! Continuing on our heading now. Navigation instruments seem normal now. I am puzzled over their actions. Attempt to contact base camp. Radio is not functioning!

1130 Hours- Countryside below is more level and normal (if I may use that word). Ahead we spot what seems to be a city!!!! This is impossible! Aircraft seems light and oddly buoyant. The controls refuse to respond!! My GOD!!! Off our port and starboard wings are a strange type of aircraft. They are closing rapidly alongside! They are disc-shaped and have a radiant quality to them. They are close enough now to see the markings on them. This is fantastic. Where are we! What has happened. I tug at the controls again. They will not respond!!!! We are caught in an invisible vice grip of some type!

1135 Hours- Our radio crackles and a voice comes through in English with what perhaps is a slight Nordic or Germanic accent! The message is: Welcome, Admiral, to our domain. We shall land you in exactly seven minutes! Relax, Admiral, you are in good hands.

I note the engines of our plane have stopped running! The aircraft is under some strange control and is now turning itself. The controls are useless.

1140 Hours- Another radio message received. We begin the landing process now, and in moments the plane shudders slightly, and begins a descent as though caught in some great unseen elevator! The downward motion is negligible, and we touch down with only a slight jolt!

1145 Hours- I am making a hasty last entry in the flight log. Several men are approaching on foot toward our aircraft. They are tall with blond hair. In the distance is a large shimmering city pulsating with rainbow hues of color. I do not know what is going to happen now, but I see no signs of weapons on those approaching. I hear a voice ordering me by name to open the cargo door. I comply.

Soon after this the admiral is taken to what appears to be an incredibly beautiful crystalline structure where he meets who the locals call "the Master." He is greeted by a humanoid being and the following account is now taken directly from Admiral Byrd's personal diary as written after the incident:

"Have no fear, Admiral, you are to have an audience with the Master."

I step inside and my eyes adjust to the beautiful coloration that seems to be filling the room completely. Then I begin to see my surroundings. What greeted my eyes is the most beautiful sight of my entire existence. It is in fact too beautiful and wondrous to describe. It is exquisite and delicate. I do not think there exists a human term that can describe it in any detail with justice!

My thoughts are interrupted in a cordial manner by a warm rich voice of melodious quality,

"I bid you welcome to our domain, Admiral."

He is seated at a long table. He motions me to sit down in one of the chairs. After I am seated, he places his fingertips together and smiles. He speaks softly again, and conveys the following.

"We have let you enter here because you are of noble character and well-known on the Surface World, Admiral."

Surface World, I half-gasp under my breath!

"Yes!" The Master replies with a smile.

"You are in the domain of the Arianni, the Inner World of the Earth. We shall not long delay your mission, and you will be safely escorted back to the surface and for a distance beyond. But now, Admiral, I shall tell you why you have been summoned here.

"Our interest rightly begins just after your race exploded the first atomic bombs over Hiroshima and Nagasaki, Japan. It was at that alarming time we sent our flying machines, to your surface world to investigate what your race had done. That is, of course, past history now, my dear Admiral, but I must continue on.

"You see, we have never interfered in your race's wars, and barbarity, but now we must, for you have learned to tamper with a certain power that is not for man, namely, that of atomic energy.

"Our emissaries have already delivered messages to the powers of your world, and yet they do not heed. Now you have been chosen to be witness here that our world does exist. You see, our Culture and Science

ET, Phone Home

is many thousands of years beyond your race, Admiral."

I interrupted, "But what does this have to do with me, Sir?"

The Master's eyes seemed to penetrate deeply into my mind, and after studying me for a few moments he replied,

"Your race has now reached the point of no return, for there are those among you who would destroy your very world rather than relinquish their power as they know it."

I nodded, and the Master continued.

"In 1945 and afterwards, we tried to contact your race, but our efforts were met with hostility, our 'Flugelrads' if you will, were fired upon. Yes, even pursued with malice and animosity by your fighter planes. So, now, I say to you, my son, there is a great storm gathering in your world, a black fury that will not spend itself for many years. There will be no answer in your arms, there will be no safety in your science. It may rage on until every flower of your culture is trampled, and all human things are levelled in vast chaos. Your recent war was only a prelude of what is yet to come for your race. We here see it more clearly with each hour. Do you say I am mistaken?"

"No," I answered, "It happened once before, the dark ages came and they lasted for more than five hundred years."

"Yes, my son," replied the Master, "The dark ages that will come now for your race will cover the Earth like a pall, but I believe that some of your race will live through the storm, beyond that, I cannot say. We see at a great distance a new world stirring from the ruins of your race, seeking its lost and legendary treasures, and they will be here, my son, safe in our keeping. When that time arrives, we shall come forward again to help revive your culture and your race. Perhaps, by then, you will have learned the futility of war and its strife and after that time, certain parts of your culture and science will be returned for your race to begin anew. You, my son, are to return to the Surface World with this message."

With these closing words, our meeting seemed at an end. I stood for a moment as in a dream, but, yet, I knew this was reality, and for some strange reason I bowed slightly, either out of respect or humility, I do not know which.

Suddenly, I was aware that the two beautiful hosts who had brought me here were again at my side. "This way, Admiral!" motioned one. I turned once more before leaving and looked back toward the Master. A gentle smile was etched on his delicate and ancient face.

"Farewell, my son," he spoke, then he gestured with a lovely, slender hand a motion of peace and our meeting truly ended.

Quickly, we walked back through the great door of the Master's chamber and once again entered into the elevator. The door slid silently downward and we were at once going upward. One of my hosts spoke again,

"We must now make haste, Admiral, as the Master desires to delay you no longer on your scheduled timetable and you must return with his message to your race."

I said nothing. All of this was almost beyond belief, and once again my thoughts were interrupted as we stopped. I entered the room and was again with my radioman. He had an anxious expression on his face. As I approached, I said, "It is all right, Howie, it is all right." The two beings motioned us toward the awaiting conveyance, we boarded, and soon arrived back at the aircraft. The engines were idling and we boarded immediately.

The whole atmosphere seemed charged now with a certain air of urgency. After the cargo door was closed the aircraft was immediately lifted by that unseen force until we reached an altitude of 2700 feet. Two of the aircraft were alongside for some distance guiding us on our way. I must state here, the airspeed indicator registered no reading, yet we were moving along at a very rapid rate.

As you can see from this interaction, the admiral had an encounter with beings more quantum and ethereal than that of an earthly disposition. These are the original notes from his encounter that have not been indoctrinated. More interestingly still are the notes from his personal diary upon coming back to the US and meeting with intelligence. Here is the original text from his personal diary:

March 11, 1947

I have just attended a staff meeting at the Pentagon. I have stated fully my discovery and the message from the master. All is duly recorded. The President has been advised. I am now detained for several hours (six hours, thirty-nine minutes, to be exact.) I am interviewed intently by Top

Security Forces and a medical team. It was an ordeal!!!!

I am placed under strict control via the national security provisions of the United States of America. I am ORDERED TO REMAIN SILENT IN REGARD TO ALL THAT I HAVE LEARNED, ON THE BEHALF OF HUMANITY!!! Incredible! I am reminded that I am a military man and I must obey orders.

30/12/56 – FINAL ENTRY

These last few years elapsed since 1947 have not been kind. I now make my final entry in this singular diary. In closing, I must state that I have faithfully kept this matter secret as directed all these years. It has been completely against my values of moral right. Now, I seem to sense the long night coming on and this secret will not die with me, but as all truth shall, it will triumph and so it shall.

This can be the only hope for mankind. I have seen the truth and it has quickened my spirit and has set me free! I have done my duty toward the monstrous military industrial complex. Now, the long night begins to approach, but there shall be no end.

Just as the long night of the Arctic ends, the brilliant sunshine of truth shall come again . . . and those who are of darkness shall fall in it's Light . . . FOR I HAVE SEEN THAT LAND BEYOND THE POLE, THAT CENTER OF THE GREAT UNKNOWN.

(Admiral Richard E. Byrd, United States Navy, 24 December 1956, original account.)

The other very interesting account of this experience comes at an earlier date. Olaf Jansen was a Norwegian sailor who with his father decided to explore further into the Arctic reaches than anyone he had known before. Olaf and his father decided they would take a trip as far north in a boat as they could. In doing so they accidentally sailed into what is potentially the same world Admiral Byrd discovered. Upon going to Agartha, he returned with similar stories to that of Admiral Byrd. The accounts he told upon return were not well received with audiences, calling him insane. As a result he was put into psychiatric care for some time. It was much later in his life when he was a very old man that he met George Emerson, an American writer who decided to publish his stories in a book in 1908. This is one of the first accounts that has similar details that align with Byrd's accounts. The book was named *The Smoky Sun*, due to the underground sun that is believed to actually exist in the hollow Earth that illuminates Agartha itself. Here are some extracts from the original book published in 1908. Olaf Jansen until his time of death stood by these accounts as real and the book *The Smoky Sun* was published as a factual work that still exists. Here is an excerpt from that account:

I lived near the Arctic Circle in Norway. One summer my father and I made up our minds to take a boat trip together, and go as far as we could into the north country. So we put one month's food provisions in a small fishing boat, and with sail, and with a good engine in our boat, we set to sea.

At the end of one month we had traveled far into the north, beyond the Pole and into a strange new country. We were very astonished at the weather there. Warm, and at times at night it was almost too warm to sleep. Arctic explorers who penetrated into the far north have made similar reports of warm weather, at times warm enough to make them shed their heavy clothing. Then we saw something so strange that we both were astonished. Ahead of the warm open sea looked like a great mountain. Into that mountain at a certain point the ocean seemed to be emptying. Mystified, we continued in that direction and found ourselves sailing into a vast canyon leading into the interior of the Earth. We kept sailing and then we saw what surprised us a sun shining inside the Earth!

The ocean that had carried us into the hollow interior of the Earth gradually became a river. This river led, as we came to realise later, all through the inner surface of the world from one end to the other. It can take you, if you follow it long enough, from the North Pole clear through to the South Pole. We saw that the inner surface of the Earth was divided, as the other one is, into both land and water. There is plenty of sunshine and both animal and vegetable life abounds there. We sailed further and further into this fantastic country, fantastic because everything was huge in size as compared with things on the outside. Plants are big, trees gigantic and finally we came to giants!

They were dwelling in homes and towns, just as we do on the Earth's surface and they used a type of electrical conveyance like a mono-rail car, to transport people. It ran along the river's edge from town to town.

Several of the inner Earth inhabitants—huge giants—detected our boat on the river, and were quite amazed. They were, however, quite friendly. We were invited to dine with them in their homes, and so my companion and I separated, he going with one Giant to that Giant's home and I going with another Giant to his home.

My gigantic friend brought me home to his family, and I was completely dismayed to see the huge size of all the objects in his home. The dinner table was colossal. A plate was put before me and filled with a portion of food so big it would have fed me abundantly an entire week. The giant offered me a cluster of grapes and each grape was as big as one of our peaches. I tasted one and found it far sweeter than any I had ever tasted outside. In the interior of the Earth all the fruits and vegetables taste far better and more flavoursome than those we have on the outer surface of the Earth.

We stayed with the Giants for one year, enjoying their companionship as much as they enjoyed knowing us. We observed many strange and unusual things during our visit with these remarkable people, and were continually amazed at their scientific progress and inventions. All of this time they were never unfriendly to us, and we were allowed to return to our own home in the same manner in which we came—in fact, they courteously offered their protection if we should need it for the return voyage.

It is possible that whatever is in fact at the North Pole, or within its vicinity, has also made an impact on the commercial flight routes of passenger planes. None of the approved civil polar routes come closer than about sixty nautical miles from the Pole. Is there more to this? This builds a picture of flights around this part of the globe that show a distinct avoidance of the area. Planes also reserve flying around this part of the world due to its strange magnetic anomalies!

Angels

Angels are the final beings that we are going to cover in this chapter. They are very special and unique for many reasons. As discussed previously, angels cross into the description of physicals and nonphysicals. This means that they are able to take the physical embodiment of a person and also exist in spirit form. Often angels work in the higher realms and dimensions that are not readily available to our human field of vision; they also work in multidimensional ways as ETs do. Angelic beings are often working in the higher densities holding all the lower densities together like divine glue.

Angels have become confused with other beings and experiences and it is important to discern which you have experienced as real angels. For example, there are ET experiencers who have had real-life encounters with physical beings from the Pleiades—beings that were humanoid, tall, very beautiful to look at, and that emitted a radiance of light and unconditional love that to behold could be seen as angelic. It could be said that they had an almost celestial feel/presence, although were not angels themselves.

In other circumstances there have been recorded experiences involving exorcisms. There have been reported cases among nonreligious people and spiritualists possessing medium capabilities who have helped in the process of exorcism; for example, exorcising a child that had become possessed by entities working in the nonphysical realm that are harmful. When the spiritualist called upon entities to help remove these beings, it was in fact high-dimensional Arcturians who came into the fold and helped remove the attachment. These were not angels, although it was experienced as an angelic presence. In essence it is important to understand the frequency of beings and spirits around you. Some of the beings in the higher realms/frequencies might feel or have energies of unconditional love and light and might be seen to glow and become visible, but it is important to discern what is angelic and what is a higher frequency nonphysical.

Angels are very special in that they are completely nonjudgmental and cross over all religions, faiths, and beliefs. It is thought by those that can connect with them that everyone on this planet has a guardian angel no matter who you are or what faith you practice. That means that if there are seven billion people on Earth at this time, then there are seven billion angels also here working at this time, whether you are aware or not, all of them looking over all people at all times. They do not grow tired or weary and are with you the moment you enter Earth up until the moment you leave loving you unconditionally at all times.

Young children and more often babies are partial to seeing these messengers of God. As young humans transition onto the Earth plane, the angels stay close as transitioning from spirit to an earthly vessel can be traumatic. This is especially so for humans as other beings such as Pleiadians are more readily born into a physical vessel with knowledge of who they are and their previous lives. They have a predisposed sense of knowing oneself already and of remembering lessons learned from other incarnations.

This is not the case with humans on Gaia. We are cloaked in a vale of amnesia regarding spiritual essence and there is a level of isolation from creator/God in which we must work the puzzle and find ourselves again. This is why angels are on Earth, to aid and protect us especially in the young arriving in baby bodies. Have you ever looked at a young child or baby who is smiling at an unforeseen thing in the room, almost interacting with it, but you were unable to grasp what they were looking at? Often this is the cord that is still attached to the other side of the veil in which the young child is still able to visually see their angels, who are at all times standing by and loving unconditionally. Perhaps next time you see an infant smiling into the great unknown, or finding entertainment from a seemingly empty space in the room, reach out and speak to the angel and give thanks. Perhaps you will get more of a response than you had thought, and remember, just because you lost your powers when you were young, it doesn't mean that those that still have theirs aren't real regardless of their age.

Over time this cord is slowly released as the soul in its new human vehicle integrates into the lower densities and distractions of the third/fourth lower reality until the ability to see or have direct communication is lost. It is at this point that angels find other ways that are more multidimensional to communicate. This could be in the dream state whereby you dream something over and over. This could be a message from your angels of a direction you should take or a warning, both of which are to serve your greatest good. Angels are also able to manipulate surroundings in the most subtle ways as not to frighten you by putting items or sudden ideas in your path. Some people call these epiphanies. Was it really you or did it come from somewhere else?

For example, you might be in traffic sitting in your car not moving when all of a sudden you look out of your window and there is a taxi or commercial car advertising a picture on it that directly answers a question you have been waiting to get confirmation on. Angels are the masters of making sure you are helped into being in the right place at the right time using your own free will. Angels do not experience human emotion and life frustrations. They will continue to give you signs and help even when their signs are ignored; they will persist. Working with your angels is important. Remember, "Ask, and thou shalt receive." It is important to be aware spiritually while staying open to the universe and the messages it sends you. An angel's energy is regarded as seventh dimensional and above. There are, of course, many dimensions but for the sake of easy understanding we shall put it at the seventh as the sixth is one of physicality, and going beyond this often entails leaving a vessel. For humans, the happier your state of being and clearer the state of mind you are in, the easier it can be for angels to communicate with you as you are resonating closer to their frequency. When you pull out of the darkness for just long enough, you find a moment of clarity and answers seem to flow.

Angels are actively waiting for you to communicate with them. They are by your side at all times. Have you ever sat in a car and wondered while you are driving to work whether you are alone? The truth is you are never alone, help is always there waiting for you. The law of Earth is that of free will. No angel or being that is benevolent can communicate with you unless permission is given. They are not allowed by universal law to break the rule of free will that is given unto the people of Earth.

Often angels will spend a lifetime with a person waiting for that breakthrough moment when a person finally asks, if you are there, give me a sign, let me know if you can help me! It is understood by mediums who contact angels that the angelic presence at this point bursts with celebration when finally, through free will a person has granted permission for their angel to take their hand in life and begin the journey together. Some angels will wait a person's entire lifetime to make contact and be given permission, and if it is not given that angel will continue to love you unconditionally regardless and hope that in the next lifetime they might get the chance.

Angels are very wonderful and mysterious beings and in times of great need or danger they will make decisions to actively participate in your life for just a moment. Many stories have been told regarding strange happenings, be it climbers on mountains or people stuck in remote areas suddenly encountering help that seemed impossible at the time. Strangers have materialized who miraculously disappeared just as fast, thereafter never to be seen again. To best understand this, let us explore the famous case of Suzie Thompson, who at the time was a resident in Florida.

In Florida exists one of the most dangerous highways in the USA. The I-4 runs from Tampa to Daytona Beach and has one of the highest counts for fatalities than any other road in the United States. The large majority of these fatalities occur near a town called Sanford south of Lake Monroe. To the southwest of the lake is St. Johns River, which feeds into the lake, which is crossed by a well-known bridge called the St. Johns River

Veterans Memorial Bridge or otherwise known as the "dead zone." Most of the lives lost or accidents on I-4 happen within this area and local residents are famously known to take a much longer route round the bridge in order to skip this treacherous area of historical disaster.

Records vary, but they detail anywhere from 1,500 to over 2,000 accidents occurring upon the opening of the highway in 1963 with many resulting in death. Approximately 440 accidents happened in the dead zone between 1999 and 2006, with 44 of those accidents resulting in sixty-five people being injured in a twenty-four-month period between 1995 and 1997. Many locals and drivers passing through have reported strange activity in the area regarding electrical interference and car radios behaving abnormally or completely dying. There is historical evidence that the government decided to build this bridge over an old gravesite without moving it. The dead zone sits directly on top of this area. It's possible this has an impact on the high rate of fatalities in this quarter-mile stretch of road although to some it is debatable; however, it does not explain the high fatality rate and strange anomalies that happen there.

In 1994 native Suzie Thompson was traveling on her way to see friends in Daytona Beach on a day measuring very high temperatures between 100–110° F on the road. She had driven through this area before many times but had always felt uneasy. As she drove near the famous quarter-mile stretch the car began to become unresponsive with the radio and motor cutting out completely. Panic began to set in as the day was approaching scorching temperatures and the next junction on the road was some distance away. She had no supplies and little water, and with no phone available was unable to call for help. Ms. Thompson decided the only foreseeable thing to do would be to walk the great distance to the nearest filling station, where a phone call could be made for help.

After some time in the incredible heat, she began to feel scared while walking alongside the busy road and the heat was slowly getting the better of her. No car would stop, and help seemed far from view. In a very panicked state Ms. Thompson continued the long walk along the dangerous road with dehydration becoming a possible factor. How could it be that she thought that a simple road trip to visit friends could potentially turn into a hazardous or even life-threatening episode? She recounts how cars were passing by with the drivers shouting at her and offering little in the way of help, some even hurling abuse.

As Ms. Thompson continued, she began to feel helpless with little hope until something strange did happen. An eighteen-wheeler pulled up alongside her, the only passing vehicle to offer help. The huge truck came to a stop on the side of the road and a well-dressed man opened the door. His very first words were, "Suzanne, it's ok, come with me."

She had never met the man before and could not understand how he might know her name. Famously Suzie Thompson is reported as describing the man as having a "good presence" and that she somehow intuitively felt safe in his company. In that instance she made a decision to climb into the cab of the lorry which she describes as being "meticulous." She later describes him also as meticulous with the cab being perfectly clean and air conditioned as if it were brand new, with all the chrome dials polished and glistening. She had the feeling she knew the man but couldn't place how.

The man then drove her to the nearest filling station and pulled on the side of the forecourt. She thanked him kindly and hopped out of the eighteen-wheeler as it sat with its huge engine idly purring on that hot July day. As she took a few steps away from the lorry, silence suddenly fell. There was no engine sound whatsoever and she turned round one last time to thank the stranger and he along with the huge vehicle were gone. How had such a large object vanished in only seconds of time? She is known for saying, "You don't just lose an eighteen-wheeler truck every day!" Before finding a phone, she inquired within the filling station if anyone had seen a large truck. The attendant explained that they had not seen one all day. Suzie Thompson still struggles to explain to this day what happened but believes more and more that help came in a way that she will never be able to comprehend. This often is how those looking after us on the other side manifest. Some have called them angels at work. They come when you least expect, in ways you never thought possible and at times of greatest need.

There is a passage in the biblical text of Hebrews 13:2: "Do not neglect to show hospitality to strangers, for thereby some have entertained angels unawares."

Angels perform miracles around us every day of all sizes. When you need a miracle just ask and hold your faith unwavering until a sign or the miracle comes. Give passage for miracles at all times and always keep your heart open. This is the teaching that Lorna Byrne, an angel contactee, teaches.

Lorna Byrne is an international number-1 bestselling Irish author with more than a million readers around the world. Her books, *Angels in My Hair*, *Stairways to Heaven*, *A Message of Hope from the Angels*, and *Love from Heaven*, have been translated into thirty languages. She has shed light on angels in a wonderful way that can be found in the public domain.

She explains how she speaks to them in thought form and gets visualizations of images that help her. At a young age she was diagnosed as being extremely dyslexic and struggled to read or write even into adulthood. She received messages from angels that her work was to write books on the subject. Lorna Byrne was unable to understand how this would happen, but help came and people fell into her life in order to facilitate the books she has become so well known for. Lorna Byrne is still able to see angels physically and explains that there are many among us both in physicality and nonphysicality doing work in different ways that make many people's lives wonderful.

Angels are said to be God's personal workers. They are a presence keeping harmony in check. They were in creation long before the Earth existed. At this time in ascension beings in the angelic realms are also helping to raise the vibration of Earth such as Michael and many more. Different religions have given different names throughout history, but the energy is the same. It is important to understand that other beings in higher dimensions are aware of angels and work with angelic entities. Angels are not just Earthbound. Through many years of research there have been Andromedan changelings whereby they explain they have worked hand in hand with angelic beings such as Michael to rid the Earth of low or bad energies. The Andromedans have even referred to Jesus as "the favorite son." So you see that in the higher realms various energies and entities cross paths and are aware of each other. It is only on Earth that humans put these energies into boxes and have them separated.

In more recent times those who work with angels have delved deeper into the way they work as the veil becomes thinner. Angels who have been channeled through people recently have given more clarity than ever regarding their operating on multidimensional levels. It is said that Archangel Michael is in fact not just one individual but a group of individuals working together in collective consciousness. There is also understanding that it was humans that have used gender to explain these beings when in fact they are neither male nor female such as God the creator. Humans have been stuck in linearity for so long that in order to comprehend something out of our stratosphere, we have taken cosmic beings and put them into a box with a label. Religions have done this with these energies for a long time. Increasingly there is direct contact from angels at this time who suggest that they are genderless. They are celestial beings and gender is not a necessary label for many of them.

⁎ 4 ⁎
The Densities Explained

The densities are a means of organizing different planes of existence according to their vibratory rate, explained as high or low energies that dictate the awareness based on a vibrational frequency in that energy. This is why different vibrations are called densities so that one can be designated from another. Often the denser a vibratory environment is, you will find a lower consciousness present with a conscious awareness that is less advanced. Each density has certain sets of laws and principles that are specific to the frequency of that vibratory rate. The inhabitants of each density operate within that plane because their consciousness vibrates in resonance with the frequency of that density as does their perception and use of that reality within their immediate existence.

Dimensions, however, are better used to describe parallel realities that exist in coherence within the now, the past, and the future existing simultaneously until something or someone changes that timeline due to an action or thought. Simply put, dimensions are equated better to timelines and their various fractals that are ever expanding and changing within the space time continuum. Densities are the conscious awareness within those dimensions. The two do work and play together, however. As you raise your consciousness to a higher density, you might find yourself becoming in alignment with higher dimensional timelines and this is how manifestations work.

The higher you are to the highest density, which we will set at twelve, the closer you are to the creator God and are

The Densities Explained

a creator God yourself. That is the basic concept. We are ever working to become closer to God/creator and to become godlike ourselves, without the ego! It is important to understand that I set out the energies within a framework of twelve in order to begin a simplified process of understanding these vibratory rates. However, within multidimensionality there are many, many levels working within the quantum soup of all that is in this universe including the densities that operate within them.

The densities have been referred to in many different ways and as many different things in the past, but they have also been known as the layers of the universe and the different realities of the world we live in. Mathematically speaking, there are various descriptions of the dimensions and its densities that express what they are in more linear terms, but they do provide much conceptual room for existing within these different levels and how one might process them emotionally. Let us begin this process with simple math, first using scientific language. For example, the first dimension would be a line connecting two points. There is no depth and no height, only a width. You can call this the x-axis. Consciousness on this level would be extremely basic and as far as science is concerned, both mathematically and spiritually, there is little or no consciousness in the first dimension as it is only a building block giving us a foundation upon which to begin, basic some may say, but an x-axis, if you will, is a starting point and there must always be a beginning.

For the second dimension we have added height or the y-axis. Think of any flat figure, like a triangle or a two-dimensional shape like a square that you might look at on a flat piece of paper. It is in the second density that life begins to take shape. Everything we perceive in our world appears to have length, breadth, and depth. However, scientists have for many years now played with the idea that the universe is in fact a massive two-dimensional hologram with illusional qualities similar to the third density. For example, in our present technological time we are able to create holograms on a flat 2D platform that appear to have length, breadth, and depth. When you visit a museum, you see these on the science floor or perhaps in the small hologram which

∴ 207 ∴

exists on some credit cards these days. When you look at these 2D holograms, be it a face, you walk around the room with the face appearing to move and peer at you as you move around the room. This is known as motion parallax. So as you move your gaze, things in the foreground seem to move faster than things in the background giving you a stereoscopic view which creates the illusion of depth, in turn looking 3D-like.

Various scientists around the world have explored that mathematically the universe could be two-dimensional. It can be explained that on top of the third-dimensional quality protruded by a flat 2D surface that color also can be drawn from this. If you look at an audio CD, you can see various colors of the rainbow appearing due to refraction from light waves. So perhaps with all of this in mind you might be able to construct a matrix based on a flat 2D foundation. What would it be like to actually live in that kind of reality? In the 3D world humans have lived in for so long we have become accustomed to a very wide and dynamic variety of emotional feelings and responses. Would living in the 2D illusion of length, breadth, and depth hinder the way we see the world? Would we only have limited perceptions of the world and would we feel only positive or negative feelings with little in between? This would equate to fear and love and nothing else. This would be a basic reality. It isn't proven completely that we live in a 2D matrix and is far less likely, however the science does ask some interesting questions.

The third density simply includes volume and the ability to obtain cross-sections from objects. You can think of this dimension as space without time. Things contain volume and mass. They are tangible to the touch. There are theorists that claim this is still illusionary and we are in a matrix-style simulation. This is the physical world we are used to living in such as the physics of the air we breathe and laws of nature as the sciences which are taught early on at schools around the world. One can feel objects in three-dimensional reality. You pick up a pencil and write on paper. There is action and reaction to various elements and the way they bond to each other atomically.

Over the past century, the quest to describe the geometry of space has become a part of a larger quest in relation to theoretical physics with experts such as Albert Einstein embarking to explain the forces of nature as byproducts of the shape of space itself. Space has often been seen as having three dimensions while general relativity paints a four-dimensional universe. It becomes increasingly complex as you enter into the world of string theory with its ten dimensions and eleven if you take an extended version otherwise known as M Theory. Other variations have been conceived by mathematicians that include twenty-four and even twenty-six dimensions. So there is some debate as to the exact number. There is a general consensus that rests nicely at twelve among some scientists and New-Agers. When ETs have left messages, they have also hinted at twelve.

Einstein played a great part in the story of dimensionality when in 1905 he published a paper describing the world as a four-dimensional setting; miraculously he was unknown to the world at that time. In his "special theory of relativity," time was then added to the three dimensions of space that are known about. In the mathematics of relativity, all four dimensions are bound together. This is where the term spacetime was born.

Einstein found that in turn mathematical tools came into being that radically transcended Newton's physics, which enabled him to predict the characteristics of electrically charged particles. In his 4D model of the world, electromagnetism is accurately described. It has been said that the fourth dimension is also knowing an object's position in time that is essential to plotting its position in the universe. However, what does physics look like outside of these ideas and did Einstein take into account other dimensions and their properties?

As we increase into the fifth and beyond densities/ dimensions, we start to see the rules of physics and mathematics begin to morph. There are the possibilities of multiple Earths simultaneously existing on different timelines, to the point of multiple universes that are infinite. What of living in these realities and the direct influence it would have on life sociologically and psychologically, how would it affect our world and the way in which we evolve in terms of consciousness? As you transcend through frequency, vibration, harmonics, acoustics, and electromagnetic fields, not only intensity but also spectrum broadness begin to transform. The possibilities begin to unfold. Imagine raising your vibration to a place whereby you look at a rainbow in the sky and see colors unseen before as you perceive visual stimulus in the color spectrum that was unobtainable at lower densities. For this reason, most of humankind find it somewhat difficult to express from a 3D point of view what fifth-density reality might be like, with the comparison being that you ask a man or a woman to describe a color they have never seen before. We do, however, have direct information from other beings both nonphysical and physical who have come from these places who describe in eloquence what these realities feel like, and increasingly people on Earth are accessing these energies like never before. On top of this, there are also some very enlightened spiritual people on Earth who have transcended to higher vibrations and given accounts throughout history and in modern times of all of the densities.

We have described the concept of ascension that is linked to the raising of awareness while transitioning into higher realms. Another way that this could be explained is like the ocean. Imagine the ocean floor. It's dark and there are many atmospheres of water pushing down on all physical things at great pressure. Things down there are sluggish and what life dwells down there has learned to survive. There is little thriving down there. This could be said for the current 3D reality in the past of Earth. As you transcend up out of the depths there is an increase in light and less pressure and new worlds open up, with life and different ecosystems. The fifth density would be parallel to raising oneself out of the water entirely and experiencing life in a way that is inconceivable due to the previous conditioning. We wouldn't be swimming; we would be floating and thereafter flying. Since 2012 it is widely regarded that we crossed the marker into lower fourth density with increasing pockets of fifth-density energies depending on your personal spiritual and ascension status. Confusing? Let us take a deeper look into how these worlds work starting with the third density.

The Densities Explained

There is some confusion on how the densities operate in real time. Various theories have been argued and some say you can only be in one density at a time, which is contradictory to the phrase "multidimensional," which implies simultaneous, or dimensions all happening together at the same time. Therefore, you are only able to see in the density you are in or part of the next, while the enlightened being at the top may look throughout all the levels as they have full cosmic awareness of all timelines and have full awareness throughout them all. After many years of research speaking to people and listening to channeled data from angelic and galactic beings, it has become apparent that there is a common thread.

Third-density realities can be lived only within a body operating at lower consciousness. As consciousness increases, awareness rises into lower fourth density experiencing the parameters of both with dualistic qualities. However, once fifth dimensionality is completely achieved, all the dimensions/densities then become available simultaneously depending on which aspect of consciousness you are dealing with. Divine order and unity are not about separation like the third and fourth densities, which still have heavy characteristics of duality, being light and dark. Another way to understand this is a building. Imagine we discuss this on the assumption there are twelve dimensions/densities and twelve floors acting as stories of the building. All the floors are in the building simultaneously. Once consciousness exceeds the confines of the third and fourth floor you get the key to the elevator and you can begin to travel up and down to all the floors that have always been there all existing at once depending on your consciousness awareness. For example, an ego-driven Reptilian isn't able to adapt to the fifth-density qualities of unconditional love and often does not ascend past higher fourth, whereas a Pleiadian can traverse over and uncap the rest of the dimensions to some degree.

What you have is a system whereby you have three to four and then the rest of the densities working in much higher cohesion without the polarities that humans face in the crumbling matrix system. This is why the more advanced multidimensional beings find it harder working in or visiting lower densities under the fifth as it is the equivalent to our previous water metaphor. They would be returning back to the dark murky depths of the ocean with multiple atmospheres pushing down. This is why the physiology of ETs is different from human anatomy. Some are built for lighter, less dense environments often with different bone tissues as their worlds and environments have different attributes regarding physics and its relation to biology. This knowledge comes from whistle-blowers such as Emery Smith, who worked at underground bases.

Smith operated as a chemical warfare specialist, biotech warfare specialist, medical doctor, and surgeon for various black military funded projects in various underground bases. He has since become a whistle-blower for the ET community, exposing the work he did on real-life ETs. His story, like many others, can be found on the Internet and YouTube.

The ETs themselves through channeling have discussed twelve levels of density when explaining to humans often with beings becoming nonphysical seven upward. More commonly three to seven beings engage with a biological vessel or body in order to operate. Let us now explore how the densities affect our lives directly and how they progress outside the laws of physics as we know it.

Third Densities
Soul > Thought > Emotion > Action > Manifestation

We will use Earth and humankind to cover the experience of this realm as it will help ground the understanding of the consciousness that is experienced in the third dimension. The third is a particularly interesting dimension as it is a place of great duality. It can accommodate light but also great darkness. This is why beings and angels often express so much love for us as they see the struggles we go through in the dualistic light and dark realities of Earth. Enlightenment is hardest to reach in the third as there are great illusions of separation of spirit and creator in

The Densities Explained

this place. Who is God and why can't we see him? Perhaps it is a charade?

In higher consciousness awareness it is easier to manifest things and bring them into reality. In 3D consciousness awareness there is a longer time delay in receiving the thing you are trying to manifest, you could call this a delay of sorts. In an old 3D world with a lower consciousness awareness it took many years to achieve goals and create manifestations. As Earth moves up in vibration itself along with the starseeds, manifestation and the delay in which it takes to receive that creation begin to quicken. You receive it faster. This is also relational to time. In a lower density, time begins to go slowly and feels more arduous. In a higher density, time begins to speed up. This is why time flies when you are having fun because from a standpoint that is felt emotionally, you are at a higher frequency.

Love and joy are high-density emotional frequencies. Fear and resentment are low emotional frequencies. This is partly why an arduous office job you hate seems to deliver days which are long and when you look at the clock little time has passed. This also means that if you are in a job that leaves you in low emotional states/densities, you will find it many times hard to access higher dimensional timelines where you create or obtain the thing in your dreams or desires. This is why in life it is important to find the things you love or are interested in. This also explains why those moving into a higher density will have to leave jobs and relationships that only served in a lower density, otherwise that person will become conflicted leading to mental or physical issues. This is why as you move into higher densities and dimensional realities there are fewer constraints within that paradigm with the universe working for you and not against you. In turn this creates less stress for the emotional and physical body and adds years to your life. In an older energy the system was set up to create many constraints and systems that governed the 3D matrix where consciousness awareness was limited and lives were shorter. You can see this in the records of countries where technologies and societies have evolved. This becomes evident of life spans and increased life expectancy.

We come to Gaia taking an earthly vessel and are conditioned early on regarding constructs of human structure and society with the old 3D world. We forget we are souls from the spirit realm and feel lonely at times. Upon awakening to the truths of the universe, souls often find it hardest to leave the third behind much like an inmate of a prison after many years who has become institutionalized. Internally there is fear of enlightenment. Souls wishing to stay in their comfort zone have been known to deliberately stay in the closet not wanting to rock the foundations that have been created over the years or even lifetimes.

At this point we begin to adventure into the great unknown of higher vibration without knowing what it even is, transmuting fear into love. As we transmute, we learn much about ourselves regarding humanity and the rose-tinted spectacles are ripped off, so to speak. You begin to see the truth in the matrix as Neo did in the film self-titled *The Matrix*, and in turn either distance yourself or educate those mentally who are not "awake" yet.

The third dimension is best explained as the material world of fear. This is a double-edged sword loaded with duality. This encompasses fear of not having possessions and fear of losing them while trying to accumulate as much as possible in this life and keeping tight control over every aspect of our existence and the fear of losing that control which in turn is all governed by the ego. Within a third density, manifestations often originated out of fear and survival with the mentality being: "What will people think of me unless I have this or that?" or "How will I exist without these clothes and this money?" In turn this creates a lack of self-worth through fear, which in turn creates a lack of trust as others could take away from us both in the present or the future, creating divide, which in turn is overcompensated by yearning for more domination over others including status creating a cycle that can be destructive to oneself and others. This becomes a self-defining destructive cycle. We struggle to connect with God/source and therefore struggle to connect to all that is and the universe and continue to create from a place of lack of abundance in order to fill that hole or attachment, believing that once we manifest that desire, we will feel whole again with the end result often leading us back to square one.

Early on we are conditioned to believe death is a dark finality, which in turn creates desperation to achieve all we can in this short life having been told we live one life and that is all with nothing after but our decaying bodies in the ground. Archaic constructs such as religions have been created in this energy and in turn used as further control historically, or in other words, "conform or you will go to hell." In third dimensionality, there is a sense of lack and scarcity and in true egoic action we fight for what abundance we can acquire with the fear that there are only winners or losers and the winner controlling all outcomes. The ego can be so protective over our reality buffering physiological harm that we lie and do all that we can to promote our own beliefs over others while promoting that we are always right. Self-induced ego control within the 3D density is almost blinding and it is easier to sell lies within the 3D matrix than awaken people to them as the ego takes over the higher self, keeping us in lower dimensional timelines regarding the choices it makes for us. Other truths and realities become irrelevant as the ego only wants to see what it wants. Viewing life from an observational and impartial place of balance is almost impossible as the ego constantly needs its addictive self being fed in delusional opulence until it becomes too late.

There are dualistic beliefs that men are the strong providers and women the weaker sex whose role it is to procreate and look after the home; however, as consciousness advances, the roles begin to balance, especially in the new Age of Aquarius, which is a more feminine era regarding energies. Added to this problem we feel we can't be whole as God created us but can only be fulfilled by another person in our lives without first loving ourselves. For many humans the only time when masculine and feminine energy balance fully is during sex, which is why sex is craved so much, becoming the root cause for desire, which in turn is used for deception and influence upon which it sells. The duality of the third pushes the human to lust after sex as a need instead of using it as a tool for sharing love. We fear loving ourselves as this is concieved as being egotistical when the opposite is the case. Loving oneself too much creates selfishness, again another duality. Balance is hard to find in third density.

We have learned not to question the ego, which often is running wild with our thoughts questioning the past and fearing every aspect of what the future holds. The ego constantly needs to know everything that is happening without letting go and living in the present. There is a constant battle between the higher self and the ego in the third density with the ego craving outcomes that feed short-term fixes while the higher self is drowned out, removing an expanded and more abundant fuller experience that takes us out of our comfort zone and teaches us how to be our best selves.

On the whole the third dimension is one of low vibrations acting as a catalyst for separation of self, others, God the creator, and the universe, including free will. Often the higher self which is the part of our soul on the other side of the veil urgently attempts to give us intuitive thought and guidance but isn't able to ground to the human through the thick sludge treacle like vibrations of third density, which is especially difficult when our body's spiritual chakra points are blocked or not aligned. Have you ever heard someone say, "I knew the answer to that question but I didn't go with my instincts, I wish I had." This is the higher self offering us life's answers and the ego sweeping them away.

We lose our true sense of self, often drifting through life sometimes in the wrong job or relationship not expressing fully who we are or finding our true potentials of self-expression. As we incarnate into the Earth vessel, our ego mind increasingly takes over in order to survive, forgetting who we were spiritually and internally. As discussed, the Akashic record will carry this data, but it is hard to access in 3D and many have no idea it is even there.

Often we use our heads and not our hearts through conditioned survival and in turn the connection to the soul within is blocked. When true intuition comes through to us in a flash of light or inspiration, the rational ego mind steps in to use logical rationale to discredit what could have been a moment of innovation or an enlightening idea or path, shutting us down once

The Densities Explained

more as we then struggle to validate if what we felt was right or wrong.

In light of all of this, we become so confused that we feel we can only find happiness from external stimuli from the environment outside of ourselves ever accepting the 3D illusions that are sold to us as reality, and there is little or no escaping. We see it in others around us and in the way they live, which confirms this even more. This is not the case unless you are an exceptional being surrounded by other exceptional beings, but for the masses this is the norm.

In turn we learn to bury questions about ourselves and our true purpose, perhaps who we really are. Historically, those who dared to question reality and the concrete constructs put in place were discredited or labeled insane or hopeless dreamers, while the masses enjoy their seemingly secure realities in shielded delusions and ideas that have been created for them, trapped in the system with egos that are programmed early on with false beliefs.

Ultimately, we struggle to see the matrix with its fear-based control, which is hugely beneficial to the rulers of a 3D world, because this way the majority are far more controllable and profitable while ending up policing the minority free thinkers as this is incentivized by the rulers at the top to propagate further submission.

Huge amounts of money are made with fear: the pharmaceutical industry, insurance, and others, for example. The fashion industry promotes images of how to look and discredits those who aren't in season or of the time and so on. Fear leads us to spend our money to fit in and control our fears, adding further to the addictive part of the ego. We must have the new phone, the new shoes, the new car to fit in, not realizing who we are as an original person is more than adequate in many scenarios. We shift all our attention onto material things as it distracts from who we are and what we are going through.

Through all of this we are like addicts in total dependency at all times. It is not until learning to choose love and love of oneself and others that we begin to break these old paradigms.

It is at this point our frequency raises, balancing the ego and using it more as an observational tool and not an object to rule us. Through this we learn to trust our intuition, listen to our hearts, and spend less time in our heads finding true happiness without strings or attachments. It is the balanced soul not living in duality that becomes enlightened. The balanced soul lives in harmony with the big picture not getting caught up in the small dramas of everyday life and the hearsay that is sweet seduction for the ego.

Ultimately the 3D matrix is a place where free will can most easily be manipulated, a place where everything on Earth has inverted backward to control becoming the polar opposite of a 5D reality where love originates thought and reason first. This is a place where illusion is most powerfully created by those you have means and the abilities to make people think they are being given free will while undermining it at every step. Earth is transitioning out of this as the awareness of the collective sees out of the box that was provided.

(Some of the ideas in this section have been inspired by the article by Gaia Sophia, https://awakeningthelove.wordpress.com/shift-in-consciousness/.)

Fourth Densities
Soul > Thought > Emotion > Manifestation

Dreams. They happen to all of us. We spend a large amount of time in our lives sleeping as the human body needs to heal and rejuvenate. Every night when we sleep we dream and yet we think little of it or even remember what we dreamt. Eight hours of every day we sleep and dream and yet this large proportion of our time is discarded as having little or no relevance of any kind as we stay locked to the physical world only trusting what is physically touched. We spend much time discussing our waking hours but very little taking into account what happened during sleeping hours and contemplating why it happened. We only discuss what we have comprehended within waking hours using our six senses, not taking into account the incredible work the subconscious is

The Densities Explained

computing at night, showing us solutions in metaphorical ideas and working through issues.

The fourth is otherwise known as the astral or dream realm. It is the in-between place between third and fifth. Often in the path of enlightenment one seeks to reach the fifth and the fourth is a bridge we must cross to get to the other side. There are interesting qualities to this vibration both in waking and sleeping states.

It is less dense and more vibrational while still hosting 3D illusions of duality, allowing the ego to play freely within this realm. It is an energy field hosting time and its various lines and potentials. Those who are practiced at the art of astral traveling can visit other countries or places in their dreams and recall these places with accuracy as if they had actually been there. Remote viewing is a fourth-density ability. Once a person has enough acumen this can be done during waking states and out-of-body experiences can take place whereby you are floating above your body looking down watching yourself without dying. It is open information that intelligence agencies use remote viewers and this information is in the public domain.

Ayahuasca is a shamanic tool used to induce ego death and travel these realms in a trance to find the truth of oneself or the world at that time. Going into an induced trance or trip can be a frightening experience for some as your survival mechanisms are temporarily stripped from you while reality in its true duality is truthed to you without buffers. Used correctly the fourth density can be a very reflective place to find knowledge and truth of oneself. It is on the fourth that we are much closer to the higher self and knowledge can be passed across the veil more fluidly. For those who are not awakened, the sleep state is a good time for angels and spirit guides to show conceptual or visual ideas. This is because when we sleep the mind is quieter and the ego is calm enough to let ideas and visions come through its filters without it trying to control what it is seeing.

This can also be a dangerous place for people who have not yet set healthy auric or energetic defenses or set out or taken ownership of their vibrational space. As your light begins to shine and increase so too does the potential for some entities within the lower fourth astral to want to attach to you for various reasons. Some of these beings will be parasitic and want to diminish your light. These entities will be part of the older energies that have plagued Earth that are still lingering or not of the light yet. Other entities will want to attach to your light to use your light as a conduit to get back to the light themselves. Spiritual practitioners have a variety of weapons in their toolbox, including imagining being submerged in a purple cloak of violet flame. The imagination becomes real in the fourth and what you envision begins to manifest but also is seen by nonphysical and other beings which become reality to them when your intention creates it. Imagine layers of protection around you and it will be seen by nonphysicals as it becomes real to them. Often those having an awakening or broadening of their senses for the first time begin to see the "shadow monsters" out of the corner of their eyes as they slip into the lower fourth for the very first time. This stage passes and not all go through it; many do, however.

This is where dark or black magic can come out to play, feeding off fears and insecurities. Sometimes this can manifest physically as sleep paralysis with the body becoming temporarily paralyzed while the individual dreams a nightmare and the victim feels unable to wake or move. Sleep paralysis can be induced by negative ETs, bad astral entities, witches or warlocks who from afar are psychically attacking you. Remember a dark consciousness or magic is no match for the light that is inside of us now at this moment in time as Gaia herself goes up and so does all vibration on Earth. Psychic attacks can be resolved more easily than ever. Contact your nearest spiritual person for help as resolve can easily be found in the newer, lighter energies.

For more awakened souls who are able to anchor their light this is not an issue as their light absorbs the darkness much like a light going on in a dark room. For beings that are increasingly ascending, dreams become more memorable as the veil becomes thinner and remembrance of all the aspects of the dream more easily digested. This is because the human synapses of the brain linked to memory are used to activating in the third density

The Densities Explained

but historically not the fourth. This is why some people never remember their dreams as they are still too heavily reliant on their logical 3D memory which quickly forgets where it has been in the astral. Other humans at this time will have soul contracts that dictate they forget all their dreams, which will be blocked for that person's own safety should someone else try to remotely view the astral work they are doing.

In recent times many lightworkers and starseeds have been activated and are busier than ever in the astral at night closing down old timelines, helping others cross into the light, and working with others and the grids of Earth in the great collective mission in regard to ascension. This is partly why some lightworkers are more tired after a night's sleep as you have been busier battling the dark and correcting time fractals and other astral clean-up jobs. So fastidious are some souls at night at present, that they are regularly meeting others from their soul groups and doing work with them and their star families including returning back to ships at night. This will translate into the 3D waking reality as meeting someone and having the strangest feeling that you know them or have met them before. This of course will be correct as in the astral you did! For those that are elevated in the soul/ET hierarchy, they will have this happen on a far larger scale as those souls are working with larger groups of souls every night.

Time becomes more fluid in the fourth density, and it can seem to either dramatically speed up or drastically slow down depending on your outlook and the perception you have with your current moment. There is less time continuity in waking hours. In much the same way you can dream a dream which felt very short, but upon waking have surprisingly transitioned through an entire night or eight-hour cycle wondering how the dream was so short and yet so much time passed.

People who have already ascended into 5D do not suffer the duality of nightmares as they are vibrating at a resonance higher than that of fourth-density shadows or dark magic that often try to distract or sabotage those ascending who are not practiced in spiritual defense. It is the fourth density that houses the lost souls and demon-like entities that became stuck as nonphysicals

∴ 221 ∴

including Reptilian entities that will cloak themselves as members of your family sometimes or other human characters.

Some beings and traumatized souls can stay trapped in the astral for long periods of time in a state of confusion or sometimes carrying out and concluding unfinished business or protecting loved ones before moving on themselves.

Spiritualists have viewed 4D as the bumpy road to enlightenment. However, with proper knowledge of protection and holding your light, there is no reason any harm should ever come to anyone in 4D. It is in the fourth that people are able to begin to experience higher levels of multidimensionalism for the first time resulting in the first signs of what is called the Clair Senses. 4D is the beginning stage of using new senses outside of the six ordinary ones we use for animal survival in a 3D world. These are abilities that most humans on Earth are capable of and yet are completely unaware of. Can you now begin to see why the rulers of a 3D world want us shut off from our true selves and divinity?

Imagine a society of fully active beings all who have the following attributes switched on. Corruption, deceit, lying, and manipulation would cease to exist overnight, and the people would be in control of the few and not the other way round. This is why the rulers of a 3D matrix keep humans in a box that is controlled via some of the tools we have discussed already including the toxins in the food we eat.

The following are all terms with origins that date back to the French language. This is a list of the clair abilities that begin only in the fourth density. These include:

Clairaudience (Hearing): The faculty of perceiving, as if by hearing, what is inaudible.

Clairvoyance (Seeing): The ability to gain information about objects, people, locations, or physical events through extrasensory perception.

Clairsentience (Feeling): The ability to physically feel, to receive messages, emotions, and feelings externally without any aid.

Clairalience (Smelling): The ability to smell scents, people, or objects that existed in the past, present, or future.

Claircognizance (Knowing): The ability to acquire psychic knowledge by means of intrinsic knowledge.

Clairtangency (Touching): To handle an object or touch an area and perceive through the palms of one's hands information about the article or its owner or history that was not previously known.

Clairgustance (Tasting): To taste a substance without putting anything in one's mouth. It is claimed that those who possess this ability are able to perceive the essence of a substance from the spiritual or ethereal realms

through taste.

This density is the beginning place to the magical world. Other personalities or people who identify in the energies of this realm are the magician, druid, witch (black-grey-white), sorcerer, enchanter, psychic, healer, past-life regressionist, and my personal favorite, the starseed.

It is important to state that as a higher density to 3D, manifestation, synchronicity, and other such occurrences such as déjà vu and coincidences can happen more fluidly and at a faster rate than 3D. The veil to the "other side" has thinned out a lot more and energies are able to pass through much more readily. In turn it is also where light and dark clash more frequently before the ultimate push into the light, which is fifth density and above.

Fifth Densities
Soul > Thought > Manifestation

This is a place of wonder where beings like the Pleiadians and

Adromedans dwell. It is a place of purer etheric light where very little fear exists at all. All life upon the fifth density lives in the unity consciousness of spirit, but there is still an experience of "I" as an individual member of the group. Linear time and space do not bind consciousness here, and there is no illusion of separation or limitation. Instead, there is a constant experience of the Oneness of God/All that Is. Judgment, guilt, or negativity toward self and others are drowned out by forgiveness, acceptance, positivity, and love, which is the key component to fifth-dimensional awareness. Love for self and others. Perceptions within this state can seem more dream-like although still being physical.

This is a place where reality is created and inspired from within first, which then manifests into the external world. If you are full of creative and inspiring ideas that are within, a soul will then create these into their external world which run parallel with emotion concluded in a state of inner knowing and inner understanding.

This is the polar opposite of the 3D world, which on Earth has been a world of external stimulus first both negative and positive which then affects us internally both emotionally and in the things we decide to create in our lives, as a result generating confusion within that person or being as the external has dedicated first without the true essence of the person being utilized inside using the soul. This is often why souls on Earth come here and feel so lost as an external stimulus governs the light inside that is trying to get out. An unawakened soul will struggle to find their authenticity as they are not connected to themselves internally but more likely to the external reality. In higher densities beings are far more able to adapt into their own authenticity, in turn making better life decisions regarding what they do in love and business, in turn having more success or luck, as some call it!

In 5D most souls are governed by the light from within and this gives a great sense of self stability and calmness, which in turn overrides many of the external triggers life brings to us. This also explains why unawakened souls in 3D live in a drama-filled existence and are constantly triggered as they live a life ruled completely by external issues with little happening inside

The Densities Explained

and no connection to the soul. For the same reason, a fifth-density being lives in balance and sees the external only from an observational point of view. Triggering issues for a 5D person are like water running off a duck's back and used merely as signposts to navigate faster into innerstanding of what is being presented in that moment. The 3D person will see a trigger as something literal with the ego drawing its sword in readiness to attack while the 5D being has worked through much duality and trauma held Akashically and there is a great control of person emotional response as a result leading to mastery.

All around the world there are UFO sightings, and many of them differ greatly. It has been argued that the US industrial military complex has had reverse ET technology since 1947 including antigravity craft which sometimes can be recognized by its triangular or cigar-shaped appearance in the sky. There is a great debate on which UFOs are real. If there are both man-made craft and extraterrestrial craft in the sky, how do you tell them apart? This is important to explore as not only emotional perceptions change in 5D, but also physical things and their physics!

Man-made craft often have metallic or moving parts that can be seen, and to some degree look very advanced but still seem to have a physicality to them that appears solid. Fifth-dimensional upward crafts appear more like an ethereal ball of light in the sky materializing and non-materializing at will transdimensionally. There are seemingly no moving parts. The sheer size of them can be astronomical ranging from one to twenty miles across. In a higher density you have more scope upon which a craft or ship can be created and used, including the consciousness of that ship, which is alive itself!

The fifth dimension is a place where dreams and thoughts manifest much quicker and the vibration is high. It is the realm of pure/unconditional love where consciousness can affect matter and physics in ways that humans aren't able to fully conceptualize. Imagine being in a craft floating in space and moving the ship with just your mind.

This is a place where DNA and hidden strands become

almost fully activated. For example, the Pleiadians' DNA works at 70–80 percent while humanity's DNA has worked at 30 percent and below for a long time. This is rapidly changing as DNA upgrades take place during the evolution of beings on Earth at this time. It is at this resonance that beings begin to really get closer to pure light and harness source/God energy. There is far less duality in this vibration, and darkness or ego-driven mentalities do not live in this space easily. This is partly why so many beings of a dark variety are leaving Earth as their mind principals easily become exposed in the increasing light along with the illusions that kept them in existence.

Time works in an entirely different way within the fifth dimension. Beings in this density are able to experience more timelines and different aspects of themselves all at once. The past, present, and future become accessible instead of having an only now moment. Imagine a human who is very in tune with ETs and is able to channel their energy and let the beings or being communicate through them. It is quite possible that during the channel the ET speaking to them might be three hundred Earth years in the future while speaking to the human in the time that is our now. Time does not affect fifth dimensionality. This is why sometimes beings from the fifth dimension need a little more effort to communicate with us during our ascension as they have to find our now from wherever they are in the time continuum. From the human perspective it can be experienced in the state of deep trance or when the soul molecule (DMT) is smoked through a pipe. It sends the user into a conscious state that pushes perception into higher vibrational states often known as a breakthrough where time begins to bend and perceptions are far beyond daily perception.

To understand time in 5D and the higher dimensions and densities, here is a channeled message from the Arcturians,

Dearest souls and family. We call you family as you are connected to us in many more ways than you are

The Densities Explained

able to comprehend at this moment in time and there are many of you who have been us in what you call your past. We would like to have the pleasure of speaking to you about time and the frustration it causes you in your world.

You understand time as a linear constraint that is finite like a piece of string. In your world you would cut a length of string and lay it straight on a surface and imagine a time measurement that is relative to the start and the end of that piece of string. The middle part would be the duration of events and experiences upon which soul growth is attained by coming and going back and forth from your planet and visiting others in the meantime. Upon this piece of string you often enjoy labeling markers like dates and you follow its straight and linear line marking information and moments from now. You are always recording from your moment in the now. That is your point of view of time. Going from A to B and marking what happens in the now while you travel along it starting at the beginning and finishing at the end. You have always gone from A to B, but could you imagine starting at M or jumping to another alphabet?

To understand in linear terms how time works outside of the constraints that you have, would be for us to take the piece of string and attach one end to the other forming a circle whereby there is no end or beginning and watch time moving all together in a circular fashion. We would be marking within the circle of time as well as the piece of string itself. Long distances in time can become folded in on itself also. This is partly how great distances can be traveled within the universe in relatively small periods of duration.

Now imagine that your earthly piece of string was very long. You were not able to see the ends because they were out of your vision. This is the frustration

∴ 227 ∴

that some of you experience regarding your ego as this part of the mind wishes to see the end of the piece of string to help formulate what will come next in terms of helping you plan for circumstances that will better help your growth and experiences from that viewpoint.

Now imagine again our point of view whereby we link the string's ends and seal them together again. A circle lies before us with the past, present, and future going round and round laid out before us. We are recording time as a whole, not in the now. This allows us to set the highest and greatest timelines and perceive how they will play out as the consequences come around again affecting the past, present, and the future as a whole.

This is where so much frustration accumulates on your planet in the past as you have a temporarily limited vision of what is and what will come around again as you feel the train on the track has left the station never to return. On the track we envision the train will be coming around again and again with nothing lost but elements where other moments are instead happening which can be influenced through the power of intention.

We feel your level of frustration regarding timelines as the multidimensional element of yourself begins to waken and remember the circular piece of string subconsciously while still having to work out of the box which says linear time, the result of this being that you wish to compensate this by experiencing everything in the now as that is the only perception that is obvious to you within the current limitation you are working out of. This will change. Have patience.

This can result in you comprehending moments in your life that do not have the maturity yet in perception regarding how to work for the outcomes of every person on the planet and Gaia herself.

∴ 228 ∴

The Densities Explained

That is why there are 9D collectives and angelics working for your ascension process who can perceive many timelines all at once and be in all of those places working simultaneously in what you call a now moment, or for us, working on many different parts of the piece of string that we have before us as a circle. Your work is so important at this moment in time on Gaia and we ask that you do not get too (as Alex would say) bogged down with timelines as this can formulate unnecessary expectations that are second best to the outcomes that are actually coming to you.

We understand the frustration of working out of an only now moment-to-moment paradigm and wanting everything in that now including dates of coming events. However, this can blur your understanding of creation and what is needed for Gaia and the collective regards highest outcomes affecting the past, present, and the future which are working together simultaneously in every moment.

There is a silver thread holding realities together that is delicate. That is why galactics wish not to offer timelines and dates as it would do more harm than good. Not all of you see that your collective consciousness is creating a new Earth and timeline every time you awaken and begin your day collectively. We as much as you want to be a family reunited together again in what you call disclosure and you want it now. We know this and it is closer than ever; however, it must arrive at a time when it is best for the collective and not the few as this will create the highest outcomes and the least damaging consequences for all and Gaia herself. To suddenly move from aeons of deception into full immediate truth would be more harmful than helpful. This must be done incrementally; however, the speed at which this is happening is greatly moving in pace, beyond even our expectations, dear ones!

Working within the now can slow some dear souls'

perspectives on outcomes for the collective. For example, have it now, think about the consequences later. Working from a now only perspective leads to the needing of instant gratification without understanding what the consequential timelines that will follow this instant fix in the now will be. This includes when they will arrive or how you will deal with them when they have overwhelmed you at a later stage which are all issues you face when working from a limited field of perception. Please trust in the plan, dear ones. We are working hard on the other side although you do not see it. This light has won, but it takes time to filter through to your reality as you see only a fraction of what is yet to come, and what is to come is wonderful, dear ones. A world so far removed from what you have had to put up with.

To finish, as your cellular and consciousness energy begins to speed up vibrationally, so will your time along with other physics that you have not yet mastered in your world. Eventually your time will speed up with fewer hours in your day with the two ends of string that will eventually match creating a circle upon which you will look back and wonder why you were rushing like addicts substituting first place for second place because you had to have it all in your now never wondering what the greater picture was.

We ask you to focus on your own self-exploration during this time and less on the collective timeline regards these larger matters as ETs arriving on your planet while having confirmation from your leaders would be satisfying for a smaller group of you, but not helpful in dealing with immediate issues requiring action in your world at this moment in time that are more pressing. This also, dear ones, is why we do not give dates as it upsets so many of you when the date passes and your expectation has not been met. This is also partly down to the collective manifesting on

The Densities Explained

your planet accessing more lines than you have had available for a long time. So we ask that you walk before you run and relax into your reality before you can fly. A calm state of mind is productive and slowing down facilitates clarity which is what you call on Earth, working smart, or the ability to achieve more with less. We are with you at all times and love you more than you know or understand and are working with the collective and each and every one of you that calls upon us at this moment in time.

Everything that is happening is necessary for the great evolution. You are like a teenager with one foot in adulthood and one foot in childhood not knowing where to turn and wanting everything in the now and overcompensating for this with impatience. This we understand and will change in your timelines soon. Allow the growing process to happen, dear souls.

This is a message to say, trust the plan, the light has won, you cannot perceive the full mechanics of it all in much the same way you do not question the engine in your car, you simply get in and drive!

Call upon us. The future on Earth looks wonderful from where we are as you will enjoy these fruits of your labor in this lifetime and many lifetimes to come should you decide to stay and enjoy all you sowed. We are in service to you at all times. We are your family, your brothers and sisters, and much more."

The Arcturians
(Channeled, Alexander Quinn)

While the Arcturians live in multidimensional time, humans on Earth often have only experienced extreme time distortion from the effects of hallucinogenic drugs such as acid and DMT. Users have expressed extreme time loss, describing the experience as having taken many minutes or hours when in fact they have been under the influence only sixty seconds. Others have discussed witnessing the incredible foresight that they beheld spiritually regards sacred geometry and viewing objects as not real but made up of god particles and geometric etheric shapes. This has flowed over into other visual depictions in modern and historical times such as various mandalas and the rose of life, a geometric circular pattern. We also see sacred geometry produced here on Earth directly by 5D beings known as crop circles. The intricacy of these designs has sparked much revelation into their meaning and manifestation.

The vibration at which beings live in this plane is much lighter and as a result have different biologies and cellular structures that are less dense and more crystalline. Illness, pain, and fatigue are quenched by wellness, radiance, and feelings of being energetic. This is because the cellular activity is different and there is a meld between soul and body with self-healing becoming operational via a genetic coloration that is switched on. This is different to the 3D reality where the human lives in a body and hopes for the best while the physical vessel goes unchecked and mismanaged allowing it to go in any tangent it is left to, creating sometimes negative or life-threatening issues.

In this space the higher self is far more integrated within the soul and there are few or little veils and barriers. The soul is operating as one, allowing cosmic intuition. This cannot be done in 3D bodies as they are very dense carbon-based vehicles which would likely end up being destroyed on a cellular level due to the very high vibration within some vibratory fields of 5D energy. In fifth density the soul is very connected to the energies of the universe, and there is a complete trust in the flow of acoustics and the soul's journey at this point. There is no ego controlling outcomes or demanding answers but the higher self giving direction on the highest outcomes each time. What will be, will be, and there is unconditional trust that everything that is needed will manifest along the journey, or as some say on Earth, reading the signs and going with the flow.

Thoughts and actions are based first in love and not fear. Beings are at one with each other and telepathy begins to take over as there is a calmness and quietness in the mind and the field that acts like a conduit around us all in the soup of God. Group consciousness is more prevalent and beings are all connected with little space for deceit or lying. A lifetime in this energy encompasses clarity, transparency, and infinite expressionism, a place where all beings find their true path in life and there is joy and happiness becoming aware of who you are, your eternal soul, and all your past lives.

The heart is a place where all thoughts originate first instead of the head and all the chakras in the body are much more aligned. Telepathy with beings in places many light years away is achievable as the very cellular structure and consciousness is interconnected within the domain of the universe breaking down distance and time.

Sometimes when people in 3D become ill it is because they have too many toxins or because the cellular structure is not working correctly as a person's frequency is very low or depleted. Five-dimensional cellular reproduction is more economical with lives in this energy that are far longer and healthier. Disease and cancerous cells are no energetic match for the high frequencies of this space and therefore die or fail to create at all.

Some cancer patients who have made miraculous spontaneous remissions have claimed that they had spiritual moments or felt total connectedness around the time they were healed. Being in a pocket of pure 5D energy can do this as illness disconnects and fails in high-vibration consciousness physicality. The feminine and masculine energies have become much more aligned and beings from this place can appear completely androgynous or unified in sexual appearance. Sexual appetite changes also and beings can experience combining energies together without physicality if they wish, which is very euphoric. Sex is a part of sharing and not a desire or lust. Beings can harmonize and bring in the highest souls to reproduce using their consciousness only if they choose. Once ascension is reached it begins with 5D consciousness. Beings in 5D have far higher IQs and can think in high conceptual terms often computing many things at the same time like a computer. Language takes on new forms such as holographic shapes that can portray many times more information than a simple linear word on a page can.

Beings living in this space can find it hard to enter back into 3D consciousness densities without issues or help. Perhaps the director Ron Howard knew this when he filmed his masterpiece *Cocoon* where Earth people are taken to a fifth-dimensional reality and are warned not to come back or they will suffer illness. Fifth-dimensional beings live in the light and attract little or no darkness of any kind. Their light is so anchored into their physical and etheric being that dark simply does not want to live in its presence. As we have discussed before, you turn on a bright light in a room and the darkness vanishes, and often with only the smallest amount of light.

Being in this vibration is to operate within different harmonics, electromagnetic fields, and frequencies which are often not seen and felt by lower dimensional beings who cannot experience or see past their own visual light spectrum. This is how angels or some ETs, for example, operate. They are seen if they choose to be seen by us. Thoughts are very carefully processed at this level and there is discipline of mental projection as thoughts manifest very quickly. Winner-takes-all mentality vanishes and competition and status dissolve into greater good for all and not the self. There is a plentiful supply of abundance, sharing, and gratitude. This is the beginning of the God plane, the heaven existence or heaven on Earth where true enlightenment is first reached. It was believed that Jesus was a fifth-dimensional or higher being as were many of the other masters who still work with and for Gaia at this time.

To get a further understanding of beings from this dimension is to understand how some of them view us. They know that we were them in the past. We are the new civilization growing up. They look upon us as children that they love. When they see us hurting each other and creating drama they are nonjudgmental, and they see us going through the growing pains of puberty of leaving junior school like a human parent would. They appreciate that we are all in the soup of the universe and linked one way or another.

If you were to encounter a high-vibrational being or

The Densities Explained

witness a channeled message that doesn't promote love for the ascending human or is very judgmental then raise your caution as to who is really speaking the message and where it is coming from. 5D beings do not behave this way by projecting any type of fear within their messages. In the same vein, increasingly, governments have planned for years fake invasions of ETs and done their best to either disprove them or tell us they are evil or dangerous often through the guise of Hollywood. If these very evolved civilizations were evil, they would have completely destroyed us already with technologies that would make Earth vanish instantly. The new beings helping unearth the darkness on Earth at this time mostly are 5D+ beings.

Diet in the fifth is drastically different. Eating low vibrational food such as meat or animal products that still carry the animal's fear signature upon slaughter are completely repugnant. Plant- and fruit-based foods on the whole are the preferred diet and the fifth-density body carries little or no toxins such as animal proteins, GMOs, heavy metals even at trace level, nicotine, alcohol, and other chemicals that humans pepper themselves with via cleaning products or aerosols that we spray daily under armpits. The Pleiadians have a physiology that is far more economical at using the food that is taken in, and there is very little waste at the other end that needs to be secreted.

There have been a great number of encounters of humans with ETs and angelic beings over the years. People who have come into contact with these beings have described such an incredible feeling of overwhelming unconditional love when either in their presence or having been touched directly. There are accounts of various people having near-death experiences while on the operating table and coming into contact with angels who wrapped their arms around them and explained that it is not their time to leave yet. Patients have come back from complex operations speaking of this indescribable unconditional love they felt that human words could not explain that had subsequently changed their lives. This is the fifth-dimensional energy. Darkness cannot be sustained here.

❖ 235 ❖

Sixth Densities
Soul > Thought > Manifestation

Sixth-dimensional consciousness is oneness with all souls and all life created by God felt everywhere throughout the cosmos. It is the consciousness of "Us" or "We" and not the self known as "I." It is oneness with every divine God-created aspect within the cosmic design. Another way to explain this is the electrical and etheric fields of the body which are used like a light interface within the body's energy field like a spiritual internet where everything is connected simultaneously conducting cellular consciousness. In this system there is a direct interface among light, the cells, and the electrical fields of biochemistry.

One can seek, find, and know absolute illumined truths about anything if intention is focused on it whether it be past, future, present, person, or even cosmic objects like planets and their vibrations. To operate in this density is to have unity conscious oneness with God and all souls. When manifesting the divine energies, workers of God respond instantly to sixth-dimensional intentions in the highest or most divine way, creating designs that inadvertently are also the higher good of every soul involved in that intention.

This is where group unity consciousness becomes present. Often beings that are channeled from 6D upward begin to communicate as collectives or councils of beings. Sometimes this can even be the collective intelligence of AI or self-thinking technologies, however not as often. In basic terms, one can feel and know the thoughts of all others in another galaxy should they decide to place their intention there. A good example of this is a direct message from the Sirian High Council based in the Sirius star system. In the following transmission, they allude to the beginning of our ascension and their sixth-dimensional perspective of how they feel us in our shift:

As Gaia rings, as Gaia strums the chords of her

The Densities Explained

heartstrings, her song ringing throughout the Universe, the music of the spheres resounds with the lights and sounds of your solar deity in transformation. The Earth, your planetary family, your sun, that brilliance that is the galaxy in which you currently appear all are tuning their instrument to the higher octave in the Universal chorus of life.

Your planet is ringing new frequencies into the cosmic sea and all intelligence is attuning to the cosmometric proportions that are woven into the light strings of love holding us in the Oneness. Ours is a distant lens upon Earth affairs, yet we are so near to you that we can feel the warmth of your breath and hear the thoughts that delight or torment you. We feel great compassion for those who are drowning in that sense of hopelessness and dread, as all the outer realities that have appeared to be secure are disrobed of the illusion and seen for what they are through the dim light of those who would manipulate events to control you.

Interconnectedness becomes interplanetary in sixth density onward. The very vibrations and tones of a planet can be felt including their own personal frequency and sexual orientation. For example, Earth is a feminine planetary consciousness. Mars has a male persona. Beings begin to live in realities like the butterfly effect. This means that on initial conditions in which a small change in one state occurs, a deterministic nonlinear system can result in large differences to a later state, person, or place. In other words, one action could have various consequences in other parts of the universe far or close to the original proximity.

As you begin to enter 5D, the past, present, and future begin to enact simultaneously. In 6D this is still the case, but there is a higher perception of timelines, their potentials, their effects, and their outcomes across them all. There is a sensitivity to this as empathy love is a primary motivator, meaning that actions encompass the greater and best good for all viewing all timelines simultaneously. You see a Dr. Strangelove in *Avengers: Infinity*

War carry out a similar process. He begins to view all timelines and their potentials in order to grasp the best course of action before fighting Thanos.

In sixth density, one can relocate or consciously experience dual or more realities at the same time if needed mentally or physically.

The higher self is almost completely integrated into the physical light body, and the third eye chakra is fully open at all times allowing for very psychic abilities directly reading another's soul including their Akashic records and genetic information. In turn this eliminates deception, lies, or barriers as there is full acceptance of all. This is a place of absolute truth where deception cannot be created as easily as it can in lower dimensional plains—especially the third! The higher self is so interconnected that divine guidance is at hand changing social structures radically. Management systems and governments are now not needed, and there are only councils or more experienced beings who are groups of representatives. Imagine you are working in a corporation where all people have an exact knowledge of what is to be done and how it will be done at all times without needing confirmation, instruction, or management. Where there had been lack of communication, there would be knowing; where there had been structural or managerial weakness, there would be total harmony and cohesion filling the void.

For many ET races in this energy, there is no forced punishment socially (as we know it on Earth) as everything is soul growth and accepted as meant to be or the law of just being. That is not to say that bad things do not happen in this dimension, however. Other than punishment, soul work is carried out on the individual when they are out of alignment.

In 5D, beings begin to speak telepathically with few speaking verbally. In the sixth density, there is only telepathic communication. Technology is also very advanced, and telekinesis is very common. Thoughts control physical things including their physics. Time travel is available, and beings travel in and out of galaxies and all around the universe in high-tech craft accessing different parallel dimensions and realities. This

The Densities Explained

in turn leads to more exposure of different races and more DNA being mixed leading to communities not only being interracial, but also having different species or mixtures living and mixing genetics harmoniously together.

The ego as we know it has completely vanished and the barriers between the conscious and subconscious mind are lowered at free will allowing high-functioning computing within the brain. Brain barriers such as right and left are redundant with full brain capacity working and firing in all previously unused places. This allows for not only the use of multidimensional abilities, but the comprehension of ideas and their realities felt in real time that humans at this present stage can't begin to comprehend yet. Imagine looking at another human and feeling the essence of their genetic code and reading their Akashic record telepathically from close up or even off-world and knowing all their lifetimes at once. Comprehension within this space can manage many existing realities in different places at the same time very efficiently. Whereas the linear human mind tends to solve one problem at a time step by step in an orderly regimented fashion, when ETs download information into the human synapse they do it in small bite-sized chunks. The ET mind can take the whole volume in one go. Whereas the human mind tends to be logical, the ET mind could be likened to a conceptual supercar. This is partly why these beings have so much compassion for our current corporeal brains/bodies as humans find it harder to manifest realities that are needed or wanted in lower vibrational energies. Imagine master painter Pablo Picasso looking on lovingly at a small child, aged six, painting on a canvas and trying the best they can with the abilities and tools available.

Physiology changes, also, with the body becoming much more crystalline and much less dense. The higher self-light body is almost completely integrated, and the being's energy is a closer match to light and photonic vibrational energy. Little sleep or nourishment is now needed within a body that holds more light.

Seventh Densities
Soul > Manifestation

This has been referred to as the angelic realm or vibration of celestial consciousness. There are more elements to the seventh, but for the sake of explaining it in easy terms we will begin with the angelics. Group consciousness becomes interplanetary and even intergalactic and beyond. Beings in the angelic realm use unimaginable laws of physics to create or change form, completely leaving their body and returning at free will as they choose. This is the space whereby those that work directly with god creator energy exist, but they are often not in physical vessels. The seventh dimension is the vibration upon which a body isn't required; however, a form can be materialized if necessary and the physical form is fluid depending on environmental needs. For example, seventh-dimensional Arcturians exist as energy only in this field. If you were to visit an Arcturian base/craft they would take form in order to interact with lower dimension beings so that interaction was more accessible and real. This could be in etheric form or physical. It can be said the same of the angels. They can manifest physical form, but they usually operate in their natural etheric light form that often can't be physically seen. Beings also embody orbs in these energies allowing themselves to float as different colored light.

In seventh-dimensional consciousness, most technologies and computerization has been done away with as there is no need. Pure creator energy is used to manifest anything or create portals to places if and when necessary.

Beings in this energy are endowed with greatness that if used in divine will, stays within the seventh energy. It can be said that Satan, a fallen angel, was cast down from heaven as he wanted to use his powers for personal gain against divine will. This is a biblical metaphor; however, there is truth that only angels or direct servants acting in divine will to god/source/creator can operate in this energy. The angels do not have free will in the terms that humans do on Earth. They must use their abilities for the creation and protection of God's souls on Earth

The Densities Explained

and the various timelines created that have yet to be lived or seen. Angelic beings are not human and never have been. They are God's creation, carrying out its personal work keeping balance in the universe and holding the lower dimensions together like glue. It was said that in the universe God created many angels manifesting realities by discovering the possibilities God had created but not yet observed. God uses the angels to implement the will in these manifested realities.

It is the beings and angels in this energy that organize coincidences and boost synchronicity in your life for your divine highest path. When you are born onto Earth you enter with an entourage who are there throughout your life, each helping you in different ways. In general, people call these spirit guides, but they can be ET entities, celestial beings, ancient spirits from the beginning of the universe, and sometimes family within soul groups. These beings are all working in the seventh and above densities. Entities can sense the consciousness of planets and parts of space itself and are the creators and manipulators of many realities themselves. In older pre-2012 energies, man felt that manifesting things took a long time. It felt like you were slowly pushing a large stone up a hill. From 2020 onward, the veil is going to be much thinner allowing for these beings/energies to help pull the stone up the hill alongside you. Your unseen spiritual helpers are now acting beside you more than ever as there is a greater landscape of light in which they can maneuver to help your cause. There is so much help on the other side, one must trust this, but more importantly, your spirit guides cannot break laws of interference. You must ask out loud for their help and you will receive it. Everyone has spirit guides, some only two or three; others might have up to twelve, depending on a far-ranging set of attributes and characteristics relational to soul growth, importance, or mission focus on Gaia at this time. They will also join you depending on issues or events in previous lifetimes. This higher self also works from these upper realms. That is why it is so important to distinguish between listening to lower density ego and higher vibration over soul self.

Imagine an inventor sitting in his laboratory trying to

come up with ideas. Suddenly he conceptualizes something never thought of before by earthly man and begins to put this idea into physical creation. One must ask, was this entirely his idea, or was the inventor subconsciously listening to the whispers of angels or his higher self? This idea has been argued at length, and there is fierce debate. This can also be said for Nicola Tesla. Many have stated that he was in touch with higher forces allowing him to conceptualize ideas that were far beyond the 3D matrix at the time. The same can be said for various mechanical inventions and machines across the world such as man taking flight or scientists finding breakthroughs in the field of chemistry and physics. Very often in history we see great inventions whereby one nation has proclaimed that they had invented something while a team in another country completely isolated from any knowledge seemingly also comes up with the same invention only weeks later being narrowly pipped to the finish line. It is peculiar that great ideas for inventions can come almost at coincidental timelines without each party ever having knowledge of each other or their ideas. Furthermore, has humanity been "gifted" these concepts and inventions within the last hundred years that has led to such a great advancement in the lead up to ascension and 5D dimensionality? And why the extreme advancement in the past hundred years in comparison to a very slow last thousand years? Perhaps some of these great ideas would not have been gifted in older, denser energy as three-dimensional humans would have done their best to weaponize them?

From some angelic and celestial testimonies there are vivid accounts detailing the rise of the Internet from as early as the 1970s. Beings in this density have for years spoken of gifting Earth a technology that would allow people everywhere to communicate faster in readiness for the great ascension evolution so that the starseeds and lightworkers could unite and share light at the rate needed to pass the great marker. Many of these channeled messages spoke of a network allowing instant communication for every soul on the Earth at little cost on a global scale. Within the '70s the Internet had not been conceptualized yet in the form that we have today and those messages were being handed down

The Densities Explained

before its existence.

To think in seventh dimensionality is to have a new impartial objectivity based on experiential understanding. Imagine you are in school at a younger age. You are learning various lessons and you are "in" the experience itself having an inner view of the school consciousness. You view your experience happening to you with you in it. Then imagine you have left school as an experienced professional in your trade returning to school as a visitor observing the pupils at work having an outer experience that is impartial and comprehensive. One experience was inner and the latter was outer. You can give guidance to a pupil as you are removed from the situation and can give far greater direction with experiential and conceptual ideas looking at the overview position. This is in line with seventh-dimensional thinking. They are having a nonphysical outer impartial experience helping those in the lower dimensions and using unimagined laws of physics to create divine manifestations of higher timelines not only for that individual, but timelines for others around that person. In other words, will this be better for him/her and the resulting effect on the people around them? If so, let us gently at first nudge this person into this timeline and if they are becoming destructive, give a harder nudge!

Have you ever been removed from a timeline, situation, or place by circumstances that seemed out of your control and looked back and said, thank god? Then you have experienced this. Be thankful for these moments in life or god only knows what troubles may have become of us along the way!

For this dimensional existence one does not necessarily need to inhabit a craft or a home. It is a consciousness that is everywhere at all times. At this point you are your higher self in totality and can simply be without any physical connection or constraint. You are everything throughout spacetime.

It is important to understand that free will is always upheld and beings seventh-dimensional upward are not allowed to interfere with lesser dimensional or earthly beings unless grave peril is apparent or help has been asked for consciously. One must ask for help and only then can an angel or being take your hand as it were to help you. Many angels will watch an unawakened being, never connect with them, and still love them unconditionally. Angels especially are working with god/creator to help humanity and when a person finds silence and connects with their angel or talks directly, there is said to be a great celebration on the other side of the veil as the limiting realities of 3D separation have finally been broken. Often when humans have been in turmoil or great danger and have asked for help, there have been unexplainable happenings that defy all understanding. This is the power of seventh-dimensional beings or angels who can bend time, circumstance, or the rules of physics in order to help a person for their highest good, in turn also serving the greater good of everyone else. This is the place where strangers will seemingly within perfect timing enter into your life at just the right moment in order to help facilitate a goal or save you. Some will be orchestrated, and others might even be your angels working for you in broad daylight.

There is also great belief in the fairy world around this density with many believing this is the place where beings from the Fairy Kingdom exist. This includes nature beings such as the divas in the forests and the sprites. These beings from the fairy realms can also operate in physicality within the fourth through seventh energies, but they are rarely seen.

Eighth Densities and Beyond

As we go up the dimensional ladder, we become further detached from the current reality that we exist in at this present moment. There is information regarding these higher dimensions although it is scarcer. The entities that exist in these places express very lovingly that it would not serve humanity at this present moment to venture into this knowledge with the view being that humans could get very stuck trying to "figure it all out" while not comprehending what any of it really means. When we fly to a holiday destination via a plane, must we know everything about the plane's engines and how to fly it? We simply hop on and away we go. There is a part we all play in the great puzzle of life and

The Densities Explained

not everything is meant to be known within certain roles at certain times.

Some of the highest and most potent hallucinogenic experiences ever recorded on this planet are said to be from "crossing over" on a very large dose of DMT. You are propelled sometimes even violently into higher dimensions and often the mind isn't ready to conceive of it. To cross over into the much higher dimensional spaces of consciousness would be deemed something far beyond DMT. The human mind as it works in evolution currently isn't able to comprehend some of these incredible realities yet and if they were explained, we might not understand them anyway. Some of the most spiritual people on Earth have crossed over into planes of existence and returned to an array of questions regarding what they felt and what it looked like with the answer being, "There are no human words for what I felt, saw, and experienced."

As you push up beyond the eighth to the ninth dimension, you begin to encounter Arcturian Councils and Pleiadian collectives that are nonphysical pure collective consciousness often operating as hundreds or thousands. In these higher places, you begin to see collective beings who are guardians of civilizations and stewards of specialized cosmic operations such as managing a planet's ascension and balancing its energies for the millions who inhabit that world. Angelic beings reside here, and Archangel Michael is present at these high places knowing all that is and answering the fears and questions of all simultaneously while being bilocated in other places and listening to the voices of millions.

Some have speculated that the harmonic convergence that began on 16 August 1987 was aided by great magnetic beings who helped in the cause. Dimensionality upward of eight and nine is a place of creators of worlds while maintaining them energetically. It is understood that some of the great grids such as the crystalline (which we will cover) were placed on Earth by beings of this nature. They are the guardians of soul transition and concepts that will take time for humans to fathom. At this time the people on Earth have much to get on with, without the worries of conceptual things that will soon come again into purview when we leave the human body for the next wonderful adventure before returning again.

✺ 5 ✺
The Crystalline Grid

In many ways the Earth has its own similarities to humans regarding its energies and the way it continuously moves and grows. Starseeds are the external energy coming into the planet, raising energy in the form of people and the good they do at this time on a vibrational level. They are anchoring the energy onto Earth, but how? Where is this energy going? When I have a BBQ on a sunny day and friends are invited over and we make our merry way into the day or perhaps have a spiritual meditation if you are that way inclined, does it drift off into the air or the Persian rug you are meditating on? Perhaps the juicy salmon steak you are eating is holding this resonance that you just plucked off the BBQ? Is the secret in the salmon? What's going on?

Sadly, salmon alone can't heal the world, but that's a nice idea. The answer, dear beloveds, are the grids of the Earth. Souls come into Gaia and Gaia's grids hold the energy. In the same way that human DNA holds a record, so too does the Earth. The crystalline grid is Earth's record holder in answer to the humans' Akashic record. Both hold energy and the vibration of things past and current. The crystalline grid is named as such due to some of the interesting correlations that crystals on the Earth both in the ground or in a crystal shop hold. It has been scientifically proven that crystals hold vibrational energy. Perhaps this is why people who are in tune with energies or New-Agers will hold a crystal and feel its resonance much like a musician will hold an instrument and feel the emotion of a particular chord or tone when strummed or blown.

The crystalline grid of Earth holds energy in the same way, although it is very different. Crystals are physical; the crystalline grid is nonvisible, but yet is present and covers all the Earth as a geometric pattern that science also sees as various energies. You might begin to ask yourself, is this really possible, can this really be so, is the author of this book having a laugh, is this another tall fishy salmon tale?

Love is something we feel that is so incredibly strong and yet, can we see it? Of course, we can see the results of love and loving actions in a loving relationship, but can you see the very essence of love itself without its effects? We can't see the pure essence of love, and yet we feel it so deeply that we know it must exist because it changes who we are. It changes the way we carry out our lives and interact with people day to day. When you look in the mirror while combing your hair, do you see love, or is it something that is only inside?

In much the same way gravity is acting on us all the time, we feel it, we can see the effects of gravity, but aside from effects on things, can you see gravity itself without a machine? It is there at all times; you have come to live with a force that is unseen every day; and yet you accept it as your truth because science has told you so and you see its effects, you trust regardless. These are all quantum energies as are magnetics and time. You can't see either time or magnetics, but you can observe their effects and create measurements in ways that put them on scales and charts.

There are forces around us at all times that we can't see but we feel. This is true of the crystalline grid. The people of Earth hold their vibration and put it into the very Earth we stand on, helping Earth herself rise in harmony. Let us explore this a little more in terms that anyone can understand. Exploring this concept is key to understanding the simple basics of the crystalline grid and how it works.

At some point we all have experienced the crystalline grid whether you are aware or not, and perhaps you have even pondered in your most reflective moments what it might have been that allowed you to feel what you experienced at that moment in your life that seemed so surreal or ethereal. With

The Crystalline Grid

many concepts and metaphors, stories illustrate the beauty and capture the essence, so we will begin with real life stories so we can outline the landscape while you paint the picture with your own colors.

I remember sometime in the early 2000s when dear friends of mine were on vacation in the Far East. Upon being in this part of the world, they decided they would visit various locations including the wonderful buildings new and old and the cultural delights that exist in the surrounding areas. It had come to the attention of the couple in question that Cambodia was on the bucket list of attractions and, sure enough, they found themselves in this beautiful part of the world visiting ancient monuments, sampling the finest Cambodian cuisine and culture that the charming people of this country exhibit. I shall not mention the hotel for fear of reprisal nor its location; however, this information does not detract from the nature of our story and it is a true story.

With weary heads and empty stomachs, the couple found a respectable hotel to stay in for the night and made their way to the reception desk in order to find room and board for the evening. To their absolute delight they not only found a room but had been upgraded at no extra cost to a suite. What better way to end a perfect day and relax in comfort? The porter asked the couple if they might wait in the foyer downstairs while the bags were taken to the suite, which, of course, they were happy to oblige. The porter shot off with haste carrying all the luggage to the room and within minutes arrived back to the foyer to greet the couple with their room key and an open palm in which silvers or a discrete tip was exchanged. Night was falling and the man and woman made their way to the suite in readiness for a warm shower and a fresh change of clothing. They finally reached the room they were to stay in, put the key into the door, turned the lock, and pushed the door open to a beautiful suite superbly executed in wonderful color and decoration. The large rooms were laden with antique and historical furniture and there was a taste of the old with a twist of cosmopolitan. What a joy! you might say to yourself.

Prior to the service of dinner was a rest period whereby

❖ 249 ❖

the couple embarked on some initial refreshments in the room. Soon exhaustion and the excitement of the day began to dull and there was a heaviness in the room. The wonderful memories, sounds, and smells of the day had all but disappeared like dust into the wind. Positivity and the physical attributes of warmth were extinguished as the room seemed to detract from all the good that had been experienced that day. There was a subtle void of negativity sucking all life away and the couple began to feel it, so much so that they began to discuss having another room for reasons they could not explain but felt it somewhere deep inside. They could innately feel the emotion of the room, and it was far from an energetic match. The couple hastily walked back to the hotel reception, explaining that the room simply wasn't for them and requesting alternative accommodation post haste. Eventually another room was found that was to their liking and a warm feeling of relief and intrigue fell upon them that seemed poles apart from the feeling of the previous room.

During dinner the couple discussed the strangeness of the situation that had unfolded and how a room could detract so vastly from the excitement of a colorful and happy day.

While they sipped their wine and finished their meals they began to speak of other things and listen to the melodies that a musician was playing on a piano in the dinner hall that night. Dinner service ended and so did the musician's set, and various guests made their way back to their rooms for the night and a few collecting at the bar for night caps and coffee. The couple found themselves at the bar with a round of coffee having completely forgotten the previous events of the evening at which point they were introduced to the pianist that had played in the hotel that night and conversation of various multitudes ensued. The three of them laughed and shared stories until it was time to say good-night and part ways. The pianist wished the couple farewell and casually asked which room they had the pleasure of staying in that night. It was at this point the couple relayed the chain of events to the musician who listened very intently, not speaking once to interrupt. The following is the conversation I had.

Couple: "Wasn't that strange, we simply could not be in that room for a minute longer. It gave us the chills. We felt spooked in that room and it simply wasn't for us, we had to change rooms. It was unexplainable."

Pianist: "There was great unrest in Cambodia years ago when the Khmer Rouge were in power led by Pol Pot. At the time his government forced and relocated many of the population into the countryside to work in what was known as collective farms. Anyone deemed to be against the Khmer Rouge, including the Buddhist monks and ethnic minorities, were murdered. There were many killings, malnutrition, poor medical care, and nearly two million people were wiped out. Some of the old-timers still call it the Cambodian genocide. Your room, the one you left, was at one time Pol Pot's office when he was operating in the area. He would work from that suite for a while during this period including potentially arranging many murders while working from that room."

This is an example of the crystalline grid. It is an energetic footprint that lingers. In much the same way a crystal can be coded or programmed, we leave our imprint into the grids of the Earth. It is often imprinted with the record of things that have happened in the past which stay their course through vibrational and emotional charge. This is why non-sensitives or anyone of a nonspiritual disposition can walk into a haunted house or place with history and actively feel the pain or negativity that endures.

This applies to the great battle fields across the world where the energy of war lingers, be it in the poppy meadows of France or the fields of Gettysburg in the US. These are the places where one can walk and somehow still feel the very essence of what happened long ago. There are many stories of people walking on old Civil War fields and still hearing cannon fire and smelling the gunpowder at unexpected times or during the night when all is quiet.

There are two types of spirits that appear on Earth, some that are active in the interaction they have and others who are a remembrance written into the grids of Gaia. Ghosts work in much the same way. They are a remembrance of an energy, often repeating over and over like a needle stuck on a broken record player. Often when these souls are contacted, they repeat the essence of what happened, but less in terms of what the future will bring as it is a historical recording captured on the grid only. This will happen regarding a place or a smell, a person, or a feeling as if it were still there. The deed was done long ago or the soul has moved on, but the essence is recorded, making it seem that the soul is present when in fact you are experiencing their mark on Earth. Human emotion is one of the strongest forces within the universe, and when amplified through focus or particular events, can be sown deep into the crystalline grids.

You can tell when you are dealing with an entity and a crystalline grid remembrance as the entity will be able to communicate more fluidly about the present and the future, whereas a ghost or remembrance on the crystalline will show perspective very much on the past with little ability to shed light on present issues. This is representative of the world as we know it. There is a push-pull energy. Energy is being put into the Earth, and energy is being pushed back out.

This is why there is such a bias regarding the psyche of world news and social thinking. Having had a bias of dark destructive energy on Earth for so long, it has affected souls who are stuck in the old energy prior to 2012. You will hear lightworkers of the new age express their fears at World War Three and other impending dooms which are yet to happen, when in fact they are foretelling a future based on the old bias that does not exist anymore! This old energy is beginning to steadily clear and there will be a time not far in the future when even the most sensitive of people will walk the old battlefields and places of suffering feeling nothing more than the love of Gaia because the areas have been cleared. As souls clear their karma, unfinished business and trauma within their Akash, so, too, does Gaia clear out her grids, which are full of war, famine, and nations taking

The Crystalline Grid

each other in a constant bid for world domination.

Those who practice the dark arts and the cabal are aware of the grids of Earth and often build great animal farms and slaughterhouses on the main arteries of ley lines and grids in order to fuel constant fear into the vein of Earth that will in turn continue further negative energy into the land we live on. Satanists and occult leaders will carry out rituals upon ley lines and grid sites in order to make sure more dark is circulating than light. For those that are sensitive to this transferable energy, it keeps holding light in an older energy far more difficult.

This is yet to come into the understanding of many New-Agers and some spiritualists who are still smudging continually around the house, burning sage and other herbs, and carrying out all manner of the old operations that used to clear darkness in the old energy. This is the same for crystals. You will see people putting crystals all round their house for protection, not understanding that the crystalline grid and energies of the Earth have changed. That is not to say crystals don't have a place in the world because they certainly do, and they hold wonderful resonances that can heal and bring happiness, but not so much in accordance with fear and protection, not like before. Crystals are tools that aid us; however, it is critical to understand that no crystal or burning of sage will now match the light shining from the starseeds and lightworkers at present when they are in their power. Their light can now shine brighter than any tools used in an old energy and where lightworkers walk, darkness will scatter in this new energy. This is the very reason they are here. Starseeds and lightworkers are anchoring their light deep into the grids of Earth and nothing matches it. So I say enjoy your sage and the wonder of crystals, but know that your light is unparalleled and cannot be surpassed when it is switched on. You are a beacon shining in every room you walk in now and darkness will run from you, it has no choice anymore. Trust that in everything you do.

The Earth has resonated in a dark bias for so long that you see it in the news, the papers, it is everywhere. As all of these energies are cleared, the media will change, also. Viewers will be in receivership of light, positive news, and fear-based or

∴ 253 ∴

panic selling will become something we laugh at. We will hear more stories about how things are always improving as opposed to constantly getting worse. Reporting murders and rapes on the lunchtime news will be obsolete, and positivity will be the new stage that the news anchors dance on. All of this will be anchored in the crystalline grid which will kick it back out as light that is felt by all. What we do on this planet is felt on a conscious level. What you put in, Gaia gives back out. That is why if you are having a spiritual awakening or feeling like you are opening up to something wonderful in your life, it is especially important not to get sucked into the old energy fear-based news. It is there for a reason and one reason only, to drag you down. Stay on your own timeline and keep spreading love and light. World War Three is not happening. Fear is control. Control eats at your mind and your mind is your sovereignty. Take back the control and laugh in the face of darkness, because it is running and hiding more than ever before.

As more and more light hits the Earth, more darkness will be exposed as light empowers the grids of Earth which have not been seen in a long time. This is why certain places in the world will draw you as the energies in the grids begin to change. You will feel a calling to go to certain places, towns, or villages that whisper to you when you are not there asking you to return. When you put your feet directly into the ground you are connecting not only to Gaia but also to her grids. This will explain why, as the grids clear and energies in places around the world change, families will feel a conscious pull to move to those new places. It is also happening with the animal kingdom, but for other reasons that are more specific that we will cover shortly.

How does light draw out the darkness and interact with the grids of Gaia which interface with people?

Imagine a commonly used surface in your house, perhaps the kitchen cabinet. You look at this surface while you are operating around it with nothing appearing out of the ordinary. Yet it is not until you shine a UV light onto this surface that you begin to expose the germs and dirt lurking there in plain sight. It is at this moment that light exposes the dirt, or what we

The Crystalline Grid

shall call the dark. This is the dark that has always been lurking there without the light to expose its existence. You see this in Hollywood, political systems, financial institutions, and religious circles where children are systematically abused in the name of religion. Where there was no compassion, integrity, and light before, there will be now. Times are changing and this means things are harder for the darkness to cover up. People will walk in a place and feel darkness that was hidden before, and it will become more obvious where evil is lurking and how to avoid it. You see it more and more in the news, the stories of powerful and influential personalities who for decades left a wake of terror regarding their victims.

The grids of the planet are cleaning themselves. Like never before the souls of this planet can walk into dark areas and the dark will run as the light/dark quota is tipped in favor of light. This is why people are rebelling against old paradigms and demanding change across the world. You can see it in Hong Kong as the people there have had enough of the old energy and are ready to build the new with marching in the streets and protests. This is partly why many healers and mediums around the world have felt like their "power" or energy has gone. They have lost their "magic," even creative people. The magic is still there, you just need to tune to the new radio channel, and this time, dear beloveds, you will find the return for your efforts is far more impressive!

To some of you this might seem a little overly esoteric. Let us find some historical and scientific grounding before we hit the crescendo at the end of this chapter. Take my hand as we walk more slowly through this and let's join this path together.

We discussed that the crystalline grid gets its name due to similarities that occur in the transmutable nature of physical crystals. For example, quartz is very commonly used in technology today and it is quite possible you have heard of liquid crystal displays in TVs and computer screens. Quartz has an interesting ability in transmuting energies. When put under pressure it can create an electrical charge, which with help can be focused. This is known as the piezoelectric effect. The word piezoelectric comes from the Greek word piezein, meaning to squeeze or press, and piezo, which is Greek for "push."

This also works in reverse. If you apply an electrical charge to a quartz crystal, it converts electrical energy into a mechanical form of energy, which allows the quartz crystal to receive and process energy while transmuting vibrations outward. In other words, if you place a "piezoelectric" material under pressure or mechanical stress, you shift the positive and negative energies taking place in the material, resulting in an electrical field pushing out externally. When done in reverse, an outer electrical field either stretches or compresses the "piezoelectric" material. You have a kind of push-pull energy. The Earth is made of various crystals with quartz being the most prevalent. You also see quartz used in the home in the forms of orgonite, sometimes in the shape of a pyramid often used with other metals and a tesla coil inside in order to stop EMFs. So you can see that there is in fact science in the mechanics of the crystalline grids which display themselves in quantum ways.

All around the Earth, physical energies and nonphysical energies are being created. There is a great deal of scientific research to show that the "bioelectrical" resonance of the human brain is linked to and works in relation to the magnetic and electrical fields of the Earth. This is shifting the planet's vibration with what we put back into it which corresponds with a transformative effect on human consciousness. In essence, you put darkness into the planet, it puts darkness back out. You flood it with light, and light resonance is felt everywhere until there is no darkness left. This is partly how the crystalline grid works. It is a field covering the Earth in nonphysicality that is interacting with us every day.

It works in positive forms, also. Perhaps you walk into a historical music venue and you can almost feel the music. The same can be said for all other arts and creative endeavors. The intent and action of the energy is imprinted on the Earth itself. The idea is that when you have enough people flooding the crystalline grid with light consciousness, it creates a ripple effect like a pebble bouncing off water and the rest of humanity is left in the wake of the ripples. You begin to have a cumulative effect. Some sources say that only 5 percent of the Earth's people or less need to be completely enlightened/awakened/light beings/have high consciousness to tip the Earth from its light/dark quota in order for the ascension ripple to become contagious.

This resonance is divine geometry. When you map out the resonance, it creates shapes. You see it in nature often. You take a drop of water frozen in nature. When under a microscope the water particles shape into beautiful geometric patterns known as snowflakes. You place iron filings or a material of many small parts on a conditioned material and play acoustic sounds from underneath and you see geometric patterns forming depending on the frequency. The crystalline grid of Earth is like this and the people of Earth have known about it for a great deal of time. Let us explore a little more of the science behind this first.

There is discussion among ancient astronauts and starseeds that the ancient Egyptian era was potentially influenced by "outside" intelligence or cosmic energies that would equate to the Sirian race of beings. In much the same way, Arcturians are said to have influenced ancient Greece with its incredible advanced understanding of mathematics and geometry.

In more earthly historical terms we go back to the time of Plato, born in ancient Greece around the time of 300–400 BC. He is regarded as one of the first major players in Western philosophy and spirituality who later went on to educate his most famous student, Aristotle. Plato theorized that patterns and grids on the Earth's structure could potentially show the energies around it. This evolved from geometric shapes in various guises. These shapes became known as platonic solids, which he envisaged as being superimposed around the Earth, almost like an energy field. Below are the shapes and their geometric proportions. This is important as we will come back to these shortly.

Tetrahedron = 4 faces
Cube = 6 faces
Octahedron = 8 faces
Dodecahedron = 12 faces

Icosahedron = 20 faces

These concepts were collated into a text called the *Timaeus*, which associated each shape with one of the elements, Earth, fire, air, and water. He went on to superimpose these various shapes over one another to create a grid system regarding the various energy patterns and the fields that encompass the Earth. These would be some of the first known human teachings that allude to energetic lines running across the Earth creating grids.

Man has since created lines that correlate longitude and latitude; however, those are relational to pinpointing places and mapping out the Earth in geographical terms only. Plato was onto something else. He had sensed the energy lines of the Earth herself in its basic terms. Some have gone on to name these ley lines. The Chinese have referred to them as dragon lines, which opens up the debate among spiritualists about who put these lines there in the first place and how old they are. In many places around the world esoteric people claim that it was a Reptilian influence in our galactic history, although they would be confused in stating this. The Chinese mystics called them dragon lines for the dragon energy of the beings who 350,000+ years ago helped anchor them, known as the Elohim, but this is more starseed mythology; back to the science for the time being.

Plato is alluding to the crystalline grid in its basic form. Throughout history humans have created templates and models or mini-Earths with the platonic shapes suggesting grid systems for thousands of years. Although it was Plato who put the geometric shapes within a recognized culture, there are in fact cultures long before that seem to have had this knowledge, and at a time when science deems man to have been primitive in the way he used tools to create and sculpt things.

The Ashmolean stones are five platonic structures with grid-like patterns carved in them from thirty-five hundred years ago and are another example of humans having conceptual ideas about grid systems on Earth. The stones are on display at the Ashmolean Museum in Oxford, England, and are potentially the oldest evidence of planetary grid research, with scholars who are still amazed and startled at their precise geometric proportions.

The grid system as we said can store energy like a record, but it also stores energies in various places like the human body does, although the Earth's energy points can be mapped out forming, yes, you guessed it, geometric patterns. Scientists and free thinkers throughout the ages and especially the last hundred years or so have begun to delve more deeply into this. Energy points of the Earth and sometimes even their strange characteristics have been known by man for aeons, but not necessarily mapped out in relation to each other until modern times.

Ivan P. Sanderson, a Scottish writer who later became an American citizen, began to correlate data that alluded to the Earth's grid system through work he carried out related to strange electromagnetic occurrences around the globe, which correlated also to the disappearance of various ships and planes including anomalies that happened in these regions. Using modern communication technology and statistical data analysis, he began to plot a grid system around the world known as the Twelve Devil's Graveyards; other names include the Vile Vortices. Vile in later years, however, could be interpreted as misunderstood perhaps, but it was the terminology given at the time, and often it is the way with humans who misunderstand the unknown; they attach fear to the door that says I don't know what's behind it.

Sanderson discovered the peculiarity that these energy points fit into a geometric pattern around the globe that was equally patterned creating their own grid system with triangle-shaped geometry within an icosahedron which has twenty faces and twelve points. Every point correlated to the strange activity that occurred to planes and ships within these areas around the triangular formation of the various faces of the icosahedron structure which maps out the Earth. What he began to map out were the power points of the electromagnetic and crystalline grid in basic form as it was then prior to the harmonic convergence in 1987. Stranger still, is how ancient civilizations all seem to congregate around these areas of the planet and then vanish or move without a trace.

The areas listed below are other areas of interesting

seismic activity and places where planes and their whereabouts historically became distorted regards time or, in the case of Malaysia Airlines Flight 370 in modern times, disappeared completely. The North and South Poles are said to have many anomalies regarding electromagnetics and even time distortion in some cases.

1. Easter Island megaliths
2. Wharton Basin
3. Indus Valley, City of Mohenjo Daro, Pakistan
4. Devil's Sea, south of Japan
5. Hamakulia Volcano, east of Hawaii
6. South Atlantic Anomaly, east of Rio de Janeiro
7. Great Zimbabwe mines, structures, and megaliths
8. Algerian megaliths, North Africa
9. Loyalty Islands
10. Bermuda Triangle
11. North Pole
12. South Pole

In later years this work would be continued by three Russian scientists, expanding the idea and giving further credence to a grid system on Earth. It began with Nikolai Goncharov, who was historically fascinated by the ancient world and its relevance in the past. He found geographical interest in the positioning of these markers on Earth and soon began to mark on a globe all the centers of earliest human culture. A local newspaper was known for documenting Goncharov as having an "intuitive impulse" as to finding what might be a geometric regularity or pattern that could be relational to the various elements he was tracking while plotting them on a map.

Soon Goncharov met Vyacheslav Morozov, a construction engineer, and then later Valery Makarov, who was a specialist in electronics. After some years of work regarding these ideas suspicion soon turned into something more evidential and there seemed to be a gravitas behind the ideas the three Russians were theorizing. Their work came to the wider attention of their peers when the USSR Academy of Sciences published an interesting issue of the journal *Khimiya I Zhizn* (*Chemistry and Life*) documenting these theories under the title "Is the Earth a Large Crystal?" The Russians began to expand on the idea of various grid systems on Earth with the patterns being formulated into triangular structures within geometric patterns and mentioning Ivan Sanderson's work. Mitigating the Poles, Sanderson had suggested five distinct areas above, five below, at equal distances from the equator. The Russians were suggesting they had found nine more.

For ten years, Makarov, Morozov, and Goncharov explored the view of the core of the Earth as a growing crystal that influences what is going on with our planet. They had conceptualized Earth as having a power field around it that affected many of Gaia's then attributes, calculating the structure to be an icosahedron, or twenty-sided figure, and dodecahedron, or twelve-sided figure. It was thought that with sixty-two apexes and the middle points of their sides that many specific qualities could explain unusual phenomena around the world. Research concluded that when embossed over each other the icosahedron and dodecahedron revealed the following interesting planetary components and their attributes around the world we live in with exact details.

1. Birthplaces for human religions, philosophies, sciences, arts, and architectural structures
2. Migration routes of land, air, and sea of the various creatures inhabiting the planet
3. Magnetic and electrical anomalies, which serve as gateways into other dimensions or portals. Places where time is lost or not linear, planes or ships experiencing unaccounted-for time that can't be explained
4. Breeding grounds and genetic pool regions where new species have formed
5. Highest and lowest solar and electric influx areas, along with regions of highest and lowest geomagnetic strength
6. Fracture zones, where the tectonic plates come together

and create seismic and volcanic activities

7. Concentrations of ores and petroleum

8. High proportions of human population centers, both past and present

9. Hotspots where the internal magma surges closest to the surface

10. High and low barometric pressure areas in the Earth's atmosphere, where storms originate and move along the crystal lattices (geometric shapes and their triangular patterns)

11. Epicenters for major ocean currents and whirlpools. (For more information, see the works of Makarov, Morozov, and Goncharov as explained on www. bibliotecapleyades.net.)

Interestingly, the list also went on to include all of Ivan P. Sanderson's twelve points and many more making up the various nodes of the crystalline grid. In essence you have a system whereby the crystal grid lines are similar to those of the body, with main arteries of influence while smaller capillary energy lines run off the main system into smaller areas. What they were becoming aware of were the Pleiadian nodes and nulls of Gaia that were placed here by the Pleiadians many thousands of years ago in the hope that we would cross the marker. These are special places on Earth that have been activated as of lately which are part of the new crystalline grid of Earth. Whole books have been written on the Pleiadian nodes and they are easily researched.

The grid idea was then taken further by William Becker and Bethe Hagens, who also gave validity to Sanderson's work. Becker was a professor of industrial design at the University of Illinois, Chicago, while Dr. Hagens was a professor of anthropology at Governors State University. Later known as the Becker–Hagens Grid, they assimilated the ultimate Earth grid idea, calling it the Unified Vector Geometry 120 Polyhedron, or the UVG 120 "Earth Star."

Becker went on to explain that the Earth was like a living crystal that was apparently drawn out with precise geometric

∻ 262 ∻

The Crystalline Grid

proportions that when mapped out, overlaid onto the locations of ocean currents, the winds, river systems, and distributions of precious minerals which ancient man seemed to utilize for the locations of old civilizations and cities. Becker was feverish in explaining the major geologic features such as mountain ranges and river systems also tied into this idea and the idea other grid theorists before him had concluded, too!

With all of this in mind, we can see that there is a field of geometric proportions that energetically encompasses the Earth and interacting with the consciousness not just of the Earth, but its people. It is believed that the Earth, with all of its points of interest and energetic pattern ley lines and electromagnetic attributes, would look similar to that of the icosidodecahedron formation, that is up until 2012.

Since the harmonic convergence in 1987 when the magnetics and harmonics of the Earth started shifting, the structure has been morphing into something more advanced. Its field of energy has changed, taking human consciousness along with it. In other words, as we go up in vibration and dimensional vibration, so do the grid systems and their complexities in terms of structural shape and energetic signature. This affects the world we are living in. Volcanic activity is increasing. Weather patterns are in huge flux with major shifts in water regards flooding and droughts, rivers, and the way water collects and where it is found. Earthquakes are happening where there were no quakes before, and migration routes are changing, with birds rerouting their journeys and nesting in different places. We see it with whales and dolphins becoming lost and beaching themselves in an effort to find new routes. In the same way that humans will raise their consciousness and move to another part of the world that resonates with it, animals will follow the new and updated grids of Earth and the electromagnetic fields that resonate around them.

Whales have been thought to have biomagnetic brains with the operational parts thought to be magnetite, which in turn allows their magnetic compass to navigate the oceans. So if whales and dolphins are rerouting and getting lost, is it evidence that there is a shift as they follow new paths set within the grids?

❖ 263 ❖

Why would whales and dolphins on a global scale become lost as of late?

If you look at the geomagnetic field of the planet you can see it has been going down for some time now especially in recent Earth times. In relation to this we are seeing the Schumann resonance on average is increasing exponentially. Things are becoming more interconnected than ever before; however, the roads are very new and teething issues will be soon overcome.

The bioelectrical field of the brain does seem to be entangled to the geomagnetic and energy fields of the Earth, therefore any energy shifts in the planet would cause modifications in the consciousness of humanity as a whole. In the same way harmful radiation can cause genetic mutation within the human body, does positive radiation from Earth, space, and the sun then in turn deliver a metamorphosis regarding DNA and its evolution? We can see how radiation sickness affects the human body in cases where a person has been over exposed. Perhaps the real difference here is that we are being faced with positive radiation that is forcing the evolution of the physical body for a higher density.

We discussed the dimensions and what they might look like from a direct viewpoint as if you were living within them. So in dimensional terms there is speculation regarding how many dimensions and densities the grid can work within, plus its observable nature within those levels. There is a mixture of information both from channeled ET messages and science alluding to the appearance being different or "opening up" the higher dimensional awareness that you can view it from. The grid is said to resonate at the twelfth density.

On a more day-to-day experience it has been observable energetically by those who have made pilgrimages to various parts of the world in order to feel these energies. In times past one might have traveled a distance to India, Nepal, Sedona, or other parts of the world that hold sacred high energies. Prior to 2012 there was a sense that to be surrounded by these vibrations coming from certain nodes and focal points, one could only gain access by visiting the pyramids of Egypt or traveling to other

The Crystalline Grid

ancient monuments, for example. In more recent times there is a feeling in the "community" that one can access these high energies more freely within the comfort of your own home as the energies are more present through the Earth than before. These high energies are more accessible for all to feel and the "light matrix" is becoming unlocked everywhere and not just in localized points on the global map. So how does the crystalline grid look post-2012?

In light of what we know already we can understand that there was prior to 2012 an icosidodecahedron formation in terms of Earth energies forming an energetic crystal lattice diamond faceted structure around the Earth. Let's put this together now to explain the full picture including the final details of Earth's gravity which is linked to its magnetics.

The magnetics of the Earth create a field and this in turn creates gravity holding everything onto the Earth creating fields around it. The focus of this energy is coming from the center of the planet. Imagine you are in space looking at the energy signature of the Earth. You are viewing this as a dodecahedron, a sphere with twelve facets. It is believed this was the first energetic field that Plato began to discuss. The electromagnetic structure that surrounds the Earth is a big living bubble shifting and morphing in various regions on the globe. This we discussed as the arteries and capillaries, otherwise known as ley lines and energy vortexes. This forms the structure of the icosahedron, a sphere with twenty facets.

Joseph Jochmans is a researcher and was a leading voice in the world of esoterica who was vocal in discussing the harmonic convergence in 1987 when the magnetics of the Earth began to shift. At the time there was a feeling that his teachings were perhaps nonsense until science began to catch up and document the various energetic changes that were occurring. He has coined the understanding of how to look at the metamorphosis of the icosidodecahedron and how it has evolved into a new grid.

He explains that out of the old grid system superimposed over the Earth is a new one forming beyond the platonic series of solids and the shapes we mentioned earlier. While Earth's grid

⁖ 265 ⁖

structure worked previously as a 3D icosadodeca crystal, we begin to see new shapes morphing into alignment. Taking into consideration an icosahedron and joining all the lines together from each other point internally, you begin to create twelve pentacles or five-pointed star structures. He mentions that if you extend the outer edges of the icosahedron and join these node points together, you create a second group of twelve pentacles or stars becoming a new more complex and updated version of the grid. This in turn forms a double penta-dodecahedron, which is essentially composed of twelve double-pentacles equally spaced across the surface of the globe.

In basic terms the old operating system of Earth has been rebooted and given a new operating system. In the same way a Mac might use the OS series or a PC in the home or office might use Windows, Earth has a new operating system also. You could call it the Earth operating system 2012.

More interesting still is the work of Becker and Hagens, the three Russians, and Sanderson within this new age. Prior to 2012, the work of these scientists and many more had unity of symbiosis. The energies and places they plotted had a commonality prior to 2012. After 2012, however, the ideas that had been plotted do not seem to work coherently anymore, and the goal posts seemed to have changed. The twelve Vile Vortices are moving as is the magnetic North Pole and much more. We are entering a brand-new world with new physics not seen on this Earth for a very long time. Effectively, we will have an operating system from which we can leap and think out into higher realms than ever before.

One might ask how humans operate in this new system? We are surrounded by all the energy fields at all times but is there an interface? As humans upgrade their DNA, so does Gaia and her physical and energetic embodiments she uses in the great scheme of things.

Let us start with the Merkaba. Science has proven that the human body radiates an electromagnetic field at some level. This is why placing magnets around the body can have both positive and negative effects depending on their application. Within the field of science, the Merkaba could be described as a field of energy that is around us. In the new-age movement and spirituality this is explained as a star tetrahedron that exists within us, formed from two pyramids pointing in opposite directions so that its points are along eight axes creating an energetic field around us. This has had its place in ancient history for a long time. Does this mean there is gravitas to this? Ancient Egyptians called it the light body. Merkaba broken down translates to Mer (light) ka (soul) ba (body). The Egyptians called this energy the chariot of the soul. The Bible also expands on this idea, saying it is that which anchors the physical body with higher frequencies. This is extended to other religions, also, such as the Jewish faith, which has various texts and scriptures that speak of this. The light body is used across the board as a generalization.

In effect the light body or field around you is interacting with the energetic grid of the Earth and the two are talking and interacting with each other. If we are becoming more attuned and the Earth/Gaia is becoming more attuned, it will mean a closer relationship between the two and a greater feeling of connectedness to the Earth. We are beginning to see this in public thought regarding the preservation of the Earth. Let's take this to a higher level of ideas then.

Gaia has shifted its energies so that we can shift and grow into the next level of humanity using the grids as a network of divine intent. In synchronizing therefore with the crystalline grid, we are then able to exchange information accelerating our evolution as a race shifting the global frequency liquidating conflict and destruction on Earth.

The new grid will potentially link crystals, portals, and dimensional openings connecting our planet to new cosmic realities and dimensional worlds. Gaia's pyramids, megaliths, and mystical sites have previously been confirmed with the lines of the crystalline grid, and as Earth awakens into a few operating systems some of those portals of energy will be activated. The new Earth consciousness lexicon will also be anchored in this holographic light matrix operating system.

In other words, Earth cleared the energetic path for

humans to garner higher dimensional living and ascension to help fast track the process into a new beautiful world. On a galactic stage, it is said that all eyes are on Gaia at this moment in time as another civilization joins the neighborhood. There is a feeling off-world that we are nearly ready to become part of the cosmos. There are perhaps ETs or beings out there thinking to themselves, "Hey, welcome to adulthood, we can do business together now, what do you say?"

Summary

Throughout this book we have been on a journey. There will have been many new ideas put in front of you. If this is a completely new arena for you, then give yourself an extremely large pat on the back and herald in a small celebration for getting this far. Before touching on the future of Earth, it is a good time to have a small summary of the events that have unfolded in these pages regarding how these attributes will affect the future.

All in one go, let's put it simply. Humans have been on Earth living in a third-density cavity after a period of descent lowering their energies and abilities and becoming susceptible to influences that have resulted in control and separation from self, the creator, and the universe and Gaia herself has had to descend her own energies and grids. This has also been affected negatively by all the galactic and earthly wars that have continued for thousands of years within our galaxy and solar system, the trauma of which is still working its way to the surface within our Akash. Atomic events in the 1940s became a catalyst for souls of different origins rushing to Earth in order to undo old systems and recalibrate a new reality that is of a fifth-density paradigm for both Gaia and her grids and the inhabitants of Earth and their vibration. Old souls are awakening and people all over the Earth are asking themselves, "Am I having some kind of weird awakening and why are my ears ringing?"

Earth changes its energies, facilitating the transformation while passing through a more energetic part of space modifying the magnetics and other attributes of the planet. The crystalline grid also ascends, creating a new operating system energetically and geometrically paving a foundation for a higher reality leap board. In turn our perceptions and lives are changing with old systems crumbling and new ones coming into creation in their replacement. As the migratory paths of the animal kingdom change, so too do the lives of humans, changing jobs, careers, and where they live including old routines set in an old paradigm.

The human is gaining back abilities that were always inherent but that were dormant or controlled. Our neighbors in the immediate cosmic vicinity are aware of this, and they are preparing to welcome distant and immediate family back into the universe. As the final battle of light and dark commences on Earth, light begins to win for the first time, and the darkness knows it has lost but will attempt until the end to manipulate light in a hopeless cause which only ends in further denial. Humans are spiritually about to become adults, and ETs, nonphysical entities, and angelic beings want the people of Earth to connect with them more than ever, working toward disclosure in a way that is least disruptive. Earth is bathed in photonic light, but there are some elements of murky duality lingering and a sense of caution is still needed as the last push out of a dark era is birthed. Earth is still lingering in fourth-density duality and polarities still exist with the truth wars being a grand example of this. Explained in simple terms, my truth is better than yours, and the battle for the highest truth within the new-age communities lingers as fourth-density egoic identity of self slowly turns into unity/group consciousness where there is one collective truth going into fifth-density aided this time by the higher self with polarity of these separational ideas fading out.

⁂ 6 ⁂
The Future

Sovereignty

Sovereignty is the full right and power of a governing body over itself, without any interference from outside sources or bodies.

—Source unknown

We begin the final countdown with sovereignty. More than ever before, the world is a place in which we can express ourselves freely using many tools through communications and technology. Systems are changing and there are windows of opportunity open unlike before whereby the individual can find their own space in life without fear or condemnation. The mortal is granted more power to self than ever before in terms of ideas and expression, but it has a very long way to go yet socially. We travel this life sailing through a huge flux of distractions and controls be it legally or monetarily. The human has to navigate an array of options that were never available before, which can seem confusing in a modern world. Indoctrination via advertising, education, cultural expectation, religious orientation, political heritage, and perhaps family history or other projections are an arsenal of instruments fired at us throughout our lives. We are constantly pulled here and everywhere putting unnecessary pressure on the human soul. It is no wonder in a modern world that is so full of noise that we can quickly become bogged down and lost in a tunnel with little or no light when on top of this we are working through issues that happened away from Earth that we are often not aware of consciously.

The Future

The outer world has taken the volume knob and turned it up to full, deafening us to a degree that we become blind to who we are and where we are going. The human condition goes through the journey often never finding purpose or oneself through a constant bombardment of subversive clattering and crashing that is at times hard to escape. The human state is so entrenched in white noise that we have forgotten how to switch it off, resulting in turning left when the universe wants us to turn right.

Worse yet are the souls who are institutionalized to a degree that it has become a normalization in their reality creating comforting walls like a fortress of familiarity which lock oneself into the matrix offering a warm feeling through a blanket of deception. Upon peeling back the ego structures, one is met with indignation or irritability. This is why as time continues there will be less sitting on the fence, which in turn creates two different types of humans on Earth with the bridge becoming bigger every generation. This will manifest most obviously during and after what will be known as the global pandemic years. Those that choose to live in constant fear will live shortened lives and those that awaken to the new Earth and adapt accordingly will find talents and purposes they never thought existed. Souls awakening won't have the time for the indignation or irritability and will by default search for "others" while moving into a new consciousness. As Morpheus told Neo in the *Matrix* movie, "This is your last chance, after this there is no turning back. You take the blue pill, the story ends, you wake up in your bed and believe whatever you want to believe. You take the red pill, you stay in wonderland and I show you how far the rabbit hole goes, remember, all I'm offering is the truth, nothing more."

We have come to live in a world that is a complete externalization of everything we are not. Of course, art and music are positive forms of this which are the polarity. However, the human swims in an egotistical ocean only finding buoyancy via socially conforming, fitting in and recognition searching in forms of dopamine-driven social media experiences. It is as if the human has broken its legs and decided to prop itself up on something that isn't even real in order to get that quick fix.

The future will become the opposite of this to some degree. The enlightened human will find fulfilment internally from within, not externally. The mortal will go within for answers using one's own feelings on a situation flexing that muscle called intuition. An advanced consciousness will not need constant fixes externally but will find calm and elation internally. Loving oneself and living happily in one's own body will be the new gun fired at the starting line with the finishing line becoming a journey finding who you really are or what makes you truly happy in life. From 2020 onward will become the great age where introspection will take more governance with the time duration of 2020 to 2024 being the great years of restructuring. Checking in on yourself and your emotions while getting a higher take on what makes you feel one way or another will clear the path to plotting higher and better routes in accordance. We will become more attached to ourselves and slip out of the numbness that has dulled our experience of life.

For example, does this food make me feel ill? Does this relationship make me sick? Does this job diminish who I am? It seems simple enough, but it is a world in which the great majority sink while blindly continuing through the quagmire. There will be greater spaces for joy and fulfilment for the masses than ever before with 99 percent of the population becoming more diluted into the top 1 percent and the masses finding better ways of living.

Becoming introspective will be part of connecting to your higher self on the other side of the veil which is thinning every year. The side of you that knows you better than yourself, or in other words your intuition, which is never wrong your higher self. From 2020 onward the human will have a stronger "knowing" of where to turn next from being silent and going within for the answers and feeling and seeing the signposts the universe is showing. Connecting with yourself will not only allow you to know yourself better, but it will also allow you to take control of your own thoughts and feelings without the white noise dulling your senses. Introspection will have the result of sovereignty, permitting ownership of your own thoughts and ideas and control ultimately of your higher good for existence. Practicing control of

The Future

what you read, see, feel, smell, or experience will not become an indoctrination blindly taken as given but an option that is looked at impartially and then taken on board or dismissed depending on how lucrative it is for your life experience growth and humans will become less like cattle but more like a high-thinking Pleiadian.

Going inside will allow one to discern the deception in the news and politics and smelling when lies or deceitful propaganda is being pushed as a consensus that is subversively given as the normal. The new human will see through and outside of the matrix and know something doesn't feel right as opposed to simply going along with it because that is what everyone else has always done, especially within particular circles in music, fashion, and other industries that creatively give platforms for aspiring voices to reach the masses. You will become your own professional introspective BS-meter in terms of people, relationships, business, the news, the world, and what is being force fed to your dietary television schedule. A higher consciousness will be in control of itself first and digest information thereafter depending on the nature and content for the moment required. Simply put, people will not be rabbits within the headlights of large corporations, big pharma, big tech, and governments, in turn creating new ways and happier balances offering real transparency.

Post-2020, more nations and individuals will break away from old ideas, forming new ones in a new paradigm, be it with various political orientations which will work in more balanced ways and start taking back their own lands and governance from foreign powers.

Contemplation will lead to far higher ideas giving advanced views of systems and self. When humans begin this process of awakening, often it starts with, "What is this life really all about, what is the point in life, is there a point to my life?" For some this can be a deadly experience as the ego is quietened and the soul begins to peel away the noise that has subjugated all thoughts from the past. This will open the soul to one idea alone: life is the meaning I give it, not the meaning life is giving me, offering free will and further sovereignty of self.

In turn human-made constructs such as religion and

politics will hold less gravity on the daily lives of a human as systems change with paradigms that create duality and divide becoming less attractive than those that create commonality or togetherness. The soul who is indoctrinated is one who is spewing everyone else's truth usually out of fear for one reason or another. The new soul will have gone inside and found their own truth and more than ever will feel compelled to tell that version, becoming free of gags, and on a spiritual level cleaning your throat chakra before aligning their personal truth to the truth of that of fifth-density cohesive collective truth. A collective truth for all.

From 2020 onward will be the great years of deception coming to the surface with people finding and speaking their truth. Where corruption or abuse once thrived, you will see more whistle-blowers than ever before telling their truths in order to diminish negativity and old energies. It is becoming more prevalent everywhere we look with women talking about characters such as Harvey Weinstein in Hollywood and other souls such as Ronan Farrow becoming the interface for change and thinking outside of the box.

Great swindles, scandals, and subversions of the truth will surface after 2020 with the masses being deeply shocked at what they thought was true. This will happen in all areas increasingly and the truth, no matter how hard it is, will be the new compulsion. Once darkness thrived in chicanery and jiggery-pokery whereas light will thrive in compassion and integrity. The UV lamp will be shone onto the surface and the dirt that was unseen will shockingly appear.

There will, however, need to be caution regarding the powers that be and their practical manipulations of sovereignty. For example, while there is quality in expression regarding gender fluidity, there is also room for power manipulation from unseen forces at the top.

While practicing elements of transgenderism he/she still understands where and who she/he is with the ability to compartmentalize the different aspects. In the future the lines will increasingly become more blurred with androgyny becoming widely acceptable. The danger will be large corporations or elite

The Future

groups pushing the lines and creating trauma in a world where they have pushed your sovereignty so far that you can't find yourself anymore with the lines of divine masculine and feminine becoming weakened and blurred. It will be subtle at first but slowly the dark side will creep in and many will find it too late. Already there are large numbers of unreported cases of individuals who wish they could return to their original gender but have taken life-changing physical steps that have gone too far. This will cause further internal issues within the family structure, which is fully understood by the elites. Blurring sexuality to such an extent in the family home comes with latent issues showing signs later down the path in forms of various trauma and through trauma comes forms of control which are profitable for the remaining elite. This will be manipulated in ways yet to be cooked up. While we practice our sovereignty, there is caution in not letting outside influences push it to such a degree that we forget who we are.

The same applies for technologies. Industry is pushing us into a technological world where everything is connected and we are completely reliant on the devices we have and use at all times. This continual reliance is being drip fed into the human state with people having a device attached to them permanently or one being inches away at all times. The thought of people going out for the day and leaving their mobile phone behind has become inconceivable with some youngsters so addicted to their devices that they have no friends, world, or thoughts of their own as thought patterns are programmed into them via these devices.

Through devices, manipulation/propaganda is easily fed into the minds of youngsters via their smartphones in the home setting. Children are becoming subversively brainwashed in the home environments and companies are feeding off analytical data regarding usage and preference information. Constant use of machines is turning adults and children into machines themselves, slowing down the ability to use imagination and intuitiveness. The technological age is very slowly chipping away at a person's sovereignty cloaked with words like convenience and connectedness.

A time will come when the age of chipping will come to

fruition and it will be sold under the banner of convenience or other multitudes of nonsense that people will thoughtlessly leap into. Allowing a device that can track you at all times while being used knowingly to give impulses to your body is not practicing being in control of your own thoughts and body. It is allowing a foreign object in, which taken over by the wrong hands can open up further darkness. In much the same way operating systems can be used for good, evil can hack or find ways to take over them. Imagine becoming chipped and an external hacker taking over your chip. You would feel inclined to remove it. The question is, why bother in the first place? This will be part of the free will moving forward as the 3D unawakened souls move into more fear and more control and the 5D awakened beings will fly higher than ever before, increasing the great divide.

The drive to slowly subjugate via external and then internal tech in the body is a careful balancing act in the future and one to play with very carefully. The human soul and heart can easily be taken away by tech and people who are becoming machines. Humans are beautiful without technology and the most wonderful moments in most people's lives are not when they are using devices. Again, there will be murky shades of grey in which mindfulness must be practiced so as not to lose your sovereignty before reaching 5D.

EMFs will have potential to increase with 5G becoming 6 and 7 and so on with radio waves attaching to human brains that are not genetically evolved enough to stop the mutation of cells causing cancer due to the bombardment of radiation that in millions of years of human evolution has only crept in within the last part of the century. The lesser amounts of heavy metals that you can remove from the body will allow for less outside radiation for it to be controlled including from phone masts. The result of this will be the estate agencies seeing more people than ever moving out of the cities for the first time.

There will be potential for rebel groups in the future becoming aware of just how harmful these phone masts are with many of them getting torn down. Cases involving cancer patients who suffered living next to these masts will finally become news

The Future

that can't be hidden by large corporations, and there will be a new *Erin Brockovich* movie made, one about the cell phone industry and the pounding on the human brain of harmful EMFs from cell phones and the effect they have on the human body.

In a time that is very close there will be AI in the form of humans far beyond Sofia the talking robot. The military and other operations have had very high-level AI humans for a long time and increasingly one will see them out and about in society. They will be hard to tell apart from normal humans, but the window to the soul does not lie. Simply look into their eyes and there will be a deadness. It is coming. These are people who have had work completed on parts of their brain or melded with chips or other technologies. The men in black are said to have had this similar attribute, although these will seem more human. Remember, no one can control you unless you give your free will away. There will be many ways in the future for groups to make you openly give away your free will. It is better to keep it at all costs. Simply state out loud, "I do not give you permission to have sovereignty over me. I am exercising my free will, and I am in control of myself. I have set my intent!"

The ego is linked to many kinds of behaviors that mask or add to the illusion of fear-based programming often connected to the external world. When the ego is relaxed and introspection is exercised, you begin to see the world in a much higher dimension. When making decisions, ask yourself, is that my ego speaking or am I capable of a much higher level of thinking outside of fight and flight, survival instinct, and delusional necessities for external validation of who I am or think I need to be because of others? Future consciousness will be about listening to the higher self and increasingly doing away with ego. It will be a process that will take humans generations to perfect.

You are perfect the way you are. In fact, you are a masterpiece because there is no one like you. Christmas is forever knocking at your door and your higher self is just waiting to remove the old Christmas wrapping and expose the big fat present inside, the new you. The evolved you, a calmer higher thinking unit who is completely in control of your existence devoid of indoctrination and subversive programming. Take a second to imagine the awesomeness of how that might feel and the people who live that dream on a daily basis.

Time and Reality

Let's start with the science bit first, and then move on to what it actually looks like in day-to-day life. We are going to need a little help from our mate Albert Einstein.

One of the most interesting and innovative theories of gravitation can be found within Einstein's well-known general theory of relativity, which says that a gravitational field represents a curvature of spacetime instead of distortion of it. In very basic terms, things that carry energy, momentum, and stresses are sources of a gravitational field, or a curvature of spacetime. Einstein's theory says time is in four dimensions and also includes three spatial elements. The idea presents spacetime not as emptiness, but as the very fabric the universe is woven into. This idea is also seen to have astronomical connections with influential gravitational fields deforming space and time.

We know that spacetime can be bent as it has been seen in the cosmos. For example, the sun's gravitational field distorts spacetime slightly, bending a ray of light through a small angle as it beams past the Earth. Science has also observed that black holes influence spacetime so much that light entering a black hole never leaves.

Internal magnetic fields are part of spacetime becoming an inseparable part of spacetime fabric. Distorting spacetime will have an effect regarding the interactions of a magnetic field. Electromagnetic fields are associated with what is known as the nonvanishing energy momentum tensor, which is also another way of explaining gravity in the Einstein field equations. In conclusion, science generally says that if you could produce a field influential enough, it would become possible to get a measurable gravitational time dilation.

Taking into account the Earth is one huge magnetic entity

The Future

and the magnetics are changing along with human consciousness, what might that look like during the normal human day? Basically, time is going to speed up. What used to feel like a year might feel like months. What used to feel like weeks might feel like days. Imagine you have been away and had an incredible weekend filled to the max. Not once have you looked at the clock or worried about the day. Upon returning home, you close the door behind you and sit down with your cup of tea and think to yourself, wow, was I really away only for a weekend? It feels like I crammed in so much more as if it were longer. All that in a weekend? This is a result of time speeding up, which is what is happening and will increasingly happen in terms of our perception of it. This is related to what spiritual practitioners like to coin as manifestation. It's going to take much shorter times to manifest your thoughts and actions into reality. Increasingly, there will seem like less hours in the day, and this will drive some people to have an innate feeling of time running out, "I've simply got to get moving," but not fundamentally understanding why. This will continue as the mental facilities that work in other densities and dimensions begin to switch on and work in tandem with an environment that changes in Gamma rays, electromagnetics, and gravitational fields that will continue to evolve. This will be linked to our sun, which will evolve and change with periods of great solar flashes and ejections coming to Earth. Time and reality will over thousands of years begin to shift reality up until time has sped up so much that an event horizon has been reached whereby the present catches up with the future. This change in environmental and biological evolution will allow humans to think, see, and feel all time realities as one past, one future, and one now acting all as one as many of the ETs see and experience it.

This will in turn change the brain's reality perception of memory. You will find yourself walking in a room and not remembering the reason for entering that place as you switch between dimensions and timelines more often. Throughout the duration of the changes made by the brain, it will seem harder to remember what you even ate for breakfast on days. This is due to the new 5D memory kicking in that wishes to know all that is obtained with the field around you managed by the higher self as opposed to slower linear time that happens hours previously managed by brain activity that will become slightly less redundant in multidimensionality, allowing new areas to switch on and work in relationship to a DNA that talks to the energies around you. Simply put, you won't need to go to the Internet and learn something through repetition and have that knowledge absorbed by the synapses of the brain. In 5D upward, one will think intuitively on something and the information with come as a download from innate or the field that is around us.

Many people around the world are experiencing an awakening and surfing bubbles of connectedness and seeing and feeling these changes in small increments here and there. When your perception of the world greatly changes along with an unexplained but felt experience of time changing, the result can be tricky or bumpy going into a new consciousness. The wonderful exciting news is, never before has it been a better time to live your dreams in the world in which we live in now and watch them manifest faster with more synchronicities than ever before. That is why it is more important than ever to spend more time putting away the smartphones and dull the white noise around us so that we can watch the signposts that the universe is showing us. Set sail and see what happens this time if it didn't work before. Perhaps it's a new venture, except that it will work like never before. The energies are ripe and ready to play with you.

After practicing sovereignty, the human is going to get a vision many times more clear-cut on where to go and what to do. The future will hold much more enlightenment for people getting into the right life and career paths. Sexual partners will also change and the way they are found. There will be less time spent and few partner experiences needed to navigate toward finding your twin flame. Humans of the future will be able to by free choice have many partners, but it will not be necessary as your higher self will lead you to your best match without all the try-outs in previous years. This will lead to divorce rates going down and marriage laws will eventually change along with any or all religious connotations that went along with them from an old energy.

People increasingly in a higher mindset will spend less time getting into the wrong jobs or relationships and finding the right one for the first time. There is a huge amount written about the twin flame theory.

We discussed how the idea of clear thought and sovereignty will lead to people speaking their truths, be it on anything. People will have more of a voice than ever in the future, and it will be seen everywhere starting with certain social media outlets. YouTube in the short term will grow exponentially with the stars of the future becoming the next big thing. Everyone will effectively have their own TV channel, and there will be a huge expanse of people coming who will discuss elements of this book and high consciousness and channeling; it is already en route. You already see groups on sites growing like wildfire discussing the starseed phenomenon with hundreds and even thousands every day adding themselves to these groups while the admins look on and think, "Goodness, what have I started?!"

The psychology of social media will change in the future with satisfaction becoming attainable from more compassionate and real stories in contrast to quick fixes such as looking at my boobs, my car, or me with someone else's money. People will feel less compulsion to feed the ego by covering up their journey by looking good but sharing their real journey and watching others grow in transparency because of it. There will be less attraction to someone's wallet but more to the size of their heart and their intelligence. Spirituality will become the new sexy for 5D women and men. It will be a psychology not of a group of showing off online, but groups of collective individuals working together without the premise being ego driven. In turn, the integrity of the information shared will be different as the agenda has been removed and the content will be more real and shared by the soul/ heart than by the survival monkey mind boosted by ego.

Within starseed psychology, this has been called the two Earth theory: increasingly, one set of institutionalized people who wish to stay in the material fear reality of the third-dimensional space and the other half who ascend into a more fifth-dimensional state of reality manifesting what they want faster based on living in their conceptual heart brain and not their linear logical fear-driven mind. We are seeing it in the children being born around the world everywhere who are embodying this state of mind increasingly. It is not to say that having two Ferraris and multiple houses won't be a good thing, because abundance is your birthright, but it is to say it will be obtained with a different mindset used not to show off egotistically but used in more compassionate ways so not to belittle. Material wealth will not be as attractive as before. A high consciousness will be the new wealth and that will be the emphasis.

Disclosure

UFO sightings are more common than ever with more members of the navy and air force openly disclosing that they have either personally dealt with or been privy to "beings" or seeing craft perform maneuvers in the sky that defy physics as we know them. High-ranking individuals we have covered already such as Ben Rich, director at Lockheed's Skunk Works and regarded as the "father of stealth," who was responsible for leading the development of an F-117, the first production stealth aircraft, will come to the fore more often. Paul Hellyer the Canadian defense minister who has also brought to the attention of the public these details and others will continue to speak out. John Podesta, former White House chief of staff, openly worked recently with musician Tom DeLonge in order to begin discussing what he already knows regarding the existence of ETs, which is now open-source information on the net. Lists of high-ranking and senior employees of deep state and underground bases will begin to dramatically increase over the years with the deep state finding it harder to hide truths and technologies. In the past there was a trail of blood, however the deep state soon realized creating martyrs was making the situation worse and opted for a different maneuver. This new tactic included debunking and accusing the perpetrator of fraud of perhaps planting child pornography on or

The Future

in one's house or computer. In recent years they have softened even more, using discrediting tactics, explaining that "He or she was drunk or suffered mental illness, you must laugh at this."

The ET phenomenon has also been controlled via the deep state in each presidency handed down from leader to leader with many of them meeting ETs, such as Eisenhower with regards to the Pleiadians and the Greys. This was an event he was unable to publicly disclose. Before Eisenhower became leader of the USA he arranged a press release that stated UFOs are interacting with allied planes called Foo Fighters. It is thought that these were Nazi antigravity technology handed down by the Vril and renegade beings from Aldebaran. Later Kennedy was asked about the disclosure, saying, "I'd like to tell the public about the alien situation, but my hands are tied." President Roosevelt also famously said, "Non Terrestrial know how in atomic energy must be used in perfecting super weapons of war to affect the complete defeat of Germany and Japan, we must take advantage of such wonders that have come to us" and "The reality is that our planet is not the only one harboring intelligent life in the universe." Adam Guelch, a member of the Mutual UFO Network (MUFON), asked George Bush Sr. in 2016 when the US government would tell Americans the truth about UFOs, with his answer being, "Americans can't handle the truth."

In very recent years there have been such a high level of high-profile military and other ranking individuals coming out about such ideas that it has now become almost impossible to hide the elements that make up disclosure.

The tide has turned regarding keeping extraterrestrial life hidden and the deep state governments which often run above presidential or prime ministerial levels have been cornered into leaking details. More than this, they want the public to know as it will fuel technological events that need to come into the public domain which are linked to these beings.

We have seen it within the astronaut sector with many finally coming out that they have indeed seen them firsthand or know that they are out there. Dr. Helen Sharman made history when she traveled to the Soviet space station Mir in May 1991 when she told the BBC in 2020, "Aliens exist, there's no two ways about it," adding that "there must be all sorts of different forms of life among the billions of stars." American astronaut Buzz Aldrin can openly be found on YouTube speaking of ET-built monoliths on the surface of Mars's moon Phobos. The list is endless.

We can begin to see a lofty picture here full of senior officials, scientists, and influencers who all agree it's time to let the taxpayer know. The general public is beginning to have personal interactions with ETs in terms of channeling and other contact forms. The Hubble space telescope alone has caught huge amounts of craft and video footage in space of these extraterrestrial vehicles moving about and this footage can be found throughout the Internet.

There is a level of complexity to the disclosure movement and when it will happen and why. The ETs themselves through channeled messages as of late have discussed the idea of the great disclosure being in the years 2020–2030 with undeniable evidence seeping much more deeply into the human psyche. Governments are no longer denying such subjects but instead have begun baby feeding small trickles of information and the idea that we are going to find "life." It is the great trickle that will happen so slowly that the general public almost won't notice it; however, there is more.

Disclosure will not come from world governments and it can't for many reasons. This upsets people within various communities as they want the president of the USA to speak on live news openly admitting there are "aliens" with them landing on the White House lawn. This cannot and will never happen for two main reasons. First, world governments both deep-state and observable understand the cultural issues faced when in full open contact with a more advanced civilization regards changes in science, technology, religion, and politics as do the ETs themselves. Second, there would be an overturning of government by the people of Earth upon finding out that secrets have been kept since the turn of the century such as technologies including antigravity and free energy. This would anger the fossil-

The Future

fuel generation as it would be seen as a deliberate regression of technological advancement which has kept nations back, in turn adding to the pollution of the planet and climate change.

We have seen disclosure in forms of free energy regarding inventors, most of whom were all murdered in orchestrations to keep the oil and petroleum industrial complexes turning over trillions. Some of the oil companies themselves even bought the patents for free energy from genius inventors worldwide before humiliating those characters or removing them from the face of the Earth while stacking their ideas and patents in locked boxes with keys that have vanished. One of the greatest examples of this being Nicola Tesla, who had many of his papers confiscated by the secret government and who died without a penny to his name.

This puts the deep state in a funk. They know they can't hide anymore and have to begin the painful journey of disclosure in small trickles that can easily be digested by even the biggest of disbelievers, while on the other hand not giving too much to upset the global population in a possible uncontrollable riotous commotion becoming reality in return for the all-out lies that have been tailored for generations. The ETs understand that too much too soon can become an issue for the human collective at this present time, and they are working on a much faster turnaround putting their feet on the ground, so to speak, and working from the inside out.

In conclusion, disclosure will come from we the people who are the bearers of truth and it will have catalysts in terms of continued discussion, ascension in consciousness, and sightings and interactions that will be more obvious and more documented than ever before. There are some, however, who are still very much rooted in the old ways and have too much to lose in terms of power and money. These individuals still exist in large corporations, oil, the military, and the deep state and will do anything to stop disclosure from happening. They possess technology far greater than the public has an awareness of and are said to be planning many false flags operations. High-level leaks and intel for many years have uncovered the idea of an "event" where a preplanned or faked UFO arrival unfolds, creating the illusion that evil has come to our planet. Should this ever happen, it is to be ignored as the human mind is beginning to surpass project fear into something far greater.

Simply put, the ETs are not going to arrive just yet because we are still too dangerous. For their ships to peacefully land in numbers in public would be impossible within the confines of military structures that still exist and various controlled air spaces. These craft would be shot at and taken down upon entering into Earth's atmosphere and a hostile welcome would be unpreventable and this is why, among other reasons, they do not come. Earth as a civilization has not fully progressed beyond destroying what they cannot understand and so our galactic friends are now playing a waiting game. We as a planetary society must raise our consciousness halfway to meet theirs before they can meet us safely, and this timeline is now in the hands of humanity only.

Hollywood has often enjoyed the frivolity of movies that portray the ETs as evil, and those who wish to destroy Earth, never understanding that these beings have had the technologies to erase Earth instantly all this time and have yet, for the most part, kept it protected. The minority want disclosure and open acceptance. The ETs want the majority to become ready before they take the far greater risk of actually arriving. There are laws in the cosmos that do not allow disclosure and the arrival of ETs on foreign planets, and these are governed by federations of councils within our galaxy. The correct environment and attributes must be mutual on both sides with powers greater than the ETs themselves governing when the most fruitful timings will be in keeping with universal balance and the law of one. While we have a vague idea of timelines, you might be wondering who the first will be to arrive? It is mostly likely to be those that look similar to us in Earth in terms of physical appearance. This will lead to beings like the Pleiaidans walking among us. This is partly because they were our seeders in Lemurian times and wish to see their love creation come to full fruition.

The Future

Systems

In the 1960s they said oil reserves would be depleted in ten years. In the '70s they said there was going to be an ice age. In the '80s they said that acid rain would destroy all crops in ten years. In the '90s they said the ozone layer would be destroyed in ten years. In the 2000s they said that the ice caps would melt in ten years. Project fear especially politically will begin to crumble and fear will not cast the final vote on what people buy into mentally and financially.

Systems like big pharma will come under intense scrutiny for selling products that kept people ill for years while making trillions. The oil companies will also go this way, knowing that they had choked the air while free energy was within their oily hands all along. Financial systems, banks, and even old institutions and monarchies are going to see real change with people breaking away as individuals or nations from old controlling paradigms. It will become exponential after 2020, speeding up greatly as the public begins to realize not everything they have been fed is what has transpired. Fake news will be nothing compared to the realization of fake science and fake history. Old organizations will find it harder and harder to keep their grasp on the previously sold narratives which don't add up, either coming clean or radically changing their stand last minute.

The abomination that is missing children and child abuse within organized crime and the religions of the world will begin to come clean, and it will repulse many just at how long it has been going on for and the extent to which it was covered up. The years 2020–2030 will be when all the darkness will come to the surface in order to be healed in readiness for the new foundations to be built from. Sovereignty, truth, and integrity mixed with elements of compassion will flow through these long earthly institutions and cults like never before. This will be upsetting for some, seeing so much darkness unearthed, but it is a triumph moving forward and must be seen as such.

Financial structures will change, also. New quantum financial systems will come into play that will use their own consciousness that will be impregnable, impregnable being for the bad guys not the masses. AI within financial systems can be hacked, and some of the code used is still very old, upon which billions of dollars can be siphoned off and used in black projects. The USA has billions of dollars that are unaccounted for every year which go into these projects. New QFS (quantum financial systems) and similar structures will be set in place and will disallow illegal money laundering within government and federal organizations.

Historically it is believed that bitcoin was one of the first major currencies used on the dark web to traffic children and drugs. Its history has nefarious uses, and you will see governments in the future try to centralize crypto currencies in an attempt to move with the times. They will try to incorporate bitcoin, potentially XRP, and other digital currencies, in attempts to further control and exacerbate the FIAT monetary systems. Eventually, these attempts will fail.

New reforms will come into play including NESARA (National Economic Security and Recovery Act) and then later on a larger scale GESARA (Global Economic Security and Recovery Act) that will take control from the debt-based system and the idea that banks have been privately owned by families such as the Rothschilds and the like. Basic finance and monetary lessons will be taught in school in the future, equipping the people with the skills to manage and handle money, something that has been kept hidden from humanity. In order to work toward a system that is similar to a Pleiadian culture, we will need to take stepping-stones that will be slowly filtered down through generations. You might be wondering who is going to enact all of this. There are people right at the top within governments and above who are pulling strings as we speak. Some call them the whitehats. As time goes on, the truth will come out. Enormous funds totaling unmaintainable amounts will become available for humanitarian projects.

Here are the main points set within NESARA to give you a flavor of things to come and ways to undo old systems that were

The Future

created not for the people, but for the few. The act does away with the Federal Reserve Bank, the IRS, the shadow government. NESARA will implement the following changes when enacted fully. There is already vast evidence that people have had debts mysteriously zeroed out with more coming to the fore daily.

1. Zeros out all credit card, mortgage, and other bank debt due to illegal banking and government activities. This is the Federal Reserve's worst nightmare, a "jubilee" or a forgiveness of debt.
2. Abolishes the income tax.
3. Abolishes the IRS. Employees of the IRS will be transferred into the US Treasury national sales tax area.
4. Creates a 14 percent flat rate nonessential new-items-only sales tax revenue for the government. In other words, food and medicine will not be taxed, nor will used items such as old homes.
5. Increases benefits to senior citizens.
6. Returns constitutional law to all courts and legal matters.
7. Reinstates the original Title of Nobility amendment.
8. Establishes new presidential and congressional elections within 120 days after NESARA's announcement. The interim government will cancel all national emergencies and return us back to constitutional law.
9. Monitors elections and prevents illegal election activities of special interest groups.
10. Creates a new US Treasury rainbow currency backed by gold, silver, and platinum precious metals, ending the bankruptcy of the United States initiated by Franklin Roosevelt in 1933.
11. Forbids the sale of American birth certificate records as chattel property bonds by the US Department of Transportation.
12. Initiates new US Treasury bank system in alignment with constitutional law.
13. Eliminates the Federal Reserve System. During the transition period the Federal Reserve will be allowed

to operate side by side of the US Treasury for one year in order to remove all Federal Reserve notes from the money supply.
14. Restores financial privacy.
15. Retrains all judges and attorneys in constitutional law.
16. Ceases all aggressive, US government military actions worldwide.
17. Establishes peace throughout the world.
18. Releases enormous sums of money for humanitarian purposes.
19. Enables the release of over 6,000 patents of suppressed technologies that are being withheld from the public under the guise of national security, including free energy devices, antigravity, and sonic healing machines.

Food

Over the years we have seen the term vegan becoming mainstream. Expect this to go to the next level regarding the way we see food. More and more people will move away from animal proteins and search for other ways to grow and heal their bodies. The red meat industry especially will begin to decline with people seeing healthier ways to sustain their bodies with reports that societies are feeling better as a result. Vegetables will become more sought after, and this will affect the way we eat and buy our food in daily life. Expensive restaurants will eventually have to follow suit more in terms of their ingredients, and people will have less tolerance eating an animal that still holds the scent of fear within its meat energetically. This will suit many more food chains and outlets having a vegetarian option, with some even going veggie completely. Demand will crave it and supply will offer it in accordance.

People will read the back of a sugary drink and become repulsed upon knowing that aspartame and other toxic chemicals still exist within these drinks when the science finally proves the damaging effect these artificial chemicals have on our well-being and senses. This will include fluoride, a chemical that was sold to

The Future

generations as a savior for the tooth industry.

In all things that will happen in advancement in the coming years, there will be duality still lurking. Food sales for veggie meats will increase, and you will see supermarkets will have bigger isles for these products. Beware, however, some of these products will seem healthier but have GSM and other modified ingredients, which are more harmful than the original meat. Fake meats and other packaged foods will be full of new types of chemicals that will cause issues and there will need to be a greater understanding of what is going into these "health foods."

Some food organizations will have wildly varying ideas on what ingredients are safe and ones that are not, and the health food guru will need to check the back of their packet for ingredients more than ever before. An example is rapeseed oil. This oil has a long history of being used in industrial contexts and is not healthy for human beings. Other sources of information declass that it is safe for you. It will be more important than ever to check your ingredients as healthy eaters will become ill as much as the non-healthy eaters and not understand why. Ask yourself, why is rapeseed oil now in all foods including cream? Only you can decide, try researching it on a search engine other than Google.

GMOs and other genetically modified crops will eventually be branded as cancer causing with the statement at the time being "sorry, we didn't know." Question the food you eat and check in on how you feel. In a higher consciousness there will still be people who need an intake of meat for their genetic makeup; this is good, but the majority will be headed more and more for the vegetable route thinking that it is an external influence from the outside world when in fact it will be internal. Their body will show them the way, although many will not be intuitive enough to comprehend this notion fully so they will explain it away as cultural or environmental conditioning, not understanding that they are part of the great shift, too.

There will be in coming times the risk for those who have become spiritual to harm their bodies with spiritual diets, also.

❖ 291 ❖

One must know and understand their own deficiencies and blood types before making radical dietary changes that can have physical and mental health issues. Some will be able to make the change faster than others, and everyone will have their own timeline. You must listen to your own body first, for spiritual groups and teachers within this field do not live in your body, they live in theirs! Many times within the new-age community, groups have radically changed their diet and run into health issues. Ascension is a slow walk, not a race. Give the body time.

⁎ 7 ⁎
Final Words

The future is incredibly bright, and the opportunities are more incredible than ever before. You are loved more than you can imagine by those around you who are unseen and on the other side whether you believe in that sort of thing or not. There is a great confluence of help and progress being made on Earth at this moment in time that is going to explode into new paradigms making life better for all on the planet. Ignore all project fears and mongering of lack and war for it is not real and will not happen anymore. There will be duality to see through, however, and one's eyes must be kept open. For example, while on one hand we have this wonderful new food, what are the dangers? If we have this incredible first-time breakthrough, how will it be manipulated to garner control back? The powers that be will try all they can in their final attempts in shadow governments to take back control.

Be vigilant as the Earth stumbles through its last bastions of an old dualistic reality on its way out. No matter who you are or what your circumstances are, know that you are incredibly important and that you are on this planet for a reason. Life is wonderful! Say it every day when you wake up and begin creating a bubble around you for everyone to see. Let drama and smallness wash over you like water off a duck's back for onlookers to observe and say, "Hey, I don't know what he/she's got, but I want some of that! I can feel it beaming off them."

Many wonderful inventions and technologies are before us as are energies that allow for all things possible like never before including the advancements in medical technologies such as med beds and other facilities that heal in futuristic ways. Incredible powers of magnetism and its abilities to clean water and create magnetic clean engines are on the way, along with other free energies that have been in existence for decades. Magnetics will have more power in the future.

Now is the time to watch the children. Don't be deceived by the age of some of them; they will be the great inventors and world changers at younger ages than ever before, and this will continue to grow greatly.

Lastly, we are not alone and never have been in this huge expanse of space. You are not alone even at your hour of greatest darkness as your star family and spirits are always with you. Aloneness is a fabrication that has been taught to us. Switch on the light wherever you walk and more than ever, dearly beloved, it will be felt and seen in a way never beheld before for those that are ready.

Finally a message from the Arcturians about the future.

Dearest Family,

We congratulate you on the magnificent acclimation of energies that your bodies are successfully adopting which are then alchemized by the chemistry of your cellular DNA. As your bodies assimilate all cosmic energy that has traveled through space to your planet, you have seen the experiences of physical exhaustion including waking up in the morning to find that the extremities of your body are seemingly numb. Many of your doctors on your planet are glimpsing a higher than normal proportion of lightworkers visiting for consultation upon which little or no issues are found. In some cases your medical healers have appeared to find cases where the client is seemingly dying and are yet completely healthy. This will be passed off by large conglomerate institutions as something that is actually manmade of which you are already aware.

This is the first time in a very long time you are finally beginning to have a relationship with your

Final Words

corporeal bodies. You are becoming aware of foods that do not resonate as the physical vessel is beginning to give you intuitive feedback that is undeniable even to those who have only just awakened. In an old energy this relationship was not sustainable and the body would express pain and signs of stress usually before or up until the point of illness only. Your new bodies are becoming hybridized. If you can imagine buying a fast car, its engine will need a higher, cleaner octane fuel. This is you, dear souls. In the coming times you will eat only once a day and need far less sleep as the light body and meridians of the physical vessel align and ingratiate pure light energy in a connected way that lines your energy points from head to toe.

The new world you will live in will be a glorious place full of changes that will aid the new human. Your construction industry will eventually do away with heavy dense materials such as wood and metal. Colossal structures the size of your tallest buildings will come into creation and the walls that supply you with shelter will have their own consciousness as homes are built from crystal materials. Imagine having a conscious experience with the home you live in as it breathes and exists alongside your own consciousness in unison. A home that is seemingly alive!

You are the forerunners now planting the seeds from the stars, intuitively changing jobs, moving to new areas and starting lives that exist within the beginning of an ascended planet. Many of you who are finding the changes the hardest are the ones who will be coming back and staying to build the new ascended planet while others will incarnate elsewhere and work out their soul purpose in different ways. This is because you are the ones choosing to wake up and put your feet onto the cold floor and experience the unknown while others stay in a comatose state ever dreaming within a paradigm that has already collapsed. The way showers are running the longest mile as they are the ones energetically leading the way and building the new world and are feeling the change of pace the most. This is also testing your resolve and agreements made prior to arriving. The rewards will be yours, lightworkers and starseeds. Have no fear.

The flora and fauna of your planet have been priming themselves in preparation for the new Earth for some time also. While humanity has aided in the untimely extinction of many species of your planet, some of these changes would have created themselves within the natural world independently of themselves as new animals, fruits, and other creations come into existence that serve a new ascended planet energy. Over many generations you will come back to observe new animals and fruits emerging, and some animals retiring from the creation story as has happened through the existence of your planet throughout the last four billion years. This perplexes the Earth seeds and the souls who have only incarnated upon Earth as this is all they have ever known and still dwell with one foot in the old while learning to accept the newness that is coming to your planet. Change is not easy.

The octave of this entire galaxy is raising its pitch by another level also. Do not think that the energies from our great central sun only affect Gaia? However, all eyes are on you within this moment in time. Humanity is the new civilization joining our galactic family and there is a cosmic anticipation of your imminent arrival. You look upon your skies and wonder when we might arrive. We look upon your planet and see you already arriving.

We ask you to not drown in the last remnants of the old world which your news outlets will be fueling for a while yet.

Focused thought will manifest in reality, dear ones, and we need you all in alignment for the world you are

Final Words

ready to receive.

We look upon you with the love that a parent has for its children who have just graduated. Take your time coming of age and enter the light with grace. We are your family and we love you beyond your imagination.

The Arcturians
(Channeled, Alexander Quinn)

⁂ About the Author ⁂

I was different from those at school. A black sheep and yet it had occurred to me that I might have abilities that allowed me to see beyond the humdrum 3D world and accepted attitudes that are often prescribed to us throughout the indoctrination that accoures upon reincarnating into a lower density. My mother was psychic and my great grandmother was one of few survivors of the Titanic. Upon having a premonition that the boat would sink, she alighted at Ireland and lived to hear of the tragedy from dry land. I however used my abilities within creative fields and led a more 3D life to begin with. It wasn't until later that the energies that run within my bloodline began to emerge.

I had been working as a singer songwriter within the music industry until such time that I had an accident in Nashville. I found myself awaking in a hospital having life changing perceptual and spiritual awakenings that would change me forever. Following this there were ET occurrences, lights in the sky and orbs which were now visible within rooms I would walk into followed by a strange ringing in the ears! I knew I had come to earth with a purpose, but it was not triggered until I began to follow the work of Nancy Ann Tappe (a synesthete) who diagnosed the colours of people's auras linking these attributes to their personalities and talents. Within the late 60s and 70s she became aware of a new colour aura surrounding souls arriving that had been unseen before, and named it after its colour. Indigo. Since then they have become known as the Indigo Children, Starseeds, and Lightorkers.

This led me to the phenomenon of starseeds, and why these special souls were flooding to earth at this time. Consequently, I became a leading voice within this field (being a starseed myself) exploring how humans were changing regarding their psychic abilities, DNA, and how this was related to a new kind of human being created on earth at this time alongside the new souls rushing in. It dawned on me that we were taking a huge evolutionary jump from Homo-sapien to Homo-luminous within a very small increment of time and it became my highest excitement to journal and uncover the deep understanding and secret knowledge of this time of potential human evolution.

I now live in the UK and work as a spiritual/metaphysical coach and help people on their evolutionary journey into 5D+, or more importantly, helping people connect to the power within, source energy and become their true multidimensional self. I often venture to Earth's heart chakra where I love to meditate up on the Tor within the spiritual town of Glastonbury nestled away in sleepy Somerset. I spend a great deal of time speaking about energies on youtube and follow the ascension cycles as they blow the sails of humanity into the new earth whilst watching the energies grow and grow!

For readings, business inquiries, and coaching please contact - alexanderquinn000@gmail.com

Other Books by Ozark Mountain Publishing, Inc.

Dolores Cannon
A Soul Remembers Hiroshima
Between Death and Life
Conversations with Nostradamus,
    Volume I, II, III
The Convoluted Universe -Book One,
    Two, Three, Four, Five
The Custodians
Five Lives Remembered
Jesus and the Essenes
Keepers of the Garden
Legacy from the Stars
The Legend of Starcrash
The Search for Hidden Sacred
    Knowledge
They Walked with Jesus
The Three Waves of Volunteers and
    the New Earth
A Very Special Friend
Horns of the Goddess
Aron Abrahamsen
Holiday in Heaven
James Ream Adams
Little Steps
Justine Alessi & M. E. McMillan
Rebirth of the Oracle
Kathryn Andries
Time: The Second Secret
Cat Baldwin
Divine Gifts of Healing
The Forgiveness Workshop
Penny Barron
The Oracle of UR
P.E. Berg & Amanda Hemmingsen
The Birthmark Scar
Dan Bird
Finding Your Way in the Spiritual Age
Waking Up in the Spiritual Age
Julia Cannon
Soul Speak – The Language of Your
    Body
Ronald Chapman
Seeing True
Jack Churchward
Lifting the Veil on the Lost

Continent of Mu
The Stone Tablets of Mu
Patrick De Haan
The Alien Handbook
Paulinne Delcour-Min
Spiritual Gold
Holly Ice
Divine Fire
Joanne DiMaggio
Edgar Cayce and the Unfulfilled
    Destiny of Thomas Jefferson
    Reborn
Anthony DeNino
The Power of Giving and Gratitude
Paul Fisher
Like A River To The Sea
Carolyn Greer Daly
Opening to Fullness of Spirit
Anita Holmes
Twidders
Aaron Hoopes
Reconnecting to the Earth
Patricia Irvine
In Light and In Shade
Kevin Killen
Ghosts and Me
Susan Urbanek Linville
Blessing from Agnes
Donna Lynn
From Fear to Love
Curt Melliger
Heaven Here on Earth
Where the Weeds Grow
Henry Michaelson
And Jesus Said – A Conversation
Andy Myers
Not Your Average Angel Book
Holly Nadler
The Hobo Diaries
Guy Needler
Avoiding Karma
Beyond the Source – Book 1, Book 2
The History of God
The Origin Speaks

For more information about any of the above titles, soon to be released titles,
or other items in our catalog, write, phone or visit our website:
PO Box 754, Huntsville, AR 72740|479-738-2348/800-935-0045|www.ozarkmt.com

Other Books by Ozark Mountain Publishing, Inc.

The Anne Dialogues
The Curators
Psycho Spiritual Healing
James Nussbaumer
And Then I Knew My Abundance
The Master of Everything
Mastering Your Own Spiritual
    Freedom
Living Your Dram, Not Someone Else's
Each of You
Sherry O'Brian
Peaks and Valley's
Gabrielle Orr
Akashic Records: One True Love
Let Miracles Happen
Nikki Pattillo
Children of the Stars
A Golden Compass
Victoria Pendragon
Sleep Magic
The Sleeping Phoenix
Being In A Body
Alexander Quinn
Starseeds What's It All About
Charmian Redwood
A New Earth Rising
Coming Home to Lemuria
Richard Rowe
Imagining the Unimaginable
Exploring the Divine Library
Garnet Schulhauser
Dancing on a Stamp
Dancing Forever with Spirit
Dance of Heavenly Bliss
Dance of Eternal Rapture
Dancing with Angels in Heaven
Manuella Stoerzer
Headless Chicken
Annie Stillwater Gray
Education of a Guardian Angel
The Dawn Book
Work of a Guardian Angel

Joys of a Guardian Angel
Blair Styra
Don't Change the Channel
Who Catharted
Natalie Sudman
Application of Impossible Things
L.R. Sumpter
Judy's Story
The Old is New
We Are the Creators
Artur Tradevosyan
Croton
Croton II
Jim Thomas
Tales from the Trance
Jolene and Jason Tierney
A Quest of Transcendence
Paul Travers
Dancing with the Mountains
Nicholas Vesey
Living the Life-Force
Dennis Wheatley/ Maria Wheatley
The Essential Dowsing Guide
Maria Wheatley
Druidic Soul Star Astrology
Sherry Wilde
The Forgotten Promise
Lyn Willmott
A Small Book of Comfort
Beyond all Boundaries Book 1
Beyond all Boundaries Book 2
Beyond all Boundaries Book 3
Stuart Wilson & Joanna Prentis
Atlantis and the New Consciousness
Beyond Limitations
The Essenes -Children of the Light
The Magdalene Version
Power of the Magdalene
Sally Wolf
Life of a Military Psychologist

For more information about any of the above titles, soon to be released titles,
or other items in our catalog, write, phone or visit our website:
PO Box 754, Huntsville, AR 72740|479-738-2348/800-935-0045|www.ozarkmt.com